Computer Appreciation
Third Edition

Computer Appreciation
Third Edition

T. F. Fry, ACMA, MBIM, MIDPM, FRSA
formerly Head of Department of Business and Secretarial Studies,
Cassio College, Watford, Herts.

Butterworths
London Boston Sydney Wellington Durban Toronto

First published 1970
Second edition 1975
Third edition 1981

©T. F. Fry 1981

British Library Cataloguing in Publication Data

Fry, T. F.
  Computer appreciation.—3rd ed.
  1. Electronic digital computers
  I. Title
  001.64 QA76.5

ISBN 0-408-00492-4   Dec. 81

Typeset by Tunbridge Wells Typesetting Services
Printed in England by Billing & Son Limited, Guildford, London and Worcester

Contents

Preface

When *Computer Appreciation* was first published in 1970 it was designed to cover the then existing requirements of a number of examinations. Despite one major revision in the form of a second edition some six years ago it has again been overtaken by the marked changes that have taken place during recent years in the continuing development of computer technology and in the structure and requirements of many examinations. Amongst the more notable of these changes has, on the one hand, been the introduction of the microprocessor and on the other hand new approaches to the learning situation through the Business and Technical Education Councils.

This third edition seeks to both widen and to bring up to date the subject matter with which *Computer Appreciation* was originally concerned. A number of chapters have been completely rewritten or extensively revised while retaining those that have not been subject to change but have, over the course of time, proved useful to readers.

The new text is still orientated towards the use of computers in business and also bears in mind the revised requirements of a number of examinations including BEC, The Royal Society of Arts, and professional accountancy bodies.

I have also tried to keep the style as simple and as non-technical as possible so that students and others reading for interest only will not find the going too laborious. I have also aimed at a text that will provide an appreciation of what computers are and do for those people who, while not technically involved with computers, are employed in organizations using these machines.

Finally may I acknowledge the help of the staff and students of Cassio College, Watford and express my thanks to Eileen, my wife, for her patience and encouragement and to Joyce, who typed the manuscript.

T F FRY

The development of computers

Few technological developments of recent times have had as widespread effect on industry, commerce and public life generally as the development of the electronic computer. Indeed, it has been suggested that the advent of the computer heralds a second Industrial Revolution. Electronic computers have certainly outstripped the human mind in the speed with which they can absorb information, process it and communicate the results, the reliability with which they can carry out these operations and their capacity to store vast quantities of information and retrieve any item in a very short time.

Fundamentally this book is concerned with two things:

COMPUTERS: an appreciation of how they work and the purposes they serve.
DATA: the raw material, the facts and figures that the computer is designed to process.

Explanation of terms

It would, perhaps, be best to start off with some brief explanations:

Data This is the term given to all the facts and figures that record an event, an activity or a situation. As isolated facts and figures, they may not be meaningful in themselves but may have to be marshalled and processed in specific ways to provide meaningful information. For example, we may have a number of data items as follows:

E. Smith   1167   39   £1.80   40%

Note that, as they stand, they mean very little.

Data processing This is the technique of sorting, relating, interpreting and computing data items to provide meaningful and useful information. For example, the above data items when suitably processed could provide the information that an employee

E. Smith worked for 39 hours on Job No. 1167 for which he was paid £1.80 an hour. His gross wage was £70.20. The direct labour costs of the job was also £70.20 and the job will be charged to our customer at £70.20 plus 40% i.e. £98.28. The profit on the job was £28.80. This means that, on processing, this data will give us information regarding:

Wages to be paid
Job costing
Preparation of Sales Invoice
Profit Levels

Data processing takes raw data and converts it to meaningful information.

Information   This is the basic requirement of an organization in the decision-making process in order to effectively plan, co-ordinate, direct and control its activities towards the realization of its objectives. Such information, however, must be relevant, timely, accurate and complete i.e. it must be *sound* information. In order to produce such sound information, data processing must work within a predetermined framework of rules known as a:

Data processing system   It is this that specifies the operations and procedures that must be applied to data, and which controls the flow of data in logical and defined stages to ensure the production of sound information as an end product of the system.

Computer   This is the latest and most technically sophisticated of a long line of devices produced over many years to carry out the operations and procedures of a data processing system. Its activities are governed by a list of instructions—a *program*—which sets out in detail the machine operations to be performed to carry out the data processing system.

Why data?

Earlier we said that data is all of the facts and figures relating to and recording an event, an activity or a situation. It will be evident that, as the range and complexity of the activities with which mankind is involved has increased, so the volumes and complexity of data generated by these activities has similarly increased.

Going back to early times, we find that man's activities and relationships were limited and simple. Living in a small rural community, he was to a great extent self-supporting. His identity was a matter of only local concern and trading activities were limited to the exchange of goods on a barter basis. The few records needed would probably be made by simple tally marks such as notches in wood, knots in string or scratches on stone.

As society developed, the dependence of people on one another for goods and services increased. The involvement of both local and central authorities in both the individual and his organizations became more marked and technical know-how rapidly developed.

These developments in turn generated more and more data and with it the need for agencies to record and interpret the data. Writing became more widespread and an easily manipulated number system was adopted (the decimal system). Some of the main areas in which, over the years, data volumes and degree of complexity have dramatically escalated are:

Personal data   In early years little or no recorded data existed on individuals. They were just known locally by name perhaps associated with the trade they pursued. As society developed, an ever increasing range and volume of data relating to people and their possessions became necessary. An early example of this was the compilation 900 years ago of the Doomsday Book containing data resulting from a nationwide survey of land ownership. From the first rudimentary data held on people—formal names and addresses, births and death dates etc.—record keeping has progressed until today the list of the aspects of our lives on which data records are kept is almost endless. Income Tax Records, Health Records, Employment Records, Motor Tax Records are but a few.

Business and Trading Data   We have already noted that the earliest forms of trading—barter—generated little or no recorded data. However, each subsequent development in trading and business activity brought in its wake more and more records. The introduction of currency led to keeping data on commodity values expressed in the currency as well as the flow of currency in and out of a business. Credit trading further expanded the range of data records with the need to keep records of debtors and creditors, in the form of comprehensive book-keeping systems. As businesses grew in size and complexity, the importance of effective management skills became apparent. With information the basic tool for exercising these skills, the generation and processing of data on all aspects of business activity became essential.

Technical and Scientific Data   Starting off with the need to record accurate measurements of physical properties—sizes, weights, volumes etc.—invention and innovation in these areas has progressed at an ever-accelerating rate. Not only has this resulted in a dramatic increase in the range, and therefore the choice of available products and processes but it has carried with it the need for increasingly complex specifications. For example, the volume of data relating to a penny-farthing cycle of 80 years ago bears no comparison with that generated in the manufacture of an aircraft jet engine.

Legislative Data   Again, the past century or two has seen a vast increase in the volume of data called for by both local and central government from both individuals and businesses. Some of the more well known are Census Records, Voting Register Records, VAT Records, Income Tax Records, Personnel Records etc.

All in all, when we compare today's businesses with those of only 100–200 years ago we find an almost phenomenal increase in the amount of data that has to be stored and processed, and the volume of information generated for both internal administration and to meet external demands.

Over the years man has sought to develop devices that would help cope with this increasing problem of volume with its associated problems of cost, accuracy and control. The following is an account of some landmarks in the development of these devices.

Development of calculating devices

The abacus

Some doubts exist about the origin of the abacus although it is widely believed that it's earliest use was in Egypt. It probably developed through the use of clay tablets into which grooves were cut side by side and allowed to harden. Pebbles were placed in or taken away from these grooves, as numbers were added or subtracted. Later, holes were made through the pebbles and they were threaded on wires or strings and mounted in a frame. Values were given to the rows of pebbles or beads; unit values for the top row and increasing in multiples of ten downwards. Manipulation of these beads, forwards and backwards across the wires in skilled hands proved to be a very fast and efficient method of carrying out the four basic arithmetic functions: addition, subtraction, multiplication and division.

It was not until the seventeenth century, by which time the arabic number system (decimal system) had been adopted throughout Europe, that any further advance in computing devices took place.

Logarithm tables

First published by John Napier in 1614, these were shortly afterwards adapted by Henry Briggs to a base of 10, producing the common logarithms we use today.

Napier's rods and bones

As an astronomer, John Napier was continually aware of the need to make quite complex calculations and found it difficult to find people to carry these out accurately. In 1614, he wrote commenting on 'this tedious expense of time' and the 'many slippery errors' to which these calculations were subject. 'I began to consider in my mind by what certain and ready art I might remove these hindrances'. His considerations led to the development of a ready reckoner known as 'Napier's Rods'. Using the principle of performing multiplication by the addition of logarithms, Napier constructed a device consisting of nine pieces of card about an inch wide, each divided vertically into nine squares. Each square is divided diagonally from the top right hand corner to the bottom left hand corner, and on each card is

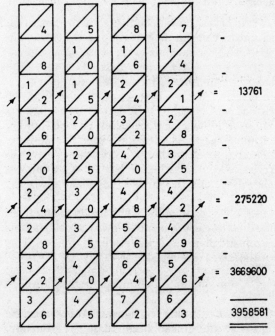

Figure 1.1   Using Napier's rods

written a multiplication table, from 1 to 9, placing the tens above the diagonal and the units below. This gives a ready reckoner capable of multiplying two numbers together. For example, Figure 1.1 shows four rods representing the 4, 5, 8 and 7 tables placed side by side to show the multiplication of 4587 by 863. Starting with the units, 3, add diagonally and carry one to the left when the sum is 10 or greater. Then proceed in the same manner with the tens and with the hundreds. The sum of the answer will give the product, i.e. $4587 \times 863 = 3\,958\,581$.

Of course it is impossible, using only one set of these rods, to work out a problem in which the same digit occurs more than once. Napier solved this by using four-sided rods, known as Napier's Bones, on which a different table appeared on each of the four sides.

Slide rules

Combining the principles of Napier's Rods and Logarithms the first real slide rule was introduced by John Gunter in 1621.

Pascal's adding machine

It was not long after Napier had developed his ready reckoner that the first mechanical aid to calculating was produced in the mid-seventeenth century. This was a machine in the sense we would use the word today with gears, wheels and dials. The son of a superintendent of taxes in Paris, Blaise Pascal wanted to produce a machine that would help his father. In 1642, at the age of 18, he produced a device that was probably the world's first adding machine. It consisted of a number of wheels each divided into ten segments and capable of being rotated through any number of these. The wheels were connected to each other by a 'carry-over' lever so that on ten being registered on one wheel a carry over of one was made to the next. The position of the wheels at any time showed the contents of the machine.

Pascal's device was, however, only an adding machine and there was a need for a machine to carry out more involved calculations including multiplication and division. It was not until some 50 years later that the first of these was developed.

Leibnitz' calculator

Working on the principle that multiplication and division can be accomplished by repetitive addition and subtraction respectively, Leibnitz, in 1694, built a machine that would carry out the four basic arithmetic rules, addition, subtraction, multiplication and division. The device made use of a drum upon which teeth were mounted, nine at one end, graduated down in steps of one, to none at the other end. A shaft was mounted parallel to the length of the drum on which was positioned a gear wheel which could be moved to mesh in with the teeth of the drum at any position. To multiply by 6 for instance, the gear wheel was moved opposite the 6 position on the drum, i.e. where six teeth were mounted around it's circumference. One revolution of the drum then moved the gear wheel through 6 teeth, two revolutions through 12, and so on. By mounting a number of these drums side by side to represent multiples of 10 and incorporating suitable carry-over mechanisms, any number could be set up on the gear wheels and multiplied by the number of revolutions through which the drum was turned.

Babbage's difference engine

The next landmark in the development of calculating machines, and indeed what is considered to be the forerunner of the modern computer, was brought about by an English mathematician, Charles P. Babbage in the first half of the nineteenth century. Babbage conceived a machine based on a principle not used before in calculating machines. This was the level difference between values computed for a formula.

The following table shows the level difference between values of y in the formula $y = x^2$.

Value of x	Value of y	1st level difference	2nd level difference
0	0		
1	1	1	
2	4	3	2
3	9	5	2
4	16	7	2
5	25	9	2
6	36	11	2

Since the second level difference is constant i.e. 2, y can be found for any value of x by simple addition. If, for example $x = 7$, then $y = 2 + 11 + 36 = 49$. Further values in the first difference can be found by successive additions of 2, from which further values of y can be found. Babbage called his device a 'Difference Engine'. However, before this machine was ever developed, Babbage became involved in a far more complex project which he described as an 'Analytical Machine' incorporating principles that are an integral part of today's computer. He planned a machine that would be able to complete sixty simple calculations a minute, that would be able to store 1000 fifty digit numbers and whose operations would be controlled through a list of instructions punched into cards. In this, then, was the concept of a machine possessing both Arithmetic and Data Storage facilities and the capacity to control it's own activities automatically through the medium of a pre-determined list of instructions known as a *program*.

Punched cards

Punched cards were originally introduced by a Frenchman, Joseph M. Jacquard, as a production aid in his silk weaving factory in Lyons. The idea was first adapted for processing data by Dr Hollerith in America who realized it's potential for recording and processing information arising from a national census in 1890. The principle Dr Hollerith used was to allocate each position on the card a pre-determined value, or meaning, and then to punch holes in the relevant positions to record the information.

From this, systems were developed to record and classify commercial data and Dr Hollerith with his assistant Powers developed a range of machines for this use. These including punches for preparing cards, sorters for arranging the cards into any required sequence, tabulators to print and summarize the information contained in the cards and to carry out some simple arithmetic functions, and later mechanical calculators that would perform multiplication and division.

Development of computers

It is now less than 40 years since the first working electronic automatic computer was completed. Up to this time, the design principles of calculating devices had hardly changed during the previous 250 years. This short life span of the computer to date has produced technical, environmental and systems developments almost without parallel in any other field. While this has been a continuing process, it is possible to identify four major stages in this process. These stages are called computer *generations* (Figure 1.2).

First generation computers

This roughly covers the period up to the early 1950s which saw the development and the marketing of early electronic data processing computers. In Britain at Cambridge University, a team led by Dr M. V. Wilkes worked on a machine known as EDSAC (Electronic

	First Generation	Second Generation	Third Generation	Fourth Generation
1944	Thermionic Valves			
	Program Plug Boards			
	Mercury Delay Line Storage			
1950	Electronically Stored Program			
1950		Magnetic Tape		
		Magnetic Drum		
		Ferrite Core Store		
		Magnetic Discs		
		Transistors		
		Multiprogramming		
		Time Sharing Systems		
1964		Realtime Systems		
1964			Family Configurations	
			Integrated Circuitry	
1970			Minicomputers	
1970				Microelectronics
				Microprocessors
				Personal Microcomputers
				Floppy Discs
				Commercial Microcomputers

Figure 1.2   Computer generations

Delay Storage Automatic Computer). The association of J. Lyons and Co. Ltd, with Dr Wilkes' team led to the production of the first computer for commercial use in this country, the LEO (Lyons Electronic Office). This became operational in 1951. Manchester University in the meanwhile had started work on MADAM (Manchester Automatic Digital Machine) the first of which, known commercially as the Ferranti Mark I, was installed in 1953. During the late 1940s and early 1950s development was going on in a number of universities and commercial companies. Birkbeck College, London, produced the first computer using magnetic drum storage, ARC (Automatic Relay Calculator) and later the All Purpose Electronic Computer (APEC) was built for the British Tabulating Machine Company. From this was developed the HEC I, shown in 1952 at the Business Efficiency Exhibition. English Electric Ltd, also working in this field, produced the ACE (Automatic Computing Engine) and from this developed in 1955, a commercial data processing machine called DEUCE.

During the same time, in America, IBM were developing general purpose computers resulting in the introduction in 1948 of the IBM 604 and the IBM 701 in 1952.

The main features of these early computers included logic circuitry based on *thermonic valves* and diodes which meant very large machines generating a great deal of heat which in turn led to a fairly high failure rate. Internal storage tended to be of low capacity based on *magnetic drum* and *mercury delay lines.* Operating speeds were within the millisecond (one thousandth of a second) range.

Second generation computers

This period in the development of computers, up until 1964, produced some major innovations in hardware and, through these, in operating modes.

In 1955, *magnetic core storage* was invented, followed in 1956 by the planar silicon *transistor.* With these, the wires and the thermonic valves of earlier machines could be dispensed with in favour of 'solid state' technology.

This period saw a dramatic increase in the number of computers in service. The first all transistor commercial machine was the UNIVAC II followed by a number of models by different manufacturers among which the better known were the ICT 1300 series, the second edition of LEO, and the most successful commercial machine of the period, IBM's 1400 series, with a virtually world wide acceptance.

Two other developments of far reaching importance occurred during this period. These were *time sharing* and *real time* computer operating modes, with *multiprogramming* facilities. In 1961, a LEO III computer was constructed with multiprogramming facilities while in 1962 at Cambridge, Massachusetts, a time sharing system was developed using a DEC PDP I machine. The first, and probably still the best known large scale real-time system was introduced in 1962. This is the American Airlines Sabre seat reservation system.

Other features of these second generation machines were that they were smaller in size, far more reliable, had a larger capacity internal storage and operating speeds were in the microsecond (one millionth of a second) range.

Third generation computers

This period, taking us up to the early 1970s saw the introduction of the first *minicomputer* by Digital Equipment Corporation, the PDP6.

An important innovation was the introduction in 1965 of the *family* concept of machines. This type of machine, rather than being a fixed permanent 'tailor made' configuration, offered interchangeable hardware options with software compatibility throughout the family. The ICT 1900 series is an example.

Integrated circuitry (electronic circuits with a large number of components built on a small *silicon chip* rather than separate components wired together) was first introduced in commercial computers in the mid 1960s. The IBM 360 series and the Honeywell 2200 series were among the first machines to incorporate this technology.

During this period, *magnetic discs* were widely adopted as a direct access backing storage medium.

All in all, third generation computers tended to be smaller in size than the previous generation although having higher capacity internal storage. With the introduction of discs, direct access storage costs were reduced, communication links to remote terminals were further developed and operation speeds of many machines were in the nanosecond (one thousand millionth of a second) range.

Fourth generation computers

The period from 1970 onwards has seen the application of micro-electronics to computer design. Based on silicon-integrated circuits using *Metal Oxide Semiconductor* (MOS) *technology* a very large number of components can be etched on a single small silicon chip. This is accomplished by using computer-aided design techniques to draw circuitry layouts and then photographically reducing the layouts by a factor of 300 or so producing a very small chip containing many thousands of circuits. It was in 1970 that Intel produced the first *microprocessor* on a single silicon chip. Micro-processors have since found their way into many applications, for example, pocket calculators, digital watches, banking cash dispensers and word processing systems.

The development of the *microcomputer* for use in commercial data processing systems entailed the provision of, in addition to the processor, a large scale internal *random access memory* (RAM) and a range of peripherals for backing storage, input and output purposes. Internal memory is again in the form of silicon chips, about 5 mm^2 by 0.1 mm thick, carrying up to 64 000 memory elements.

Microcomputers are constructed on a modular basis with silicon chips mounted on printed circuit boards which can be plugged in to the main console and provide the connections (interface) for linking peripherals and power supply to the processor. The basic processing unit will usually incorporate a visual display unit and a keyboard for the manual entry of data. Miniature magnetic discs (known as *floppy discs)* and magnetic tape in cassettes are used as additional backing storage while *matrix printers* are used to provide a printed output.

There is now a wide range of microcomputers on the market with the capacity to carry out commercial data processing operations which up until now have, to a great extent, been the province of the larger mainframe computer. For many machines, application packages are available from manufacturers, for example sales ledger, stock control, payroll, purchase ledger packages etc., although software costs tend to be fairly high in relation to the costs of hardware.

The future of the microcomputer could well be as a dedicated machine, sited departmentally to carry out limited areas of work, representing a far cheaper way of utilizing computer power compared with the large centralized machine catering for all processing needs of an organization.

Exercises

1. Give an account of the factors that have given rise, over the last 100 years, to a marked increase in the demand for data processing.
2. What do you think are the main differences in principle between an electro-mechanical accounting machine and an electronic computer?
3. Distinguish between *data* and *information*. Explain how the one can be used to produce the other.
4. Give an account of the development of aids to calculating up to the introduction of the modern computer.
5. What do you consider to be the main trends in the development of computers today?
6. What do you understand by a *microcomputer*? Suggest ways in which this differs from the conventional computer.

2

Basic elements of a computer

Before considering in detail how the various parts of a computer work, let us try to get a picture in broad outlines of what a computer is and does. This can probably best be done by breaking down a simple office job into its component parts.

What a computer does

A clerk working in a stock control section has to price requisitions passed to him from a materials store. These requisitions contain the following information:

Description and part-number of the articles issued from store.
Quantity issued.
Number of the job on which the articles are used.
Date, requisition serial number, and a signature.

On receipt of the requisition the clerk is required to enter in the relevant column the unit price of the article, which is obtained by reference to a price-list. He then multiplies the unit price by the quantity and enters the product in the £·p column. Should there be more than one line entry on the form he will have to add the column and enter the total at the bottom.

To complete this task, the stock control clerk will have to perform a sequence of operations something like this: (see Figure 2.1)

(a) Read the information appearing on the requisition.
(b) Refer to a price-list to obtain the unit price of the article.
(c) Multiply the unit price by the quantity.
(d) Enter the answer to (c) and total if necessary.

Taking a closer look at these operations we can identify them as follows:

(a) Read the information appearing on the requisition—here the clerk is accepting information for processing—we can call it the *input* of the procedure

13

(b) Refer to a price-list to obtain the unit price—this is reference to stored or filed information—we can call it *storage*

(c) Multiply the unit price by the quantity—this is the *arithmetic* of the procedure

(d) Enter the answer to (c) in the £·p column—this is the *output*.

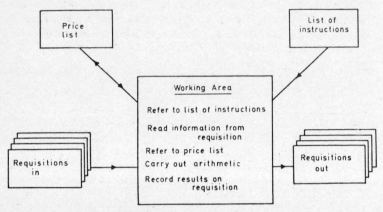

Figure 2.1   Processing data manually

The procedure then has four distinct elements:

Input   *Storage*   *Arithmetic*   *Output*

but in order to get the correct answer, the operations must be carried out in a pre-determined sequence. We could make a more detailed list of instructions, in sequence, which could well take this form:

1. Read part-number from the requisition.
2. Look up part-number in price list, read price and enter it in the unit price column.
3. Read quantity from requisition.
4. Multiply quantity by unit price.
5. Write answer to (4) in £·p column.
6. If there is another entry on the requisition start again at (1), if not carry on at (7).
7. Add the £·p column.
8. Write total at bottom of column.
9. If there is another requisition go back to (1), if not stop.

Since the correct operation of this procedure depends upon the observation of this sequence of instructions, we should add a fifth to the four elements listed above. We can call this a *program*. However, we must remember that the program is not part of the information to be processed but the list of instructions that have to be followed to give the correct answer. The name we usually give to the information for processing is *data,* and so the program is applied to the data in order to give the required results. We must also remember that the program has to be stored. If we are new to a job we may keep the program jotted down on a piece of paper to which we can refer as we go along. Later, as we become more experienced, we will probably memorize the program and carry out the instructions automatically. But whether on paper or in our head, the program is stored.

We start, then, with data recorded on a requisition form and at the end we have an answer recorded in £·p. In between them there is a 'working area' in which we refer to the program, refer to the data on the requisition and to the price list. We carry out a simple calculation and note the answer down on the original requisition.

There is still one further factor we must bear in mind. It would be most unusual to have a clerk working away on these requisitions without being supervised. Someone has to make sure that the instructions are being carried out correctly, that the requisitions are available when required, that the correct price-list is being used and so on. In other words, there must be an element of *control* over the whole proceedings.

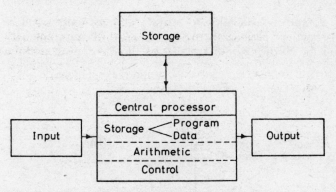

Figure 2.2   Basic elements of a computer

Now a computer works very much like this:

The original information, recorded in one way or another, is read into the machine   INPUT
The completed answer is read out of the machine   OUTPUT
And in between is the 'work area' which we call the   CENTRAL
PROCESSOR

In which reference is made to the stored data and the stored program	STORAGE
And also in which the calculations are carried out	ARITHMETIC
And the whole proceedings supervised by	CONTROL

We will see later that the internal storage capacity of the central processor is not always sufficient to hold the program required and all of the data as well, so supplementary external stores are used to which reference can be made in a very short time.

Basic computer structure

Basically then, a complete computer configuration consists of a central device known as a *central processor* with a number of devices surrounding it that are used for specialized purposes (see Figure 2.2). There are *input devices* for reading and transferring data and programs to the processor, *output devices* for accepting information from the processor and devices, usually known as *backing stores*, for storing additional data. These devices surrounding the central processor are called *peripherals* (see Figure 2.3).

For a computer installation to operate we must have a central processor and the peripherals to support it, which are commonly known as the *hardware* of an installation. In addition we need the

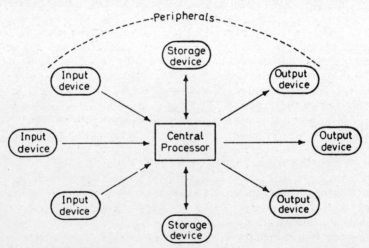

Figure 2.3   Elements of a computer configuration

programs to instruct the computer and the systems on which it will work, collectively known as the *software.*

While these basic elements of a computer are dealt with in detail in later chapters, let us now take a brief look at each of them.

Central processor

The main features of a central processor are its capacity to store and manipulate data, to store and execute programmed instructions on such data, and to monitor these proceedings through the medium of a built in overall control known as an operating system. In addition, of course, it must have the capacity to communicate or output the results of its processing.

The data on which the central processor is to work can be read into store either directly as primary information from an input device, or it can be information already stored in a device external to but connected with the processor from which data can be extracted and returned as and when required.

The manipulation of data may involve many processes as will be seen in more detail later, but will include its capacity to process arithmetic functions, comparison of data items, assembling data into a pre-determined output format, and indeed to arrive at decisions based on criteria supplied to it. However, while a computer has the capacity to carry out many processes, it will only do what it is instructed to, and the vehicle for communicating these instructions is a computer *program,* temporarily stored in the central processor to enable it to carry out a specific task.

The processor's capacity to store information is sometimes known as the computer's *memory.* However, when all is said and done a computer is only a machine, and can only retain information presented to it in the simplest of forms. In fact the computer's memory is only required to remember sequences of two distinct characters (0 and 1) and all information presented to it is coded in this form. This is a numbering system known as *binary.* Of course it would be a very laborious process if all numeric and alphabetic information had to be changed to this form by hand before it was fed to the machine, so the computer is designed to do this for itself. In the same way it will convert the results of its calculations from binary back to the numbers and letters we normally use. On the surface this may appear to be a very complex and costly method of working out what are comparatively simple problems. The advantage of a computer is in its high speed, which can process data many thousand times faster than manual methods.

Input

Unfortunately, it is usually not possible to feed data into a computer in the form that it originates. If we could feed the actual requisition mentioned earlier into the machine, get the machine to do the required 'working out' and write the answer in the correct place, then eject the completed requisition from the other end, things would be a lot more straightforward. However, there are difficulties that prevent a computer from doing this. For example, the requisitions may be of different shapes and sizes with writing in different positions. The form of handwriting may differ so much from requisition to requisition that we could well have difficulty in reading it ourselves let alone in expecting a machine to do so. To get over these problems the information must be:

(a) prepared on a standard size and type of form that the machine will always be able to accept and
(b) recorded in such a way that the machine will be able to recognize it and read it.

One widely used method of doing this is to convert the information into holes punched into cards or in a continuous strip of paper tape giving each letter, number and symbol a distinctive pattern of holes that the computer will recognize. These two forms of input are known as *punched cards* and *punched paper tape*, and are prepared on machines by an operator from the original data.

Output

While the information may be read into the computer in a coded form, such as punched cards or punched paper tape, output from a computer in a coded form of this nature would normally be unacceptable as a method of communicating the results of the computer's work. It is the function of an output device to present these results in a readable and usable form. This can be accomplished, for example, by using a *printer* or a *cathode ray tube* (CRT) (or a VDU, *Visual Display Unit*), both of which will convert the coded computer results into conventional numbers, letters and symbols.

Types of computer

Up until now, we have used the term computer in a rather general sense, as a machine that is controlled by an internally stored program, deals with all its processing in terms of binary numbers, has the capacity to store information and is able to carry out a range of processes on this information. Because it deals in discrete numbers—digits—this type of machine is known as a *digital* computer. However, there is a second type of computer known as an *analogue* computer, although to this we can add a third category known as a *hybrid* computer, which is really a machine that is a combination of the two, digital and analogue.

Digital computers

As we saw in the previous paragraph, a digital computer is essentially, as its name implies, a machine that works in discrete digits or numbers. All processing is carried out in terms of a numeric representation of the information being processed. This information, whether originating as decimal digits, as alphabetical characters or as symbols, is converted into a series of binary digits and stored in this form. All input data is converted into binary expressions. All processing is carried out in terms of 0 and 1, and output is converted back from this form to the conventional alphanumeric characters we normally use.

Analogue computers

Perhaps the best way to explain the difference between digital and analogue computers is through a very simple example. If we wanted to measure, in gallons per minute, the rate of water flow through a tap, one approach would be to place a succession of one gallon buckets under the tap, removing each as it became full. If we counted the number of buckets filled in 30 seconds and multiplied this by two, we would arrive at a figure representing the rate of flow in gallons per minute. This is a digital approach to the problem; we are working in discrete numbers. This, incidentally, would give us a flow rate for one particular half-minute in time only, and ignores the fact that rates may change from one minute to another in the light of variables such as water velocity and tap aperture.

An alternative approach would be to fit monitoring devices that would continuously measure the water velocity and the tap aperture, convert these measurements into electrical pulses and relate them in order to produce the movement of a needle over a graduated dial indicating flow rate in gallons per minute. We then have an analogue computing situation. In effect, an analogue computer is concerned with the continuous measurement of physical properties and performing computations on these measurements using the physical properties of the computer itself to provide an analogy of the problem to be solved.

A further very simple often quoted example of this analogue function is that of a car speedometer. Here, the position of a needle relative to a dial represents the speed of the car in miles per hour, but is arrived at not by computing numbers but by the continuous monitoring of shaft revolution speeds and a conversion of this through the device's physical properties, gears and cables, to give a dial reading.

Hybrid computers

This is really not another type of computer, but a machine that incorporates both digital and analogue elements.

It has the advantage of a memory in which program instructions can be stored and executed without the need for manual setting and, of course, can store physical variables by converting them to digital expressions. This entails the conversion of measurements of physical properties to digital statements and the converse of this, involving the use of analogue-to-digital and digital-to-analogue converters. For example, we may be interested in measuring varying light intensity over a given area, say a picture. First we would give a numeric value to the varying intensities, say 0–99. If we then divided the area up into a number of very small 'dots', photo-electrically scanned these dots in turn and related the amplitude of the current induced to the numeric scale, this would provide us with a series of digital expressions which could be held in store and retrieved to reconstitute the picture later on. The scanning operation is the analogue element of the process, while the storage of numbers to represent the light intensity is the digital element.

Exercises

1. A computer consists of a central processor supported by a number of peripherals. What do you understand by the term *peripheral*? Explain why these are necessary and give examples explaining the purpose of each.
2. What do you understand as the basic elements of a computer? Using any illustration of your own choice, explain how these play their part in processing data.
3. Distinguish between the *hardware* and the *software* of a computer installation.
4. What is a computer *program*? Explain why a program is essential in working out a problem by computer.

5. What are the main functions of a *central processor*?
6. What do you understand by an *analogue* computer? Illustrate your answer by describing an analogue device with which you are familiar in your everyday life.

3

Binary arithmetic

There are, in common use, a variety of *numbering systems* with which we are very familiar. For example, when measuring time we know that 60 seconds equal one minute, 60 minutes equal one hour and 24 hours equal one day. Again in linear measurements, twelve inches equal one foot, three feet equal one yard and so on. In money we know that two half-pence equal one pence and 100 pence equal £1.

In all of these systems a 'carry-over' occurs when a given number is reached:

45 secs + 30 secs	= 15 carry 1	= 1 min 15 secs.
8 ins + 9 ins	= 5 carry 1	= 1 foot 5 ins
£0·63p + £0·72p	= 35 carry 1	= £1·35p

The most commonly used of these is the *decimal* or *denary* system having a carry-over factor of 10. The value of each digit in a decimal expression is governed by its place in the expression. In the number 4695 we know that the right-most digit is equal to 5 units, the next left equals 9 tens, the next 6 hundreds and the left-most digit 4 thousands. Each digit then, reading from right to left, represents a multiple of a successively higher power of 10, where $10^0 = 1$, $10^1 = 10$, 10^2 (ten squared) $= 10 \times 10 = 100$ and so on.

$$4695 = (4 \times 10^3) + (6 \times 10^2) + (9 \times 10^1) + (5 \times 10^0)$$
$$= 4000 + 600 + 90 + 5 = 4695$$

Use of a number system based on 10 involves the use of a collection of 10 symbols, 0, 1, 2, 3, 4, 5, 6, 7, 8, 9.

The binary number system

In a computer the use of such a wide range of characters is inconvenient, and use is made of a range containing only two characters, 0 and 1. This is known as the *binary* system which, as a matter of fact we use every day when converting half-pence to new pence. For example $\frac{1}{2}p + \frac{1}{2}p + \frac{1}{2}p = 1$ carry $1 = 1\frac{1}{2}p$.

In a decimal system a carry-over occurs each time ten is reached and is indicated by moving a one to the left followed by a zero. In a binary system a carry-over occurs each time two is reached and is indicated in the same way by moving a one to the left followed by a zero.

In decimal $5 + 5 = 10$ (decimal ten)
In binary $1 + 1 = 10$ (decimal equivalent two) and
$1 + 1 + 1 = 1$ carry $1 = 11$ (decimal equivalent three)

In a decimal system place values increase by an additional power of 10 moving from right to left of an expression, in a binary system these place values increase by additional powers of 2.

Place values in a decimal system $10^4, 10^3, 10^2, 10^1, 10^0$.
Place values in a binary system $2^4, 2^3, 2^2, 2^1, 2^0$.
(remember, $2^0 = 1$, $2^1 = 2$, $2^2 = 4$, $2^3 = 8$ and so on)

This means that in the binary expression 11101, we have, reading from left to right:

$$(1 \times 2^4) + (1 \times 2^3) + (1 \times 2^2) + (0 \times 2^1) + (1 \times 2^0)$$
$$= \quad 16 \quad + \quad 8 \quad + \quad 4 \quad + \quad 0 \quad + \quad 1 \quad = \text{Decimal 29.}$$

Conversions from one notation to the other

Decimal to binary

The principle used here is to divide the decimal number successively by two until it is reduced to zero. Each time, when on division by two there is a remainder of one this one becomes a binary digit 1, and when the remainder is 0 this becomes a binary 0. The binary expression is built up from right to left.

Example: To convert decimal number 343 to binary.

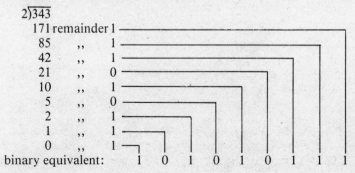

```
  2)343
   171 remainder 1
    85    ,,     1
    42    ,,     1
    21    ,,     0
    10    ,,     1
     5    ,,     0
     2    ,,     1
     1    ,,     1
     0    ,,     1
binary equivalent:    1   0   1   0   1   0   1   1   1
```

Binary to decimal

The decimal value of a binary expression is equal to the sum of the decimal values of the binary digits.

Example: To convert binary number 111011 to decimal.

$$\begin{array}{cccccc} 1 & 1 & 1 & 0 & 1 & 1 \end{array}$$
$$= 2^5 + 2^4 + 2^3 + 0 + 2^1 + 2^0$$
$$= 32 + 16 + 8 + 0 + 2 + 1 = \text{decimal } 59$$

Binary fractions

In a binary integer, successive places to the left increase in value by an additional positive power of two. In a binary fraction, successive places to the right decrease their value by an additional negative power of two.

binary fraction .1 $= 2^{-1}$ $= \frac{1}{2} = .5$ decimal fraction

.01 $= 2^{-2} = \dfrac{1}{2 \times 2}$ $= \frac{1}{4} = .25$,, ,,

.001 $= 2^{-3} \quad \dfrac{1}{2 \times 2 \times 2}$ $= \frac{1}{8} = .125$,, ,,

.0001 $= 2^{-4} = \dfrac{1}{2 \times 2 \times 2 \times 2}$ $= \frac{1}{16} = .0625$,, ,,

Conversion of decimal to binary fraction

Multiply the decimal fraction successively by two, counting each 10 carry-over as a binary 1, and if there is no carry-over count as a binary 0. Discard the carry-over for the purpose of the next multiplication. The binary expression is built up from left to right.

Example: To convert decimal fraction .625 to a binary fraction.

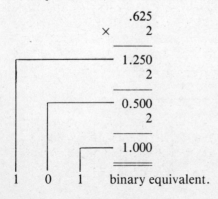

1   0   1   binary equivalent.

Conversion of binary fraction to decimal fraction

The decimal value of the binary expression is equal to the sum of the decimal values of the binary places.

Example: To convert binary fraction .1101 to a decimal fraction.

$$
\begin{array}{ll}
& 1 \quad\;\; 1 \quad\;\; 0 \quad 1 \\
= & 2^{-1} + \; 2^{-2} + 0 + 2^{-4} \\
= & \tfrac{1}{2} \;\; + \;\; \tfrac{1}{4} \;\; + 0 + \tfrac{1}{16} \\
= & \qquad\quad .8125 \text{ decimal fraction.}
\end{array}
$$

Calculations in binary

Addition

As, in the case of decimal addition, one is carried to the left each time ten is reached, so in the case of binary addition one is carried to the left each time two is reached. The simple rules are:

$$
\begin{aligned}
0 + 0 &= 0 \\
0 + 1 &= 1 \\
1 + 1 &= 0 \text{ carry } 1 \\
1 + 1 + 1 &= 1 \text{ carry } 1
\end{aligned}
$$

Example.

	decimal				binary			
	106	1	1	0	1	0	1	0
	+ 124	1	1	1	1	1	0	0
carry	1	1	1	1	1			
	230	1	1	1	0	0	1	0

Note a carry-over does not occur in this example until the fourth pair of binary digits from the right. Here $1 + 1$ equals 0 carry 1 and the carry 1 is the digit shown below the line under the fifth pair of digits. Here $0 + 1 +$ carry 1 equals 0 carry 1, the carry 1 being shown below the line under the sixth pair of digits where $1 + 1 + 1$ equals 1 carry 1, this pattern repeating itself for the seventh pair.

Subtraction

In decimal subtraction, when taking a larger number from a smaller number, one 'ten' is carried from the left and compensated for by adding one to the next left digit to be subtracted similarly in binary one 'two' is carried from the left and added back to the next left binary digit to be subtracted.

The simple rules are:

$0 - 0 = 0$
$1 - 0 = 1$
$1 - 1 = 0$
$0 - 1 = 1$ (carrying one 'two' from the left—then two minus one equals one)

Example:

decimal				binary				
150	1	0	0	1	0	1	1	0
108		1	1	0	1	1	0	0

carry	1	1	1	0	1			
42	0	0	1	0	1	0	1	0

Note a carry does not occur until the fourth pair of digits from the right when 1 is subtracted from 0. The fifth digit in the top row is brought into the fourth position where its value becomes 2. 1 from 2 equals 1, and the original 1 carried is added back below the line to the fifth position. With the sixth pair of digits the 1 has to be carried from the eighth position. It has a value of 2 in the seventh position one of which, on being carried, will also have a value of 2 in the sixth position.

Binary coded decimal

All of the binary numbers so far used have been expressed as one continuous string of binary digits or bits. This is generally referred to as *pure binary* or as *serial binary*. However, this is not the only way in which numbers can be stored in binary form in a computer.

Decimal	Binary			
1	0	0	0	1
2	0	0	1	0
3	0	0	1	1
4	0	1	0	0
5	0	1	0	1
6	0	1	1	0
7	0	1	1	1
8	1	0	0	0
9	1	0	0	1
0	0	0	0	0

Another method, known as *Binary Coded Decimal* (BCD), consists of encoding in binary each decimal digit separately, using four binary bits for each. Since there are only ten decimal digits, this gives a range of only ten different binary patterns, a combination of which can be used to represent any decimal number.

Place values in powers of 10 can then be given to these binary patterns depending on the position they hold within the decimal expression

Example:

Decimal		4	6	9	5
Binary coded decimal		0 1 0 0	0 1 1 0	1 0 0 1	0 1 0 1
Values:		4×10^3	6×10^2	9×10^1	5×10^0

Octal number system

It will be noticed that four binary bits in a group, within the range 0000–1001 are required to express a decimal digit within the decimal range 0–9. We can, however, within this range of four bits get 16 different patterns 0000–1111 which means that six of these patterns are not being used. If we reduce the number of bits from four to three we have the capacity to express a range of eight patterns equivalent to the decimal numbers 0–7, that is 000–111, and the whole range of patterns is being used. Expressing numbers using a radix of eight is known as an *octal* system, and when each digit within the octal number is expressed in binary we call it *binary coded octal*.

A decimal number can be converted to octal in much the same way as to binary, except that a division by 8 is used. Each digit within the octal expression can then, for computer storage, be expressed as a group of three binary bits.

Example: To convert 6190 to octal.

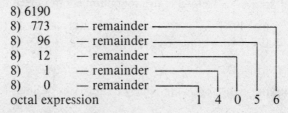

```
8) 6190
8)  773   — remainder
8)   96   — remainder
8)   12   — remainder
8)    1   — remainder
8)    0   — remainder
octal expression         1  4  0  5  6
```

In decimal terms this is now equal to:

$$(1 \times 8^4) + (4 \times 8^3) + \quad 0 \quad + (5 \times 8^1) + (6 \times 8^0)$$
$$= 4096 + 2048 + \quad 0 \quad + \quad 40 \quad + \quad 6 \quad = 6190$$

Expressed as binary coded octal it appears as:

001   100   000   101   110

Expression of alphabetic characters

In addition to numbers, the computer also has to cope with alphabetic characters and symbols. This means that each of these must be represented as a unique binary expression. There is no standard way of doing this in the sense there is a coding common to all makes of computer but the following illustrates one approach to the problem.

The 26 alphabetic characters are divided into three groups of 9, 9, and 8 consisting of A to I, J to R and S to Z respectively. Four binary digits are used to indicate the place of the letter within the group, for instance $A = 0001$ and $I = 1001$, and these are prefixed with two additional digits to show the group in which the letter occurs, say 01 for the first group, A to I, 10 for the second, J to S and 11 for the third, S to Z. This means that A equals 010001 and Z equals 111000.

However, using a four digit group in which there are sixteen different alternatives, 0000–1111, to record only nine different characters and using a two digit group to record only three different groups out of a possible four is a very wasteful process. In effect we are using six binary digits with a total of 64 variations to record a range of only 26 characters. Assuming we wish to use a 64 character set, ten numbers, 0–9, twenty-six letters, A–Z, and 28 different symbols, the obvious thing to do is to divide these into four groups of 16 each, use the 16 codings 0000–1111 to record the position within the group and the four alternatives 00–11 to indicate the group.

Exercises

1. Express the following decimal numbers in pure binary.

(a) 497   (e)   6.5
(b) 226   (f) 17.25
(c) 512   (g) 23.75
(d) 127   (h) 64.375

2. Express the following binary numbers in decimal form:

(a) 10001   (e)   10.1
(b) 101011   (f) 101.11
(c) 1111101   (g) 111.001
(d) 110011   (h) 100.101

3. What do you understand by Binary Coded Decimal? Express the following decimal numbers in BCD form.

   (a) 426
   (b) 814
   (c) 5865
   (d) 17893

4. Carry out the following additions in binary.

   (a) 11101 + 10110
   (b) 1110110 + 111111
   (c) 10101 + 110011 + 11101
   (d) 111011 + 10110 + 11111

5. Carry out the following subtractions in binary.

   (a) 11011 − 1010
   (b) 101010 − 1111
   (c) 1000100 − 101101
   (d) 1100110 − 11011

6. Express the following decimal numbers as octal expressions.

   (a) 6947
   (b) 1365
   (c) 8000

7. Show how the following octal expressions could be expressed by using binary digits:

   (a) 1745
   (b) 6702
   (c) 3645

8. Give an account of a way in which alphabetic characters could be expressed in binary for computer storage.

4

Computer input

As we saw in Chapter 2 it is, unfortunately, usually not possible to feed data into a computer in the form that it originates. It must first be converted into a form that is 'machine acceptable'. This means that data must be recorded on a medium that is physically acceptable, for example a card of standard size and thickness, or a paper tape of standard width and also that the mode in which the data is recorded must be recognizable to the machine. Broadly speaking, input data falls into the following groups:

(a) Where neither the original document is acceptable to the machine, nor the mode in which data is recorded. For example, a handwritten entry in a goods received book. In this case data must be transcribed onto a medium and into a form that is acceptable, such as *punched cards* or *punched paper tape*.
(b) Where the original document and the mode of recording are both machine acceptable. For example, data recorded in *magnetic ink characters* or *optical characters* on a document that the machine is able to handle.
(c) Where the original document is acceptable but the form of recording is not, involving a conversion to a machine-readable form using the same document. Examples of this are *mark sensing* on *punched cards*.
(d) Where there is no need to use a document as such to record the data before transferring it to the computer but where the data can be read in direct from a key-board machine, such as a *teletype terminal*.

We are now going to deal with these forms of computer input in greater detail.

Punched cards

A punched card is a piece of high quality cardboard made to an exact size and standard thickness. The accuracy of its dimensions is critical

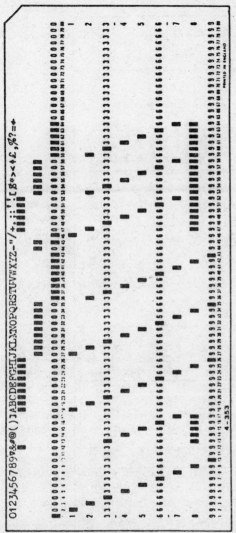

Figure 4.1   An 80-col punched card, with ICL 64
character card code (ICL Ltd)

for machine processing. Several sizes of card have been commonly
used in the past but the size in most general use for computer input
purposes is the 80 column card illustrated in Figure 4.1.

The card is divided into 80 vertical columns, each column having
twelve positions into which holes may be punched. Each column on

SYMBOL	CARD PUNCHING	SYMBOL	CARD PUNCHING	SYMBOL	CARD PUNCHING	SYMBOL	CARD PUNCHING
0	0	] RIGHT BRACKET	7/8	Q	11/8	' APOSTROPHE	10/6/8
1	1	A	10/1	R	11/9	! EXCLAMATION	10/7/8
2	2	B	10/2	S	0/2	[LEFT BRACKET	11/2/8
3	3	C	10/3	T	0/3	$ DOLLAR	11/3/8
4	4	D	10/4	U	0/4	* ASTERISK	11/4/8
5	5	E	10/5	V	0/5	> GREATER THAN	11/5/8
6	6	F	10/6	W	0/6	< LESS THAN	11/6/8
7	7	G	10/7	X	0/7	↑	11/7/8
8	8	H	10/8	Y	0/8	£ POUND	0/2/8
9	9	I	10/9	Z	0/9	, COMMA	0/3/8
SPACE	NONE	J	11/1	— MINUS HYPHEN	11	% PERCENTAGE	0/4/8
& AMPERSAND	10 OR 10/0	K	11/2	'' QUOTES	11/6	? QUESTION	0/5/8
# NUMBER	3/8	L	11/3	/ SOLIDUS	0/1	= EQUALS	0/6/8
⊕	4/8	M	11/4	+ PLUS	10/2/8	↓	0/7/8
(LEFT PARENTHESIS	5/8	N	11/5	. STOP	10/3/8		
) RIGHT PARENTHESIS	6/8	O	11/6	; SEMI-COLON	10/4/8		
		P	11/7	: COLON	10/5/8		

Figure 4.2   64 character card punching code (ICL Ltd)

the card can record one character, a number, a letter or a symbol by means of a pattern of one, two or three holes unique to each character. These patterns of holes representing characters are known as a *punching code*. This code varies slightly from manufacturer to manufacturer.

For recording the digits 0 to 9, each is represented by a single hole in the relevant position in the column. For example, the figures 0–9 are punched into columns 1 to 10 in Figure 4.1.

Representing letters creates a little more difficulty since there are 26 in our alphabet but only twelve punching positions in each column. This problem is solved by dividing the alphabet into three groups of 9, 9 and 8 letters each, A–I, J–R and S–Z. The group in which the letter occurs is indicated in one of the three top punching positions, while the remaining nine positions show the numeric position of the letter within the group. For example, the letter D, the fourth letter in the first group, will be indicated by holes in the 10 and 4 positions on the card. In the third group, however, since there are only eight letters, the punching positions 2 to 9 are usually used. The coding V, the fourth letter in the third group, being 0 and 5. In the illustration, the alphabet is punched into columns 18–43 in Figure 4.1.

Not only can numeric and alphabetical information be recorded but also a range of symbols each having its own unique pattern of holes. A number of these symbols are shown in columns 11–17 and 44–64 in Figure 4.1. An example of a complete 64-character punching code is given in Figure 4.2.

Preparation of punched cards

Cards may be prepared in a number of ways:

(a) By an operator reading the data from an original document, converting it into the required punching code and entering it through the keyboard of a card punch machine.

(b) On a card punch machine, by reading data that has been recorded on the card itself in another form (e.g. printing or handwriting), converting this into the required punching code and entering through a keyboard. These are known as *dual purpose cards*.

(c) By marking, at source, the position on a card where holes are to be punched in such a way that a machine will read the marks and punch holes automatically wherever the marks occur. This process is known as *mark sensing*.

Card punch

This machine consists essentially of a keyboard, a hopper containing a supply of blank cards, a punching mechanism to perforate the cards and a stacker to accept cards after they have been punched. The cards are automatically fed from the hopper, and progress column by column past a position where twelve punching knives are situated, one for each vertical position on the card. These knives cut holes in the card as information is entered on the keyboard. The card is then transferred to the stacker while a new card takes its place. In older types of card punch, keyboards contain only twelve keys representing the twelve punching positions on the card and it is necessary for the operator to convert data on the source document to the relevant punching code before depressing the keys. However, modern types of keyboard contain keys for a full range of characters and the machine automatically makes the conversion to the punching code.

Dual purpose cards

While the same type of machine as outlined above is used for punching, the source data is written in ordinary characters in defined positions on the cards themselves rather than on separate documents. The data can be read by the operator and keyed in to the machine. It should be mentioned that when the card is moved from the hopper preparatory to being perforated, it still remains visible to the operator. Cards of this type are usually designed so that the written data will not be obliterated by the punching.

Organization of data on punched cards

As we have seen, the basic principle used in punched cards is to give each vertical position a predetermined value and to encode all the information we wish to present in terms of these values. The same principle applies to the 80 columns along the length of the card. To make sense of all the punched holes we must give each column a predetermined meaning. For instance, if we wish to represent the following information on a card:

Reference number   Description   Quantity   Value

We must allocate a fixed number of columns to contain the reference number, a fixed number to contain the description and so on. These groups of columns on the card are known as *fields* and are usually distinguished from each other by printing vertical lines on the card and a field heading e.g. 'Description' at the top of the group of columns. The whole of the information indicated above and consisting of four data fields is known as a *data record*. When a card holds one such record only it is usually known as a *unit-record* or a *single-record* card. Under certain circumstances, however, it may be possible to hold two or more records on a single card, when we usually refer to the cards as *spread* or *multi-record* cards.

Accuracy of punched cards

An essential of any input medium is the need for complete accuracy, otherwise the results obtained from processing will obviously be unreliable. In order to ensure the correct transcription of data from source documents to punched cards, a process known as *verification* is carried out. The cards, having been punched once from the source documents by one operator are then passed to a second operator who punches them again from the same documents. If, on the second punching, a hole already exists in the position keyed-in, the card is released. If, however, no hole exists, it means that different characters have been punched by the two operators. The operators attention is drawn to the difference, a check made to see which is correct and the card repunched if necessary. It is important that cards repunched to correct errors should in turn be verified to ensure the accuracy of the correction.

Punched card reading

The accuracy of the cards having been ensured, it is now necessary to transfer the data contained on them to the store of the computer. This is accomplished by a *card reader* which senses the pattern of holes in each column of the card, and converts these into a series of electronic pulses. The pulses are in turn either stored in binary form in the computer's central processor or passed from the processor to some other form of storage device such as magnetic tape or magnetic disc (Figure 4.3).

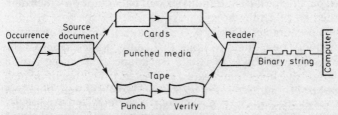

Figure 4.3   Source to machine conversion

The card reader consists of a hopper into which the cards are fed, a reading station, a mechanism for transferring cards through the machine, and a stacker into which cards are deposited after reading. The card is passed between a light source and a row of photo-electric cells, one for each punching position on the card. Where there is a hole the light penetrates the card causing a charge to be set up in the cell corresponding to the position of the hole. The position and pattern of the cells in which charges occur are recognized by the machine and translated into the appropriate electronic pulses for transmission to the store of the computer.

While the cards have already been verified to ensure that they have been correctly punched, an additional check is necessary in the card reader to guard against misreading. This is done by including a *checking station* in the reader in addition to the reading station. The checking station reads cards a second time during their progress through the machine, the data from each reading being compared before release to the computer store. One way of doing this is to add the number of holes in the card at the reading station and record this number in a register. The holes are then added again at the checking station and put into the same register as a minus quantity. If, at this point, the content of the register is zero the data from the card is transferred into storage; if not, the card is rejected. Another method is to take the total of values of the holes in to the register and to release the data in the same way if a zero total is obtained.

Card reading speeds vary from machine to machine from about 300 cards a minute in the older slower types of reader to more than 1500 cards a minute in newer faster machines. An average reading rate would probably be in the neighbourhood of 900–1000 cards a minute giving a maximum character reading rate of around 1300 characters per second, although of course the effective reading rate will depend on the number of characters contained on the cards.

Punched paper tape

Punched paper tape is a continuous strip of paper tape on which data is recorded by punching holes across its width. Each row of holes represents a character (Figure 4.4), the pattern for each character being unique. The number of holes that can be punched across the tape varies from system to system. 5-track tape, that is tape using a maximum of five holes to indicate a character, is 11/16th of an inch wide, and 6-, 7-, and 8-track 1 inch wide. However, most modern paper tape readers use 7- or 8-track tape with a standard character code of 64 or 128 characters. The Figure 4.5 shows a complete 128 character punching code.

The number of tracks on a tape will determine the number of unique hole patterns that can be used to represent different characters. On 5-track tape this number is 32, and on 6-track tape 64. Since 32 different combinations of holes are insufficient for the range of characters needed, on 5-track tape, two characters are allocated the same hole pattern and a special 'shift' code inserted to

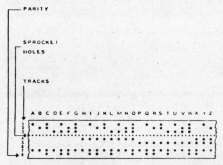

Figure 4.4   Punched 8-track (7 data bit) paper tape (ICL Ltd)

indicate which character is meant. For instance, a number and a letter have the same punching code. To distinguish between them, before the code representing the number is punched into the tape a figure shift code is inserted, and before the same code representing a letter is punched, a letter shift code is inserted. The shift code need only be used when changing from one set of characters to the other. This problem does not arise on 6-track tape where 64 different hole patterns are available.

On 7- and 8-track tape, one track is used exclusively for checking purposes, leaving 6 and 7 tracks respectively for recording characters. Thus 7-track tape will accommodate 64 different characters, and 8-track tape 128. The track used for checking purposes is known as a *parity* track, and its purpose is to provide a further safeguard against errors caused by faulty transcription of data. A hole is punched in the parity track where necessary to ensure either that every complete pattern of holes consists of an odd number of holes (known as an 'odd parity check') or that every pattern consists of an even number of holes (an 'even parity check'). These parity holes are automatically inserted during the punching process. When the tape is being read, a check is made on each pattern to ensure that it conforms to the correct principle. If this is not so—if, for instance, a pattern with an even number of holes is found in a tape using the 'odd parity' check system—the presence of an error is signalled, and an investigation must be made.

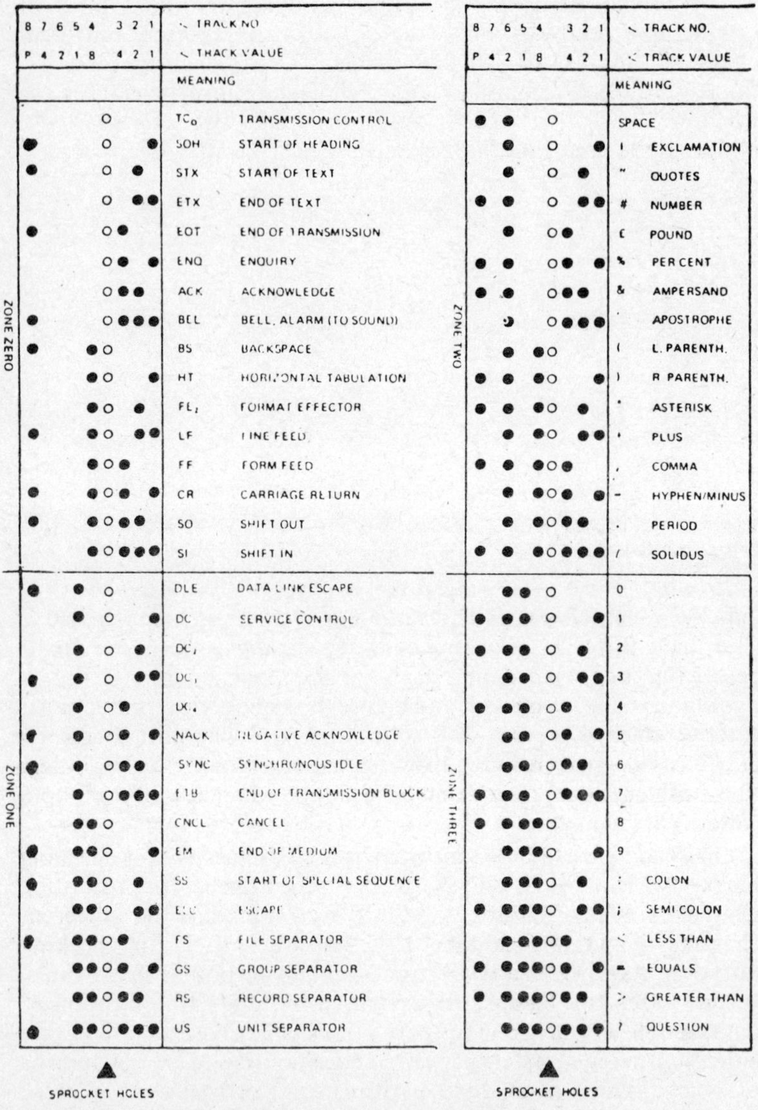

Figure 4.5   8-track (7 data bit) 128 character punching code

The figure tabulates the 8-track (7 data bit) punching code. Track numbers are 8 7 6 5 4 3 2 1 with track values P 4 2 1 8 4 2 1.

Code	Meaning		Code	Meaning
TC$_0$	TRANSMISSION CONTROL			SPACE
SOH	START OF HEADING		!	EXCLAMATION
STX	START OF TEXT		"	QUOTES
ETX	END OF TEXT		#	NUMBER
EOT	END OF TRANSMISSION		£	POUND
ENQ	ENQUIRY		%	PER CENT
ACK	ACKNOWLEDGE		&	AMPERSAND
BEL	BELL, ALARM (TO SOUND)		'	APOSTROPHE
BS	BACKSPACE		(	L. PARENTH.
HT	HORIZONTAL TABULATION		)	R PARENTH.
FE$_1$	FORMAT EFFECTOR		*	ASTERISK
LF	LINE FEED		+	PLUS
FF	FORM FEED		,	COMMA
CR	CARRIAGE RETURN		-	HYPHEN/MINUS
SO	SHIFT OUT		.	PERIOD
SI	SHIFT IN		/	SOLIDUS
DLE	DATA LINK ESCAPE		0	
DC	SERVICE CONTROL		1	
DC$_2$			2	
DC$_3$			3	
DC$_4$			4	
NACK	NEGATIVE ACKNOWLEDGE		5	
SYNC	SYNCHRONOUS IDLE		6	
ETB	END OF TRANSMISSION BLOCK		7	
CNCL	CANCEL		8	
EM	END OF MEDIUM		9	
SS	START OF SPECIAL SEQUENCE		:	COLON
ESC	ESCAPE		;	SEMI COLON
FS	FILE SEPARATOR		<	LESS THAN
GS	GROUP SEPARATOR		=	EQUALS
RS	RECORD SEPARATOR		>	GREATER THAN
US	UNIT SEPARATOR		?	QUESTION

ZONE ZERO / ZONE ONE (left), ZONE TWO / ZONE THREE (right)

SPROCKET HOLES

Preparation of punched paper tape

A paper tape punch is a keyboard machine in which blank paper tape is fed from a reel, through a punching position on to a take-up reel.

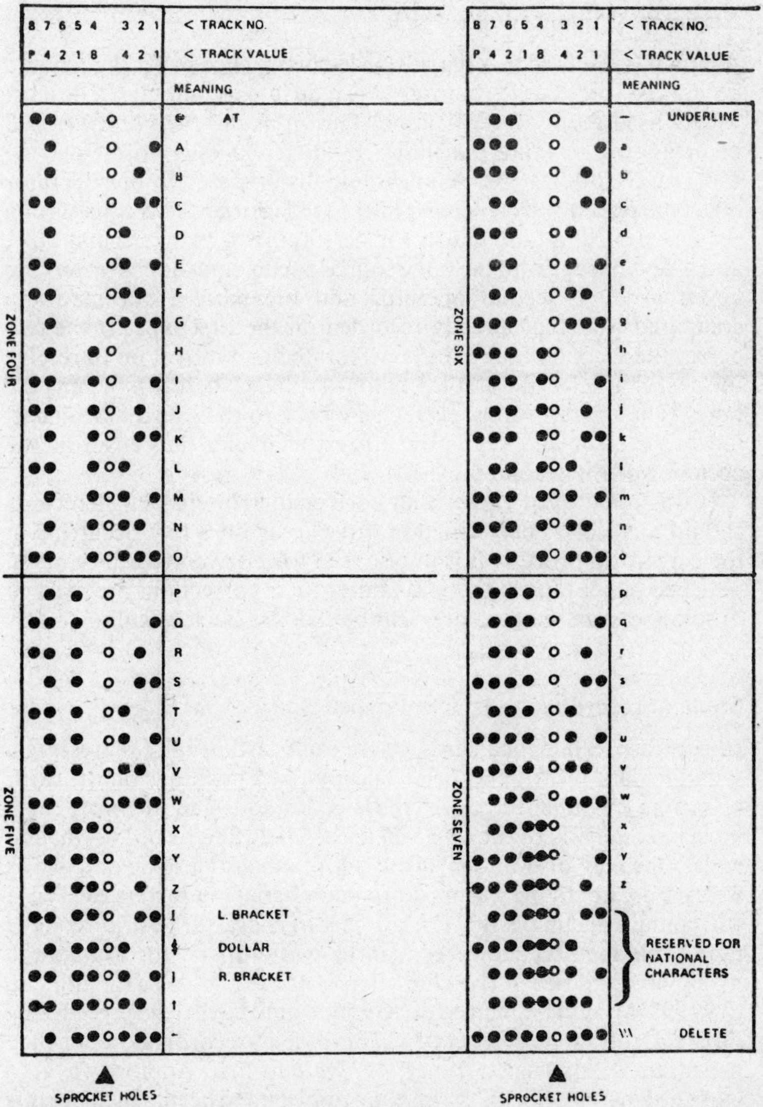

8 7 6 5 4 3 2 1	< TRACK NO.	8 7 6 5 4 3 2 1	< TRACK NO.
P 4 2 1 8 4 2 1	< TRACK VALUE	P 4 2 1 8 4 2 1	< TRACK VALUE
	MEANING		MEANING

Figure 4.5 (*cont.*)

The keyboard contains keys for the whole range of characters needed and, as each key is depressed, the machine automatically selects the correct pattern of holes to indicate a character and perforates the tape accordingly.

Accuracy of punched paper tape

Again, it is essential that data recorded in punched paper tape should be verified for accuracy before being read into a computer. The most widely-used form of verification, known as the *two-tape method*, involves two separate punchings by different operators from the same source documents. A tape is initially prepared by one operator on a tape punch and is then fed into a *tape verifier*. This consists of a reading device, a tape punch for perforating a blank second tape, and a keyboard. From the same source documents the characters are keyed in by a second operator and the pattern automatically compared with that already recorded on the first tape. If the two agree, the second blank tape is perforated and moves on to receive the next character, if not, the keyboard will lock before punching the holes. The operator must then check back to the source document, locate the error and key in the correct character thus ensuring the accuracy of the second tape.

It was mentioned earlier that corrected errors in punched cards should themselves be verified in order to avoid errors occurring in the correction process. It is impractical to verify corrected errors in punched paper tape in this way, but if these corrections are marked in some way on the tape they can be checked back visually.

Mode of recording on punched paper tape

In contrast to punched cards where each card usually represents a separate data record and fields occupy fixed positions on the card, recording on punched paper tape is continuous and therefore there must be some way of showing where each field and record begins and ends. One way of doing this is to adopt much the same practice as with cards, i.e. fixing the maximum number of characters each field will contain and allocating this number of character positions on the tape. This method, however, can be wasteful. If, for example, a maximum field size of five characters is needed, giving a quantity up to 99 999, an actual quantity of, say 56, would have to be preceded by three insignificant zeros, 00056. This type of recording on punched paper tape is known as a *fixed field length* format. Another way is to vary the lengths of fields to suit the actual data to be punched but this means, of course, that fields must be separated by some kind of marker. In the above example, instead of five character positions, of which three are insignificant zeros, only three positions would be needed of which one would hold an *end of field marker*. This is known as a *variable field length* format. In practice it is found that some fields, by nature of the data, are of fixed length, for example account number or stock item number, while others are variable, for example description, quantity, value etc. The use of a fixed field length for fixed length data provides a validity check by ensuring that the correct number of characters are present in, say, an account number. It is common practice to use both of these formats in order to combine the best features of each. This is known as a *fixed-variable field length* format. Items containing a constant number of characters are treated as fixed length fields, and data items in which the number of characters vary are treated as variable-length fields.

Punched paper tape reading

A paper tape reader consists of a feed reel, a mechanism to move the tape through the machine, and a reading station. The method of reading is by photo-electric cells and a light source between which the tape passes. Charges are set up in the cells as light penetrates the tape, and are transmitted for storage to the computer's central processor.

In modern paper tape readers, reading speed varies from around 1000 to 2000 characters per second.

Comparisons between punched cards and punched paper tape

(a) Speed of reading   There is little to choose between the two. The fastest tape and card readers available both have reading speeds around 2000 characters per second.

(b) Preparation   Key operated punches used for both cards and tape. Cards can be mark sensed for automatic punching. Card verification more positive.

(c) Cost   While both punching and verifying processes use the same card, at least two separate tapes have to be prepared. However, volume for volume of data, punched paper tape is cheaper.

(d) Flexibility   Punched cards can be renewed, replaced and rearranged in any required sequence. Tape is more rigid in that once it has been prepared the order of the data items cannot be altered and additions or deletions cannot easily be made. Cards, however, have fixed length fields. This is less flexible and more wasteful than the variable-length field facility offered by punched paper tape.

(e) Security   While strict controls should be imposed on the use and storage of both forms of input, it is easier for a punched card to go astray than a section of a reel of punched tape.

Key to magnetic tape/disc systems

Having established the need to interpose between the source document and the computer a data preparation process that will convert the data into a machine acceptable and readable form such as punched cards or paper tape, it will be conceded that this is a very time-consuming and laborious process. In an attempt to overcome some of the disadvantages inherent in these purely mechanical processes, methods have been devised over the past few years of writing data from source documents direct to magnetic media which can then, in turn, be read in to the computer at a far faster rate than punched media.

Key to tape

In principle, this consists of a keyboard very similar to an ordinary typewriter keyboard, a magnetic tape unit and a buffer store in which the data can be temporarily held after keying in but before it is written to the magnetic tape. While we have not up until now considered magnetic tape in any detail—this will be dealt with in a later chapter—sufficient to say at the moment that the mode of recording can be likened to that of punched paper tape except that the frame, representing a character is not recorded as punched holes but as a pattern of small magnetized areas.

An operator, reading from the source documents, will enter the data through the keyboard from where it will be entered into the unit's buffer store. Any obvious errors during this process can be corrected by back-spacing and re-typing. Some systems incorporate a cathode ray tube display unit on which a block of data can be displayed as it is typed and a visual check for its accuracy made. The block of data may then be transferred from the buffer store to the magnetic tape. A positive verification procedure is incorporated by re-winding the tape, transferring the data back a block at a time to the buffer store, and keying the source data in for a second time by a different operator. The original record and the second entry are now compared much in the same way as punched tape and any error state signalled for correction. Key to tape systems have been developed using magnetic tape cassettes rather than the conventional magnetic tape used in main-frame computer systems. This makes loading and handling the tape much more convenient although, of course, being fairly short a cassette tape has less capacity. The data on these cassette tapes can then be transferred to the conventional computer tape system ready for computer processing.

Advantages claimed in the use of key-to-tape systems are:

(1) It is faster than punched card or tape systems because it is less mechanical.
(2) A magnetic tape can be used over and over again whereas a card or paper tape can be used once only.
(3) Easy error correction and verification procedures.
(4) A much quieter process than punching cards or tape.
(5) Less storage space is required for magnetic tape than cards and paper tape.

Key-to-disc

This is a further method of entering data from a source document direct to a magnetic medium but this time to a magnetic disc. While again we have not considered magnetic discs in any detail, perhaps for the moment it is sufficient to say that data is recorded as small magnetized dots in tracks on the disc surface.

While from an operator's point of view, a key-to-disc system is similar in many respects to a key-to-tape system, it is, however, a rather more sophisticated system in two major respects:

(1) A number of operators at key-board stations (32 would not be unusual) can simultaneously key data which is passed through a minicomputer to one magnetic disc unit (see Figure 4.6).
(2) A validation program can be held in the minicomputer to check

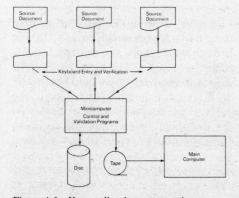

Figure 4.6   Key-to-disc data preparation

the validity of field and record formats, i.e. to check that each data item contains the right number and type of characters. It will also check that quantitative data falls within preset limits, perform check digit verification tests and generate batch totals for reconciliation with previously determined source document batch totals. This validation procedure has the advantage that fully validated data is eventually entered into the computer so saving time on main computer runs.

A key-to-disc system then consists of

(1) A number of keyboard devices for entering source data.
(2) A minicomputer in which are control and validation programs.
(3) A magnetic disc drive.
(4) A magnetic tape deck used for transferring the data from the disc to the main computer.

A typical key-to-disc data preparation routine is as follows.

(1) First operator reads from source documents keying in information through a keyboard.
(2) Information probably displayed on the display unit for visual checking when any obvious errors can be corrected.
(3) Validation checks carried out by minicomputer.
(4) Block of data written to disc.
(5) Second operator performs the verification process by retrieving data from disc and keying in for a second time the original data from source documents. Errors coming to light are corrected.
(6) Verified data written back to disc.
(7) At end of run, data on disc transferred to tape for entry to main computer.

Direct data input

Methods of computer input we have so far discussed, each involve two distinct stages: (a) preparation of a source document; and (b) the manual transfer of data, through a keyboard, to punched cards, punched tape or magnetic media.

It is evident that a great deal of time and expense would be saved if the information contained in the source document itself could be read directly into the computer. Two conditions are necessary to accomplish this. Firstly, the document itself must be machine acceptable, and, secondly, the data must be recorded in a machine understandable form.

Four ways of preparing input data to meet these requirements are mark sensing, optical mark reading, magnetic ink character recognition and optical character recognition.

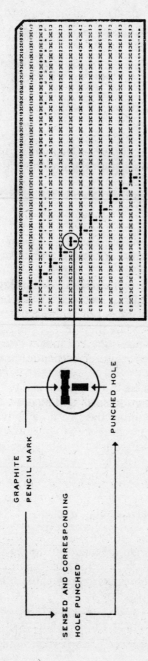

Figure 4.7   A mark sensing card (ICL Ltd)

Mark sensing

This is an application of the use of punched cards in which columns of digits 0–9 are pre-printed and each digit enclosed in a pair of brackets (Figure 4.7). Data is recorded by making a stroke through the digit and between the two brackets with a soft graphite pencil. The cards are then passed through an automatic high speed punch which will 'sense' or 'read' the position of the marks and punch holes in the same places. While this method has the advantage of obviating the need to punch the card manually, in practice a major disadvantage is the limitation in the range of characters that can be conveniently marked to those needing one mark only i.e. numeric information.

Mark reading

In principle, this is much the same as mark sensing which is usually associated with punched card systems as a means of providing for the automatic punching of holes.

Defined positions on a mark reading document are given pre-determined values and data is recorded by marking the relevant positions in black ink or black pencil. The machine will, through an optical scanning process, locate these marks and assign to them the value determined by their position. A number of vertical columns of figures are printed on the form each with a dot immediately above and below it.

These vertical columns are in turn grouped into fields, each field for recording one data item. Recording is by drawing a vertical line through the characters joining the two dots above and below. It should be noted that it is not necessary to print the vertical columns of figures in a special optical character fount, as it is not the shape of the character that determines the value but its position. An example of an Optical Mark Reading document is shown in Figure 4.8.

Magnetic ink character recognition (MICR)

This system is based on the use of a stylized set of characters printed in an ink containing a ferro-magnetic substance. This ink can be magnetized and subsequently detected and recognized by a machine.

The two most important founts at present in use are the E13B and the CMC7, the former originating in the USA and the latter of French origin. The E13B fount is most generally used in this country while the CMC7 fount is more widely used in European countries. Examples of these founts are given in Figure 4.9.

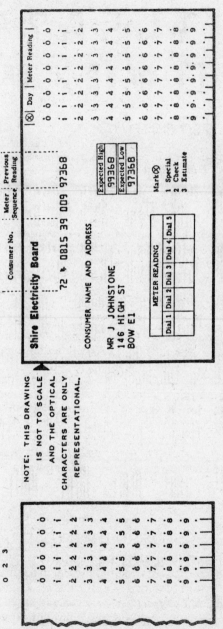

Figure 4.8   OCR mark reading document (ICL Ltd)

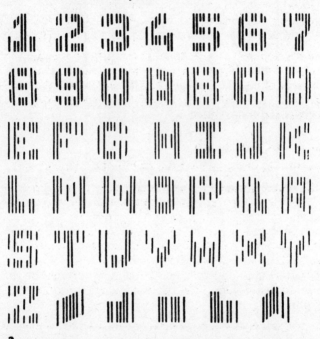

The *E 13 B* *fount*

The *C.M.C. 7* *fount*

Figure 4.9   Examples of magnetic ink characters (ICL Ltd)

(1) The E13B fount.
     The ferro-magnetic content of the ink having been magnetized,
     the characters are passed over a reading head where the
     magnetism induces a current in the reading circuit.
        Since the induced current will be proportional to the
     magnetized area passing the head, a varying current will be
     produced determined by the shape of the character. By
     comparing the pattern of this current with standards built into
     the machine's circuitry, it can be recognized as representing a
     given character.
(2) The CMC7 fount.
     Each character is built up of seven lines so as to give spaces of
     different widths between any two lines. Recognition of the
     character is by conversion into binary code in which a wide space
     represents a binary one and a narrow space a binary zero.

The main development of MICR using E13B fount has been in
banking and the tendency has been to develop specialized machines
to meet the needs of banking systems. The use of MICR in banking
systems has been restricted to a range of 14 characters only, ten
numerical digits and four symbols.

Preparation of MICR documents

Basic considerations in the preparation of MICR documents are

(1) Since the source document is also the input form, its size must
     fall within the tolerances imposed by the machine used for
     processing.
(2) The successful reading of the characters depends on the accurate
     reproduction of the character shape and constant ink density.
     This necessitates very high quality printing.
(3) The characters must appear in pre-determined positions on the
     document to ensure their correct positioning at the reading head
     during processing.

There are two stages at which the magnetic ink characters may be
encoded on the document. The first of these is after the document
has been printed but before it is used. This necessarily is limited to
non-variable data such as, in the case of cheques, the cheque
number, the branch reference number and the customer account
number. This is known as *pre-encoding*.
   The second stage occurs after the variable data has been entered
which, in the case of cheques, would be after completion by the
drawer. This is known as *post-encoding*. The method used is to pass
the cheques one by one through a keyboard machine where it

remains visible while the operator reads the data and keys it in. The cheque then passes through the machine where the characters are printed in magnetic ink. As a precaution against error the machine adds the quantitative data and gives a total for a batch of documents at the end of a run. This can then be checked against a total prepared by pre-listing before the documents were processed.

MICR reading

As was mentioned earlier, the main development in the use of MICR has been for processing cheques. This entails two main functions, sorting the cheques into some pre-determined order, say branch order for distribution back to branches, and summarizing the amounts on the cheques to give listings and control totals. These two operations are carried out on MICR Sorter/Reader. Speed of sorting and reading is round about 1200 documents a minute, which on a basis of a maximum of 75 characters on each cheque, gives a reading rate of 1500 characters a second.

Optical character recognition (OCR)

This is another way of encoding data direct on to a source document but one that relies solely upon the shape of the characters and is not dependent upon the properties possessed by the ink. It is, therefore, far more adaptable in that OCR documents can be prepared by a variety of devices such as typewriters, accounting machines, cash registers and indeed a computer printer itself provided, of course, the device is fitted with a special OCR typeface. These characters are not as stylized as those required for MICR and so are more easily read by human sight. An illustration of an Optical Character typeface is given in figure 4.10.

1234567890-*.

1234567890-*.

Figure 4.10   An OCR fount

Preparation of OCR documents

The object is the same as that of using magnetic characters: to produce a document at source that is both machine acceptable and machine readable. The same considerations relating to document size, quality of printing and character positioning apply.

   Optical recognition characters may be inscribed on the documents in the following ways. Non-variable data may be included when the document is initially printed. Variable data is added by a keyboard machine or a mark sensing process. The line printer used for computer output may print characters which can be optically recognized by the input devices. Combinations of these methods may be used, for example, in a meter reading system. Documents are prepared on the computer printer in OCR characters, containing the customer's name and address, reference number, and previous meter reading. The meter reader will enter the current reading in the mark reading area of the document which is then passed back through the computer system. The computer calculates the quantity used and prepares the bill together with a new document to be used at the next meter reading. In this example the document produced is both the output of, and input form used by the computer, and is known as a *turn-around* document.

Reading of OCR characters

Optical characters and marks are both read by being scanned by an artificial light source.

During character reading, as each individual character is scanned, the reflected light is passed through a lens system and focused on a photo-electric cell. This produces a current from the cell which varies in proportion to the amount of light reflected from the dark and light areas of the character. The wave form representing this variable current, unique for each different character, is recognized by comparing it with standard patterns in the electronic circuitry of the machine.

During mark reading, there is a photo-electric cell for each position in the vertical column. The column is scanned from a light source and a mark in any particular position will trigger off a response in the appropriate cell. This is automatically converted into a series of binary pulses representing the value of the position marked.

As with MICR, one disadvantage of optical character recognition is that it is impossible to verify individual characters, so a great deal of care must be exercised when using this system. With the most up-to-date machines reading speeds for OCR documents can be up to 3000 characters per second.

Data transmission

In all of the input methods we have so far discussed we have assumed two things. Firstly, that data originates on a source document, that these documents are collected together in batches and that the data is then converted into a machine acceptable medium. Secondly, that all this takes place in close proximity to the computer. Now these two considerations may not always apply. Data may originate a considerable distance from the computer and have to be conveyed to it by one means or another, and on the other hand we may want to enter just one isolated item of data at a time. For example, we may wish to ask the computer a question "What is the balance on A B Jones' account"?

The process of conveying information over distances from its source to a computer is known as *data transmission*. Strictly speaking this term has been associated with three different methods:

(1) When data is physically transferred from source to a computer installation. For example, when a punched paper tape is prepared at a remote point and sent by courier to the computer centre.

(2) When communication lines are used to transmit data to an off-line machine at the computer centre. For example, when data is transmitted to a paper punch which will prepare a punched tape for future entry to the computer.

(3) When data is transmitted over communication lines and is entered directly into the computer. In this case, we say the transmitting device is *on-line* (Figure 4.11).

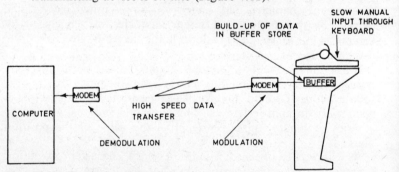

Figure 4.11   Terminal–computer link-up

However, the term data transmission is generally accepted as referring to a situation where telecommunication lines are used between the point of data origin and the computer. We saw earlier in this chapter that when data is prepared in punched form, on passing through a reader, the coded holes are converted into a series of electrical pulses known as binary bits which are, in turn, stored in the computer. Data transmission is basically an extension of this principle applied to greater distances. Transmission is by means of communication lines and it will be appreciated that the time taken to transmit a given volume of data will depend on the operating efficiency of the medium over which it is transmitted. The unit used to define the rate of transmission is known as a *baud*. A baud represents the transference of one bit per second.

Transmission lines

Data transmission usually makes use of the Post Office public telegraph or telephone networks, although, in some cases, private direct lines are used. Transmission can also take place by the use of radio links including communication satellites.

The use of telegraph lines, known as the Post Office Datel 100 service, is not generally regarded as a suitable transmission medium for computer data. As the title indicates, the speed of transmission is slow, 100 baud, and generally speaking transmission is of a relatively low quality. The Post Office telephone network offers a faster and more reliable medium at varying speeds. These are known as Datel 200, 300, 600, 2400 and 4800 services. The numbers indicate the maximum transmission speeds in baud. The transmitting device is linked to the telephone network by means of a Post Office device called a *modem*, an abbreviation of 'Modulator–demodulator'. Modulation is the process of converting the digital data (i.e. data in binary form) to an analogue representation for transmission. Demodulation is the technique of reversing this process at the computer end. It is, therefore, necessary to have modems at both ends of the link (Figure 4.11).

Another way of transmitting data, although this works at a slow input/output rate is by the use of a device known as an *acoustic coupler*. In this case, an ordinary telephone instrument is inverted into a cradle designed for this purpose which is an integral part of the

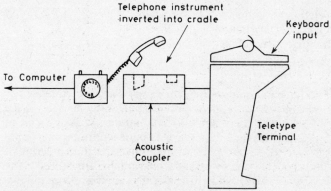

Figure 4.12   Use of an acoustic coupler with terminal

terminal. The digital signals are converted into audio signals and transmitted over the line in much the same way as are audio signals. At the computer end they are converted back to digital pulses ready for entry to the computer. Transmission by acoustic coupler has two major disadvantages (a) low transmission rate, with a maximum effective rate of 200 baud; (b) the danger of data becoming corrupted by extraneous noise picked up on the system. However, one major advantage is evident in that acoustic coupling can be used direct with any standard telephone instrument thus permitting the use of portable terminals (Figure 4.12).

Transmitting modes

There are three telecommunication modes known as *simplex, half-duplex* and *duplex* (often known as *full-duplex*).

Simplex lines transmit data in only one direction. This is suitable where the terminal is being used solely as an input device to the computer and there is no need for results to be transmitted back to the terminal.

Half-duplex lines enable data to be transmitted in either direction but in only one direction at a time. A short pause is incurred when the transmitting direction is reversed.

Duplex or full duplex lines permit data to be transmitted in both directions simultaneously.

Computer terminals

Essentially, most computer terminals have a dual function in that they can be used for both input and output purposes. While there is an extensive range of terminals available they can, broadly speaking, be classified into the following main categories:

> Teletype terminals
> Visual display units
> Intelligent terminals
> Batch processing terminals
> Specialized terminals

These all have in common that they can be connected on-line by transmission line direct to a computer.

Teletype terminal

By far the most widely used type of terminal, this consists of a keyboard similar to a typewriter into which data can be entered manually. The keyboard contains not only the usual range of alphanumeric characters but also a number of *command keys* through which instructions may be conveyed to the computer. The terminal also incorporates a printing device so that data entered through the keyboard will be reproduced in hard copy form and will also record information transmitted back from the computer to the terminal.

By definition, a teletype single-character serial printer is a slow input/output device with a maximum speed of around 300 characters per minute. It will be appreciated that if data is transmitted to the computer as and when it is keyed in, the computer will be tied up for comparatively long periods of time working at a rate far below its capacity. To get round this problem a small memory store is usually incorporated into the terminal which will accept and hold data as it is keyed in. When the computer is ready to receive this data it can then be transferred at high speed in bulk. This memory device is known as a *buffer*. This gives us a situation where a number of terminals can be linked on-line to the computer, all being keyboard operated simultaneously. The computer will then search round the terminals in rotation, transferring the buffer contents of each to its own store. Such a computer operating mode is known as *time sharing* and this search and transfer process is so rapid that each terminal appears to be in direct communication with the computer all the time.

Visual display units

This is a device on which information can be shown visually by display on a cathode ray tube. Many such terminals incorporate a keyboard for data input purposes. Data input is automatically displayed on the screen as are also the results of processing emanating from the computer. Visual display units have the advantage of a rapid response time, i.e. information is presented almost immediately rather than having to wait for a printed record, although, of course, they will not give a permanent record.

Intelligent terminals

So far we have associated with terminals just the ability to transmit and receive data. Terminals limited to these functions are sometimes known as *non-intelligent terminals*. However, some terminals are minicomputers in their own right having their own central processing unit, their own peripheral input and output devices and can be programmed. This type of terminal is known as an *intelligent* terminal and, like other terminals, is linked by transmission line to a main computer. These terminals are able to carry out simple processing tasks in a 'stand-alone' capacity so relieving pressure on the main central machine. For example, a batch processing intelligent terminal could be programmed to perform data validation and control total checks.

Batch processing terminals

As the name suggests, this is a terminal designed to process data in batch mode. It will usually consist of a reader—punched card or punched paper tape—a small processing unit and a printer with, of course, associated off-line data preparation equipment such as card or tape punches.

Specialized terminals

This covers a very wide range of device types that are intended to accept data in one form or another and transmit it direct to the computer. Examples are

(1) Monitoring devices used in process control.
(2) Optical scrutiny devices for reading encoded data on products such as bar coding techniques used for point of sale pricing in retailing.
(3) Document up-dating terminals. For instance up-dating a bank pass book as transactions are made.

Exercises

1. Give an example of a simple paper tape code and explain with a diagram how:
   (a) a character may be represented on paper tape.
   (b) the number 456 may be represented on paper tape.
2. What do you understand by a *parity check*? Explain how a parity check is incorporated into data held on paper tape.
3. Explain the safeguards that can be used in the preparation and processing of punched cards to ensure the accuracy of the data.
4. Compare and contrast the use of MICR and OCR for recording data at source.
5. What do you understand by a *source document*? Give a short explanation of how data recorded on such a document could be prepared for entry to a computer.

6. What do you understand by *data transmission*? Give an account of the hardware you feel would be required to transmit data over communication lines from a point remote from a central computer.
7. Distinguish between a non-intelligent and an intelligent terminal giving a short description of an example of each.
8. Describe three methods by which source data can be entered into a computer without the need to convert it to a machine acceptable form.

5

Output devices

In this chapter we will describe and compare various *output devices* which may be linked to a computer to make the results of its operations available for use. Here we are considering the process of the machine communicating or recording in one way or another the results of its processing. In principle, we can regard output as taking one of two forms: (a) intermediate output and (b) final output.

In the first case, the output would be written to some form of storage where it would be held until required in some further processing stage. An example of this is a sales ledger routine where customer accounts are updated day by day but a complete statement of the account is not required until the end of each month. In the second case, we are thinking of the output required for information and action by an agency outside the computer. For example, a printed set of customer statements of account at the end of the month.

The two main types of device for intermediate output are *magnetic media* and *punched media,* and by far the most important and widely used of the two is *magnetic media*. These devices are discussed in some detail in Chapter 7. Punched and paper tape can be used as an output media by using on-line punches on which cards or tape can be automatically punched under computer control. These are both very slow output forms and do not lend themselves to handling large volumes of data. However, while not popular forms of intermediate output, they do never-the-less provide results that can be filed and then re-input into the system when necessary.

One important application of punched cards as an output form is their use as turn-around documents. The card having been punched with master data, e.g. name, address and last meter reading, can then be used to record movement data, such as a new meter reading manually, and have the new information punched into the card and the card then re-input into the system for processing an account to be sent to the user.

The following is an account of those devices that are used to output information in a final communicatable form.

Printers

A printer is essentially a device that will reproduce characters on a piece of paper. Broadly speaking there are two main ways of doing this:

(1) To physically impress a type face on the paper, known as *impact printing*.
(2) To project an image of the characters, using a light source, and then to fix the image usually by *electrostatic* or *photographic* means.

Impact printers

For computer output purposes, the first kind of printer can again be of two types:

(1) Those that will print a line of characters virtually simultaneously, known as *line printers*.
(2) Those printing one character at a time in succession, *serial printers*.

Line printers

The most important feature of a line printer is, as its name suggests, that it prints a whole line of characters (known as a *print line*) simultaneously.

The two types of printer most generally used for on-line computer work are known as *chain printers* and *barrel printers*. In these, the type face moves continuously even while the printing operation is being performed.

A third type of printer is the *stylus printer* (or *dot matrix printer*) which prints characters as a pattern of dots formed by fine wire needles.

The printing mechanism in a chain printer consists of a closed metal loop or chain, which carries the type faces and revolves continuously parallel to the print line. Behind the paper is a row of hammers, released individually as the required character on the chain reaches the printing position. The speed of the hammer strike is such that a clear impression is made on the paper even though the type face is moving at high speed. To increase the speed of this type of printer, sets of characters can be repeated along the length of the chain.

A barrel printer makes use of the same principle of continuously moving type faces, but they are embossed on the surface of a metal cylinder or barrel. Each character is repeated along the length of the barrel, once for each printing position (see Figure 5.1). The barrel is revolved at high speed so that each character is presented to the print line in turn. When, for instance, the row of A's is lined up in the printing position, hammers are released simultaneously at all positions in the line where the letter A is required, impressing the paper against the type faces. Next the row of B's moves into position and these are printed, and so on through the whole range of characters impressed on the barrel. This means that a line of type is built up progressively, character by character, during one revolution of the barrel.

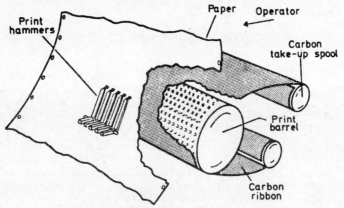

Figure 5.1   General arrangement of a barrel printer

Printing speeds of chain and barrel printers, while dependent to some extent on the number of characters in a print line and the number in a set of characters, are very high, and can reasonably be expected to produce 1200 lines a minute, each of 120 characters.

The character set of a line printer usually has a maximum range of 64 different characters: 26 alphabetic, 10 numeric and the remainder symbols (see Figure 5.2). The print line can consist of up to 160 character positions, although a line with 120 print positions appears to be the most popular.

The principle of the *stylus printer* is that the impression on the page is produced not by a solid block of metal in the shape of the required character, but by the projecting ends of a number of wires carried in an open ended box the size of one character. The shape of character is formed as a number of small dots by selecting the pattern of wires necessary to form a given character and impressing these on the paper. With a number of these boxes arranged side by side along the length of the print line a complete row of characters can be printed at one time.

The techniques for transferring and for controlling the transfer of data from the central processor to the printer naturally vary in computers of different makes and sizes, but the following general points can be made.

One area of store is usually reserved for output. In this area data representing one print line is assembled ready for transfer to the

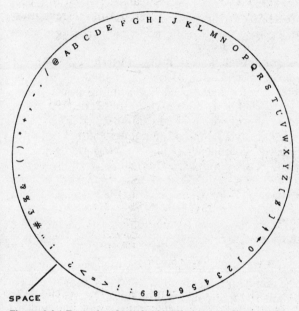

Figure 5.2   Example of a print barrel character layout (ICL Ltd)

printer. If the printer has direct access to the output area of the processor, the transference of the print line will take the same time as its printing, since the characters are transferred successively. This means that a great deal of processing time will be wasted while the program is concerned with supervising the transfer and printing of the output data. One extensively-used way of reducing the time wasted is to give the printer its own small store, known as a *buffer*, to which a whole print line can be transferred in one go. The printer itself then takes over control of the printing operation, extracting characters from the buffer as they are required. This leaves the output area in the processor free to receive the next output record while the previous one is being printed, and also permits the performance of processing instructions while printing is taking place.

While the use of a buffer utilizes processing time more efficiently, the fact remains that even with this provision data cannot be processed any faster than the rate at which the results can be output from the machine. In order, therefore, to make better use of processing time, output can be written on a magnetic tape, known as a *print tape*, when demand for computer time is heavy. This print tape will accept characters at a rate of at least 150 000 a second compared with the 2400 or so a second that the printer is able to deal with. The magnetic tape can then be printed out during a slack period.

Further considerations in line printing concern the layout of printed data and the specification of the paper used. Continuous stationery is necessary for high speed line printing, sheets being separated from each other by a line of perforations across the paper. For many output reports pre-printed stationery is used. It is important that weight, maximum and minimum widths, length of sheets and sprocket hole spacing should conform with the specification issued by the computer manufacturer. Multiple copies may be obtained by the use of inter-leaved carbon paper or NCR (no carbon required) paper, say up to six copies for the former and eight for the latter.

The arrangement and layout of data in printed form is subject to the following considerations:

(1) Printing time does not depend on the number of characters in a line but on the number of lines printed. It takes as long to print a line of two characters as it does a line of 120. It is an advantage, therefore, to get a maximum number of characters in a line by using stationery which is as wide as possible. If, however, the stationery must be narrow, consideration should be given to printing two forms simultaneously, side by side.

(2) Spacing a line, i.e. leaving a line blank, takes less time than printing a line, but the first in a succession of space lines takes longer than the others. It is, therefore, uneconomic to use too many single space lines.

(3) Wherever possible, in order to save printing time, all pre-determined data such as the title of the form and headings of columns should be pre-printed.

(4) The assembling, layout and presentation of data for printing is subject to program control. This process is known as *editing*. This involves the insertion of symbols such as £ signs in the

correct places, correct spacing of data items and arranging them appropriately to conform with the layout of the form used.

Serial printers

These machines print one character at a time in much the same way as a typewriter. Because of this they are fairly slow input/output devices and their main area of use is as terminals linked to a central computer or as a console for operator/computer communications.

The mechanics of single character printers take two main forms:

(1) Machines using the conventional typewriter print bar with a separate character embossed on each. The maximum input rate of this type of printer is around 5 characters a second with an output of about 10 cps.
(2) Machines using a wheel with a number of spokes radiating from the centre on the ends of which characters are embossed. The wheel revolves until the relevant character is in the printing position and is then impressed upon the paper. Printing speed with this type of device is far faster than with a conventional typewriter, being in the neighbourhood of 35–40 characters per second. This type of printing wheel is usually known as a *daisy wheel*.

Non-impact printers

Microfilm

As a method of capturing computer output data, this is growing in popularity as an alternative to the printer. While a number of systems are on the market, the basic principle is to photograph data displayed on a cathode ray tube. The data may be displayed as a direct output of the computer or it may first be written to magnetic tape and then the tape used to display the image on a CRT. Some systems use a roll of 16 mm film photographing 'pages' of data serially throughout the length of the film while others use a microfiche principle. This is a sheet of film say 4 inch × 3 inch on which up to 80 pages of data can be recorded.

Of course, output on microfilm can only be read by the use of a special viewing device which may incorporate a photo-copying facility to produce a hard permanent copy. Each frame on the microfilm or microfiche is indexed to facilitate retrieval and some systems are fully automatic enabling a frame to be retrieved by keying in its reference.

Advantages in the use of microfilm are

(1) Speeds well in excess of a line printer and can be up to 100 000 characters per second.
(2) Will reproduce diagrams, charts etc as well as the usual range of alpha/numeric characters.
(3) Relatively cheap.
(4) Easy to produce a printed copy if required.
(5) Very compact thus reducing storage space and cost.

Disadvantages are

(1) Some sort of viewing equipment is required.
(2) Not suitable when a printed document is required for circulation and use, e.g. an electricity bill, a statement of account, or a wages statement.

Generally speaking microfilm comes into its own for the bulk storage of inactive files to which reference is not frequently required. However, it does provide a convenient means of circulating, from a central computer to remote points, such information as, for example, car part lists to local depots or client account balances to branch banks. In these two cases, microfiche systems are generally used.

Optical printers

This type of printer makes use of the xerographic principle of document reproduction. An image of the data is projected from a cathode ray tube on to a revolving drum with a light sensitive surface. As the drum turns, paper that is continuously in contact with part of the drum surface moves in pace with it. Powder dusted on to the drum adhers to the areas covered by the projected image and is in turn-transferred to the paper as the drum revolves, it is then fixed by a heat process giving a permanent image.

Visual display units

As explained in the previous chapter this is the display of data on a cathode ray tube but does not represent a permanent output record unless fixed by a microfilm or photo-copying process as described earlier.

Other output methods

Digital increment plotters (graph plotter)

The object of this device is to communicate the output of a computer in printed graphical form such as diagrams, charts or line drawings.

The machine basically consists of a drum which moves a sheet of paper backwards and forwards. To provide accurate positioning the paper is sprocket controlled. Suspended from a slide above the drum is a drawing pen that is able to move left or right across the width of the paper. This gives movement in four basic directions, the paper backwards and forwards and the pen left and right. By altering the relative speeds of the paper and the pen, a line in any direction and of any curvature can be drawn on the paper. The dimension and shape of the lines is determined by the output data. While programming for this type of output device is very complex and the output of data comparatively slow it is, nevertheless, a very fast method of producing output data directly in graphical form.

Acoustic output

Mention should be made of one of the more recent developments in output, that involving the use of voice systems known as *acoustic output* or *voice output*. While voice synthesizers in the form of sophisticated tape or disc recorders have been in use for some time, and it is a comparatively straight-forward process to play back selected sounds under computer control, more recent developments involve the storage of sounds, words etc. in digital form. These digital signals are read out of store when required, fed through a digital to analogue converter thus producing an analogue audio signal for playing through an amplifier or loudspeaker.

A summary of output devices indicating their main attributes is given in Figure 5.3.

Ancillary machines

Having surveyed the types of output device available, mention should be made of the ancillary machines that are often necessary to deal with output after it has been produced in printed form.

Bursters

Output from a line printer is in the form of continuous stationery with a line of perforations between sheets to enable them to be separated easily. Machines designed to pull the sheets apart, known as *bursters*, operate by passing the paper over rollers running at different speeds so submitting the paper to sufficient tension to burst the line of perforations. They can usually be adjusted to take paper of various sizes and of varying strengths. An additional facility in

Output device	Extent of use	Hard copy	External distribution	Interrogation	Permanent file	Intermediate output	Turnaround for re-input	Information retrieval
Line printer	Extensive	✓	✓		✓		✓	✓
Terminal (Typewriter)	Extensive	✓		✓	✓			✓
Visual display unit	Extensive	✓		✓			✓	✓
Graph plotter	Limited	✓	Limited		✓			
Magnetic media	Extensive					✓		
Punched media	Limited					✓	✓	
Micro-film & Micro-fiche	Developing	✓ (Two-stage)	✓ (With viewing device)		✓			✓
Audio-response	Developing (limited)			✓	✓			✓

Figure 5.3   Use of output devices

many of these machines is the incorporation of cutting wheels to trim off the sprocket holes on each side of the paper.

Guillotines

These are used for cutting or trimming continuous stationery. They may be used in place of bursters by cutting either side of the row of perforations and are sometimes used in conjunction with bursters when, for instance, two reports are printed side by side and need separating by a cut down the centre of the paper.

Addressing machines

In some computers there may be insufficient storage space available to retain all the names and addresses needed for distribution of reports. If this is so a separate addressing machine is sometimes used, addresses being allocated to the correct forms by comparison of reference numbers appearing on the form and also on the addressing plate.

Decollators

These separate multiple copies of continuous stationery from their inter-leaved carbon paper and are usually used before the bursting process. The machine removes the carbon paper from the copies by winding them on to separate rollers. If it is then necessary to re-assemble the copies, this can be done on a *recollator*.

Folders and mail handling equipment

Many output reports prepared on a line printer are in a finished form ready for distribution. An example of this is a Sales Ledger Statement ready for sending to the customer. After decollating and bursting the forms have to be folded and inserted into envelopes for distribution. Folding machines are available, but a more complex machine known as a *mail handling machine* will cope with both folding and inserting into envelopes in one operation.

Exercises

1. List the main kinds of output device that are used in a commercial data processing situation and in each case give one example of an application in which you feel the device could be used to advantage.

2. Distinguish between a *serial printer* and a *line printer,* giving examples of the use of each.
3. What do you understand by a *turn-around* document? Give a description of an application that makes use of this principle.
4. What is a *visual display unit*? How can permanent records be obtained from this device?
5. Give short descriptions of three examples where you feel microfilm or microfiche techniques could be used to advantage.
6. Give an account of a system in which you would use output both to magnetic tape and to a line printer, stating at what stages in the system these two output forms would be used.
7. The output of a sales invoicing procedure consists of invoices printed in triplicate on continuous stationery. The original is sent to the customer, the first copy to the sales office, and the second copy to the accounts office. Explain how ancillary machines could be used to help deal with the distribution of these documents.

6

The central processor

In an earlier chapter, the central processor was described as being rather like the work area in a manual system into which source data is accepted and subjected to the processes necessary to achieve a required output. We saw that the functions of the central processor are, essentially, storage, arithmetic and control. In this chapter each of these functions is dealt with in more detail. However, it must be said that it is impossible to talk of a 'typical' central processor because of the wide range of types and sizes available and the different methods of organizing the processing functions. The following descriptions are, therefore, of a general nature.

Storage

One of the most significant characteristics of a computer, and one which distinguishes it from mechanical and electro-mechanical machines, is its capacity to store large volumes of data. However, it is not necessary or economic to store all this data in the central processor itself since other forms of storage are available outside the processor. All that the central processor need store at any one time is the data needed for immediate use. The rest is stored in one of the mass storage media described in the chapter on storage, such as magnetic tape, drums, discs or cards. For example, in a stock inventory system in which the stock balance for each item is to be adjusted for issues and receipts, the only data that need necessarily be stored in the processor is that relevant to the particular stock item being processed at the moment. Such a file could be processed by transferring data item by item between the external store and the central processor.

In practice, in order to get as much benefit as possible from the high working speed of the processor, as many data items as possible are transferred at one time from the external store, but the fact still remains that the bulk of the data is stored outside the central processor. A number of factors determine the size of the block of data transferred at one time (these are mentioned in the chapter on storage) but perhaps the most significant is the availability of space in the processor's store.

We said earlier that the processor need only store the information necessary for immediate use. This information takes two main forms. First the program or the section of the program that is required to control the work being performed currently in the processor and second, the data being processed. A simple analogy may help to clarify the central processor's functions—that of people going to the cinema. The queue waiting outside represents the mass of data records stored externally to the central processor. The number that can be conveniently accommodated at any one time are then counted off and allowed into the foyer. This represents the transfer of a block of records from the external store to the central processor. These people then pay their seat money one by one at a cash desk and a ticket is handed out according to a pre-determined routine. This represents the interaction of the program on the data records. Having paid their money and received a ticket the people move from the foyer to the auditorium, in the same way that having been processed the data is transferred to output. All the time this is going on, the manager is standing by to regulate the flow of people from the queue, to make sure the ticket issuing process goes on smoothly and, should anything go wrong, to get it rectified. This is rather like the control function in a central processor.

It should be emphasized that this analogy is only a simple basic parallel and does not apply in its entirety to every central processor function.

What is stored in the central processor?

Program, data and control. These three factors must be present during processing. However, if we look more closely at the data, we will probably realize that it can take different forms. This can probably best be seen by considering an actual situation.

In a stock inventory system, concerned with keeping track of the number and value of spare parts held in a factory store, a record is kept which gives the stock situation for each item, under the following headings:

PART NUMBER	DESCRIPTION	UNIT PRICE	QUANTITY IN STOCK	VALUE OF STOCK

The record is made up of five data fields which are subject to varying degrees of change. The Part Number and Description will probably remain constant all the time this particular item is stocked. The Unit Price is subject to occasional change as production costs or market prices fluctuate, and the Quantity and Value are subject to continual change as stock items are received into and issued from the factory stores.

Another way of looking at these five fields is to say that some are purely descriptive and as such are not subject to processing in the sense that they have to be changed or modified in any way. Others are quantitative and are subject to processing in the sense that the values and quantities need constant adjustment. This type of data is known as *master data* and reflects the up-to-date position of a particular activity.

Having said that these elements of master data are subject to change, obviously the change must be effected by the application of new data recording the detail giving rise to the change. In the above example the change in the master stock data would be brought about by the use of data which record the items received by, and issued from the factory stores. This data will be partly descriptive, to identify the master record to which they relate, and partly quantitative, to determine the extent of the change. Data of this type is usually known as *movement data*. Processing applies movement data to master data with the object of keeping the latter up-to-date. This is known as *up-dating* master data.

The kinds of information stored in the central processor are:

(a) Master data. This contains values that are continually changing and represent a current situation.
(b) Movement data. This records changes that are applied to the master data to keep it up-to-date.
(c) Program. To specify the processing needs in the inter-action of (a) and (b).

How is data stored?

As far as the mechanics of storage are concerned, an account of these will be given in Chapter 7. In most current main-frame computers, the ferrite ring type of store is used. Each ring is capable of being magnetized in one or other of two directions, and thus of indicating a binary 1 or a binary 0. In this section we are concerned with how data represented in this way is organized in the central processor store.

Each ferrite ring, then, represents one binary character. This is the smallest indivisible unit of store and is known as a binary bit. Furthermore, we have seen that each numeric or alphabetic character is represented in store by a group of these bits, each data field in turn is made up of a number of characters and each data record of a number of fields. All of this is represented in store in the form of binary bits. Now a store holding tens of thousands of these bits will be completely meaningless in terms of information unless we can define the beginning and end of each character, field and record. It would be rather like having a page of a book covered with completely random characters. Characters are meaningless unless they are marshalled into words, the words in turn arranged into sentences, and the start and finish of each sentence defined.

For example, unless we know the particular convention being employed, and where the characters begin and end, the binary number 10011110 could equally well represent 472, 916 or 158. As well as knowing what number a particular binary sequence represents, we have to know where in the store it can be found when it is needed.

Now at this point we should remember that there are in use many different types and makes of machine. There is no standard way of organizing data in store that is common to all central processors. In fact the methods in use vary considerably. In view of this the following descriptions are intended only to reflect basic ideas.

We start off then with two main problems: (a) to define the size of each character, each data field, each data record and so on, and (b) to be able to locate any data item in store. One solution that may suggest itself is to mark in some way where each group of bits representing a character starts and finishes, but this is not quite as simple as it sounds. What kind of mark do we use? We only have two alternatives, 0 and 1, and these are both used to make up the character itself. We might reason, why not use a group of bits with a pattern distinct from any of those used to represent characters. Here again we run into trouble. Using this method we would probably finish up with markers so big that most of the storage space would be taken up with them. In any case it would be quite a problem to know where the marker ended and the character began. Since, also, we want to know the location of each data item in store, each separate bit would have to have a unique reference. With a store containing hundreds of thousands of bits this idea can be seen to be impractical.

Having discarded this, our thinking might suggest next that one way of getting round the problem would be to divide all the bits into groups of a standard size, each group containing sufficient bits to record one character. This fixes the limits of each group which means there is no longer a need to mark where each group starts and ends. In addition to this, there is no longer a need to give each bit a unique reference, all we need do is to provide a reference for each group. Now, although we have not solved all of the problems, we can

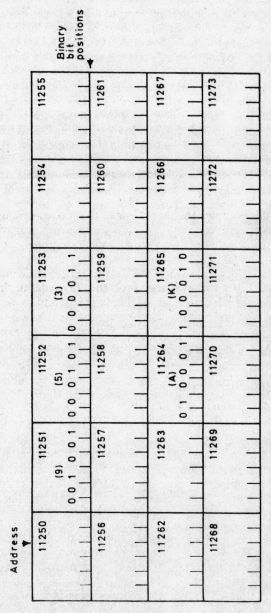

Figure 6.1   A section of a central processor's store. The number 9 is stored at address 11251. The letter K at address 11265.

begin to see in principle how the data is organized in the central processor store. It is rather like having a lot of small boxes, each having a reference number, as shown in Figure 6.1. Each box contains sufficient bits to record one character, and the character is located by the box number. The name given to this number is an *address*.

Having decided to divide the store up into groups of bits, the next problem is to decide the size of the groups. Now we saw in Chapter 3 that the number of bits required to store a decimal digit is four and the number to store an alphabetic character is six. Thus a 6 bit group would appear to be sufficient to hold any numeric or alphabetic character and since with six bits we can get 64 different characters, 000000–111111 (0 to 63), we could throw in a number of symbols as well, to give a range of 64 different characters.

Now some computer central processors use this principle of arranging bits into groups of six, each group capable of holding one character and each six-bit location having it's own unique address. These machines are known as *character-addressable* or *character machines*.

But what now happens if we wish to use a binary expression containing more than six bits? The biggest number we can represent with six bits in binary is 63, seven bits are required up to 127 and eight up to 255 and so on. One answer, of course, is to overflow from one location to the next and indeed, this can be done provided that in our programming we let the computer know we are going to use a number of locations to contain a single expression. Because of this facility for increasing the size of a location to accommodate one large binary expression this type of store organization is known as *variable word-length storage*.

Of course, another way of getting around the problem is to increase the size of the bit groups but on first thought, to do this, we would have to sacrifice the convenience of a 6-bit grouping which will hold any one individual character. Why not then have a group containing a multiple of 6 bits, say 18, 24 or 30, so that it can contain either a number of 6-bit characters or one longer pure binary expression. Many machines organize their storage in this way. For example if we decided to have groups of 24 bits one group could contain either four six-bit characters or one pure binary expression (see Figure 6.2).

As we saw earlier, numeric data may be either descriptive or quantitative with the latter only being the subject of calculations in the central processor. The construction of a 24-bit word in this manner will give the facility for storing descriptive data in BCD (Binary Coded Decimal) and the quantitative data in pure binary

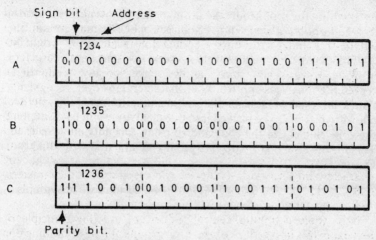

Figure 6.2   Examples of a 25-bit word

bearing in mind that more complex electronics are required to perform arithmetic on data expressed in BCD.

This arrangement, however, brings with it a further problem in that we can no longer give an individual address to each character within the group. But does this really matter? If the first character to be read always appears in the first position in the group and the succeeding characters are arranged in sequence, the machine need only refer to the address of the first character and keep on reading until instructed to stop. This can be done with a program instruction to read a defined number of characters, or by using one group of six bits to hold a special stop marker.

Perhaps it would be as well, at this point, to attempt to organize our terminology. We have been using the term *group* to indicate a sub-division of the central processing store and have seen that a store organized into six-bit addressable locations is known as a character machine and is said to have a variable word length. We have further suggested that a group may contain a multiple number of six bits. The name given to a group of this nature is a *word* and a machine with a central processor divided in this way is known as a *fixed word length* machine. The sub-divisions of the word into character locations are often known as *bytes*. Each word is addressable but individual bytes are not.

One further example should be mentioned. This is based on groups of eight bits. The recording mode used divides the character set into 10 zones, each containing 10 characters. The first four bits indicate the zone number and the second four the position of the letter within the zone group. An arrangement of this nature is known as a *zone/numeric code*. For instance, zone 0001 may contain the letters A–J and so the binary coding for the letter H would be 00011000. At first sight this may seem an uneconomic way of utilizing store space since, as we have already seen, BCD representation needs only 6 bits per character. However, recognizing that a large proportion of data is in numeric form, this method allows two digits to be packed into one eight bit group by discarding the zone element of the code and so using four bits only for each. This means a saving of two bits per digit compared with BCD (see Figure 6.3).

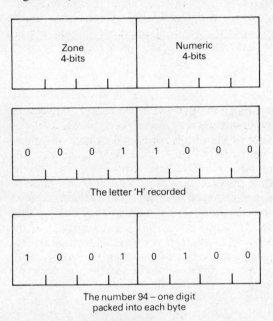

The letter 'H' recorded

The number 94 – one digit
packed into each byte

Figure 6.3   Use of 4-bit bytes

Eight-bit locations in this type of machine are also known as bytes and a machine using this kind of storage organization is usually referred to as a *byte-addressable machine* or a *byte machine*.

Figure 6.2 gives an example of a 24 bit word that can be subdivided into 4 six-bit bytes. Stored numbers may be either positive or negative, and a method must exist for distinguishing between these two alternatives. This is usually done by reserving one bit in the word to indicate the sign, 0 equals plus and 1 equals minus. For example, in the 24 bit word illustrated the left-most bit is used for this purpose leaving 23 bits to record the value of the expression. With numbers recorded in BCD, the use of a six bit byte leaves two spare bits, one of which can be used to indicate the sign.

While, as we saw earlier, calculations in the central processor are best done in pure binary, it is common practice to simplify input and output procedures by reading and storing data initially in BCD form. When data is required for calculations, the binary coded decimal characters are converted within the machine to pure binary expressions and the results of the calculations converted back to BCD for output purposes.

One further consideration arises in the storage of data in the processor. In order to provide a check on the accuracy of transferred data, additional space is provided in each word to hold a *parity bit*. A test is made on transfer of each word for an odd or an even number of bits, depending on the system used (see Figure 6.2).

Where is data stored?

In considering where data is stored in the central processor perhaps the short answer is 'Does it really matter?'. In early machines it was necessary to keep a note of the address of each data item and quote this in programming instructions. In modern machines the allocation of storage space is part of the control function of the central processor and if the processor itself records the location of each item there is really no need for the operator or programmer to know.

But for all this, specific storage locations may be reserved for specific purposes. While different types of machines use different approaches to storage, facilities will exist within the processor for the following:

(1) *Control*. The control function is stored in a number of locations reserved exclusively for this purpose. The address of these locations remain fixed.
(2) *Accumulators*. These are locations reserved for holding data upon which arithmetic is being carried out.
(3) *Data*. By and large data may be stored anywhere in the processor's store. Usually, however, one part of the store is reserved for receiving and holding input data ready for processing while another part is reserved for marshalling together and holding output data until it is transferred to an output peripheral.
(4) *Program*. Again, the list of instructions comprising the program can be stored in any part of the processor's store not being used

for any other purpose providing these instructions are stored in the sequence they will be worked through.

(5) *Operating System*. These are programs designed to generally supervise and monitor the whole of the computer operations. They are dealt with in more detail in a later chapter.

Of course, there must be the facility for transferring data from one location to another within the processor. Data may be read to the reserved input area, transferred to the accumulator for arithmetic processing and the results transferred back to an output area.

Methods of transfer vary from one type of machine to another. In some machines data is transferred bit by bit until the whole expression has been moved, while in others all the bits in a word are transferred simultaneously. On the other hand transfer of an expression stored in BCD could well be done one character at a time. The first method is usually known as *serial* transfer, the second as *parallel* transfer and the third as *serial/parallel* transfer.

Computer arithmetic

However complex a mathematical problem, if it is capable of solution, it can be solved by the application of the four basic rules of arithmetic, addition, multiplication, subtraction and division. In manual calculating, reducing a problem to these simple terms would be too lengthy a process and more advanced techniques are usually used to speed things up. However, a computer works so fast that it is easily able to cope with a mass of simple arithmetic in a very short space of time.

In fact we can make use of the computer's great speed to simplify the internal arithmetic processes even further. Multiplication can be performed by repeated addition, and division by repeated subtraction. In this way we have reduced our four necessary processes to two, but simplification can go even further. By employing a process known as 'complementary subtraction' we can deal with subtraction using additive methods. In decimal calculations, the complement of a number is that number which must be added to it to give a zero total. For example, the decimal complement of 429 is 571. When these are added, they give a sum of 1000, in other words zeros in the three digits concerned. To subtract 429 from another number, say 760, by 'complementary' subtraction we add 571 to 760, giving 1331, and as we did when finding the complement, ignore the most significant digit. This gives the correct answer of 331.

The usefulness of this method lies in the fact that the complement of a number expressed in binary form is easily obtained by reversing all of the binary digits (that is, each 0 becomes a 1 and each 1 a 0) and adding 1 to the result.

Here is an example of complementary subtraction, using numbers expressed in binary form.

110111–101101

Find the true complement of	1	0	1	1	0	1
reverse bits	0	1	0	0	1	0
add						1

$$0\ 1\ 0\ 0\ 1\ 1 = \text{True complement}$$

	1	1	0	1	1	1
add true complement	0	1	0	0	1	1

110111–101101   =   (1) 0 0 1 0 1 0

In the computer store a negative number is stored in the form of its binary complement using the most significant bit in a word as a sign bit. For example, using a 12-bit word the number $+52$ is stored as

0 0 0 0 0 0 1 1 0 1 0 0
↑
sign bit

while the number -52 is stored as

1 1 1 1 1 1 0 0 1 1 0 0
↑
sign bit

Now if we wanted to work out $100-52$ we would have:

100 = 0 0 0 0 0 1 1 0 0 1 0 0
−52 = 1 1 1 1 1 1 0 0 1 1 0 0

by adding (1) 0 0 0 0 0 0 1 1 0 0 0 0 = $+48$

Note that by adding in the sign bit the correct sign in the answer is obtained.

Since we can now produce the results of multiplication, division, addition and subtraction by forms of addition, all arithmetic processes in the computer can be reduced to the following four basic rules:

$$0 + 0 = 0$$
$$0 + 1 = 1$$
$$1 + 1 = 0 \text{ carry } 1$$
$$1 + 1 + \text{carry } 1 = 1 \text{ carry } 1$$

Gates

The central processor contains special electronic circuits to carry out the arithmetic, known as *gates*. When pulses representing binary digits are presented as input to a gate, a defined output results. The gates have names which depend on the output produced by a given input.

A two input 'OR' gate has the property of producing an output pulse as a result of the application of one pulse to either input or simultaneously to both.

Input		Output
0 + 0	=	0
0 + 1	=	1
1 + 0	=	1
1 + 1	=	1

An 'AND' gate will only produce an output pulse if input pulses are applied to both inputs simultaneously.

Input		Output
0 + 0	=	0
0 + 1	=	0
1 + 0	=	0
1 + 1	=	1

A third gate known as an 'EXCLUSIVE OR' gate, is similar to an OR gate but does not produce an output pulse when two inputs are simultaneously present.

Input		Output
0 + 0	=	0
0 + 1	=	1
1 + 0	=	1
1 + 1	=	0

The arithmetic and logic unit

The use of a combination of these gates in an Arithmetic and Logic Unit will enable the four basic rules mentioned above to be carried out as illustrated in the following example. For this purpose we will assume that one set of gates is used for each bit position in the word,

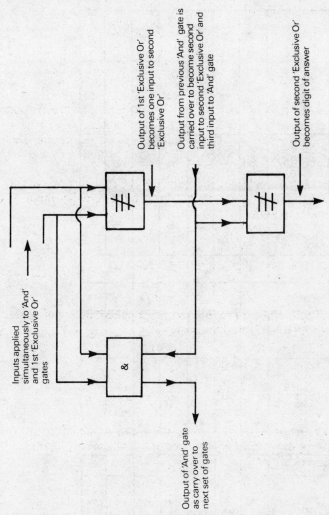

Figure 6.4 A set of adding gates

thus twelve sets of gates would be available for a twelve bit word. A set of gates for this example consists of two Exclusive OR and one AND gate.

(1) Input is applied simultaneously to the AND gate and to the first Exclusive OR.
(2) The output from the first Exclusive OR becomes one input for the second Exclusive OR.

Bit Position	'AND' Gate Input 1	'AND' Gate Input 2	'AND' Gate Input 3 (And output from previous stage)	'AND' Gate Output	1st 'EXCLUSIVE OR' Gate Input 1	1st 'EXCLUSIVE OR' Gate Input 2	1st 'EXCLUSIVE OR' Gate Output	2nd 'EXCLUSIVE OR' Gate Input 1 (from 1st Exclusive Or)	2nd 'EXCLUSIVE OR' Gate Input 2 (And output from previous stage)	2nd 'EXCLUSIVE OR' Gate Output
1	0	0		0	0	0	0	0	0	0
2	1	0	0	0	1	0	1	1	0	1
3	0	1	0	0	0	1	1	1	0	1
4	1	1	0	1	1	1	0	0	0	0
5	0	1	1	1	0	1	1	1	1	0
6	1	1	1	1	1	1	0	0	1	1
7	0	0	1	0	0	0	0	0	1	1

Figure 6.5   An addition using AND and Exclusive OR gates

(3) Any output from the AND gate is carried to the next set of gates as the second input to the second Exclusive OR gate and also as an additional third input to the AND gate. This means an AND gate that will give an output pulse if either two or three input pulses are present (see Figure 6.4).

Applying this the addition of 111100 and 101010 is shown in tabular form in Figure 6.5 and in diagrammatic form in Figure 6.6.

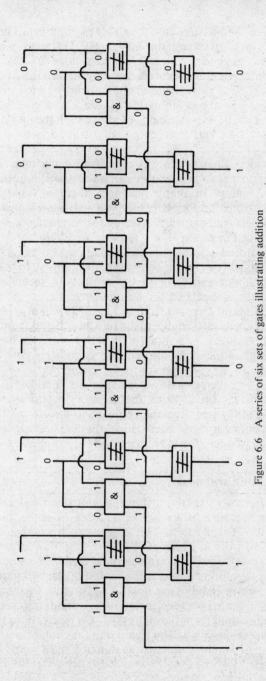

Figure 6.6   A series of six sets of gates illustrating addition

It must be emphasized that the above example is just one way, not the only way, of doing the arithmetic. Different machines use different arrangements of gates. Some machines use one set of gates only to process a binary expression bit by bit serially. In this case the output of the AND gate is delayed one pulse in order to carry it into the next stage. Again, a combination of AND and OR gates can be used, the output of the AND gate being used to inhibit the OR gate output in the case of 1 + 1 and also being used as the carry over to the next digit.

It is evident then, that a way of performing arithmetic is for the processor to pass the data through an arithmetic unit containing electronic gates. In many machines there are special storage locations, called *accumulators* to which data on which arithmetic has to be performed is transferred and which hold the results of the calculations. For example, it is required to add factor A to factor B which are stored in locations 496 and 723 respectively. The program instructions will call for the contents of location 496 to be copied into the accumulator and then for the contents of location 723 to be added to the contents of the accumulator. Factor A, now in the accumulator and factor B from location 723 will now be circulated through the arithmetic unit and the sum moved into the accumulator to replace factor A. This total can then be transferred back to either of the original locations, moved to a completely new location or retained in the accumulator for further calculations. There are some machines, however, that do not use special accumulators as such but pass the data direct from the storage locations through the arithmetic unit, and feed the result back directly to the original location, obliterating or 'overwriting' the data previously held there. This mode of operation is known as *add to storage*.

Table look-up arithmetic

As an alternative to the arithmetic unit described above, some machines use what is known as a *Table Look-Up* principle for carrying out calculations. This consists of a number of reserved locations in store in which are kept the sum of, and the difference between, every possible pair of decimal digits. The address of each location is determined by a combination of the two numbers to be added or subtracted. For example, to add 4 and 5, these two numbers would be copied from their locations in store into a special register where they would form the address 45. On reference to the location whose address is 45 it will be found that the content is 9, the answer to the sum of 4 and 5. Similarly the sum of 5 and 4 would be found in the address 54 whose content would also be 9.

To carry out subtraction, a set of difference tables are stored, addressable in the same way. The difference between 7 and 2 would be found in location 72. To distinguish between the addresses of locations containing the sums of numbers and the locations containing differences, a separate series of location addresses is used in each case. For instance, the sum of 7 and 2 might be found in location 0072 and the difference in location 0172.

To cope with the carry over from one digit to the next, one is added to the address containing the answer for the next pair of digits. To add 49 and 38 the sum of 9 and 8 is found in location 98 which is 7 carry 1. The 1 is added to the address formed by the next pair of digits 4 and 3 giving 43 plus 1. This is location 44 which contains 8.

One other essential function of the central processor from which it derives its decision-making capacity is the ability to compare numbers and to take different courses of action depending on whether one number is greater than, less than or equal to another. This process is carried out in the ALU. The two numbers are compared arithmetically and the results of the comparison placed in a register. The program then calls for a test of the contents of this register and the result determines the next sequence of instructions to be followed.

The stored program

A computer program consists of a number of *instructions* that are designed to make the computer carry out a pre-determined series of operations. In the final analysis, each instruction is expressed in the central processor as a series of binary bits, in much the same way as data, and the instructions are stored in word locations of the central processor store again in the same way as is data. Since the machine proceeds in sequence from one address to another when carrying out the program instructions, these instructions must be stored in the sequence they are required. This does not mean that they must be in one continuous sequence of addresses, but that there must be continuity between the last instructions in one series of locations and the first instruction in the next.

For example, a program requiring 500 locations could have the first 200 instructions in addresses 1401 to 1600, followed by stored data in 1601 to 2000 and then the program instructions continuing in 2001 to 2300. The contents of address 1600, however, must direct the machine to 2001 for the next instruction (Figure 6.7).

While the format and construction of computer program statements and instructions are discussed more fully in Chapter 11, sufficient for the moment to say that essentially a program instruction contains two basic elements as indeed must even the simplest instructions used in everyday life in order to make them capable of intelligent execution. One element specifies the action to be taken and the other the medium on which the action is to be performed. In a computer instruction the first of these elements is called the *operation* and the second the *operand*. In the instruction 'read a book' the operation element is to 'read' and the

ADDRESS

11250 DATA	11251 DATA	11252 DATA	11253 PROGRAM	11254 PROGRAM	11255 PROGRAM
11256 PROGRAM	11257 PROGRAM	11258 PROGRAM	11259 PROGRAM	11260 DATA	11261 DATA
11262 DATA	11263 DATA	11264 DATA	11265 DATA	11266 DATA	11267 DATA
11268 DATA	11269 PROGRAM	11270 PROGRAM	11271 PROGRAM	11272 PROGRAM	11273 PROGRAM

Figure 6.7 Store locations with program instructions

operand, 'the book'. However, if access to a particular passage in a specific book is required, the operand in this instruction is insufficiently defined. The location of the passage would need to be specified i.e. 'read line 24 on page 139 of this book'. Obviously when processing data by computer the principle of positively identifying the data required must be observed. As we know, data items are held in store in words each having a unique address. So, to identify the data, all that is necessary is to quote in the instruction the address or addresses at which the data is stored. The operand element of an instruction then, just quotes the address at which the data to be worked on is to be found.

The operation element specifies what is to be done with this data. By definition, there will be a limit to the number of functions any device or machine will perform. Since this number is finite it is a quite straight forward procedure to allocate each a code number and use this code number to identify to the machine the operation required. For example, Add = 0001, Subtract = 0010, Read = 0011, Write = 0100 etc. This list of codes representing computer functions, or the operation element of the program instruction is known as a *machine code*.

Execution of program instructions

While detailed techniques for moving and processing data in the processor will vary from machine to machine the essential steps in executing an instruction are as follows (Figure 6.8)

(1) Location of the first instruction to be carried out and its transference to a control unit.
(2) Extraction from store of the data to be worked on, the address of which is specified in the operand element of the instruction.
(3) Carry out the operation specified in the instruction on the data in (2) above.
(4) Location of the next instruction and a repetition of the above sequence.

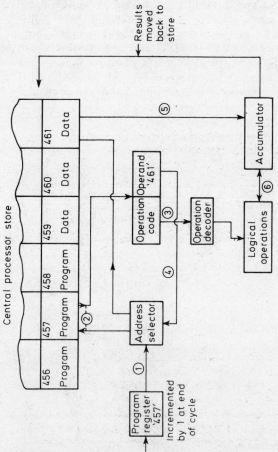

Figure 6.8   Executing a program instruction

While a detailed technical description of how these stages are carried out is not the province of this book, the following comments seek to give a fairly simple explanation of the process.

It will be appreciated that the first instruction to be executed may be stored in any location in the central processor and it cannot be identified until the address of this location is specified. The first stage then is to communicate the address of this first instruction which may be done by operator intervention or an operating system. The address is entered into a control register, usually known as a *program register*. This will now control each step until the cycle of operations for executing the instruction is complete.

Reference is now made to the address stored in the program register, through the medium of an address selector, and the instruction contained in this address read out to another register known as an *instruction register*. This register now contains both elements of the instruction, the operand address and the operation code. The next steps are to decode the operation code in terms of the circuitry to carry out the operation i.e. add, subtract, shift etc and then to move the contents of the address specified in the operand to the arithmetic and logic unit where the operation is carried out.

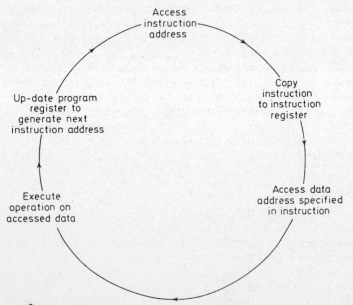

Figure 6.9   Execution cycle of a program instruction

In the meanwhile, the address in the program register will be incremented by 1, giving the address of the next sequentially stored instruction so enabling this cycle of operations to be automatically repeated.

The control and timing of these operations is the function of the program register, which by keeping in step with the processor's timing pattern will, in effect, do this routine by numbers:

(1) Locate instruction in storage by reference to the location address it contains and through the medium of an *address selector*.
(2) Locate the operand by reference to the address now stored in the instruction register—also through the medium of the address selector—and move the data contained to an accumulator.
(3) Decode the operation part of the instruction and execute it on the operand.
(4) Update the address in the program register to give access to the next instruction.
(5) Go back to one and repeat the cycle (Figure 6.9).

Control

We have seen that the central processor performs a number of different functions such as accepting and storing input data, assembling and communicating output data, re-arranging data in store, and carrying out calculations, all of them specified by its particular machine code. Perhaps the most important feature of the processor is the control function which supervises all of these processes and co-ordinates the activities of the configuration as a whole. Control instructions are stored in a number of locations reserved for this purpose, usually known as *control registers*. While the detail of the control function varies in detail with the type of machine, the following factors are generally present (Figure 6.10).

Program control

This is concerned with initiating the activities called for in the program instructions. As we have already seen, these instructions are held in sequence in ordinary store locations. From there they are copied one at a time into a control register which is, basically, a multi-position switch. On recognizing the function code the switch will set up the electronic circuits necessary to perform the function, and on reference to the address part of the instruction, will link these circuits to the appropriate locations. When the instruction contained

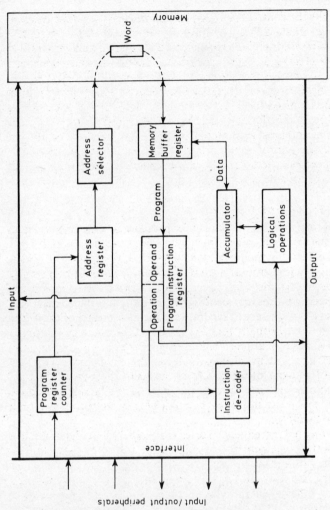

Figure 6.10 Simplified view of the central processor

in the register has been executed the next sequential instruction is copied in, over-writing the previous one, and this is executed in turn. In this way the program is worked through alternating between the transfer of an instruction to a control register and its execution, until the final 'stop' instruction is reached.

Input and output control

The activity of input and output as well as storage peripherals is governed by the control function. In response to a 'read' instruction the transfer of data from an input device is initiated and control registers will set up a 'count' to ensure that the specified amount of a data is transferred. It is also part of the control function to allocate unoccupied storage space to receive the data. In response to a 'write' instruction, the control registers will arrange to assemble the output data in the required form, and transfer to the output device issuing instructions to this device to accept and record the data.

A further and most important control function, is to identify and notify the operator of any malfunction arising in the configuration. In most machines these reports are communicated as typed messages on a control console typewriter.

Central processor working speeds

Before leaving this chapter on central processors mention should be made of the speeds at which they can perform their activities.

A computer is a mass of electronic equipment through which information in the form of both data and instructions is constantly flowing at an extremely fast speed. All of this information is in the form of electric pulses representing binary bits. In order to carry out operations it is necessary to synchronize the movements of these bits so that they are brought together in the right place in the many thousand storage locations available and at precisely the right time.

This timing is synchronized by a device that emits pulses to travel throughout all parts of the processor at a constant rate all the time the machine is working. The name given to this device is a *clock generator*, and it usually takes the form of a crystal controlled high frequency oscillator.

The timing pulse frequency varies from machine to machine. It is known as the *clock rate* and may be in the region of thousands of megacycles (million cycles) per second. A timing pulse is the smallest indivisible time unit of the computer and may, by its presence, represent a binary 1 bit or by its absence a 0. The clock rate governs the whole time scale of computer operations, each operation taking up a defined number of pulses. The minimum time interval between successive computer operations is referred to as the *cycle time*. Cycle time is measured in microseconds (millionths of a second) or in very fast modern computer in nanoseconds (thousand millionths of a second).

Exercises

1. Explain what is meant by the following terms:
   (a) Location

    (b) Address

    (c) Bit

    (d) Byte.

2. Give a short account of the main functions of a central processing unit.

3. Distinguish between the *operation* and *operand* elements of a program instruction. Describe briefly the routine for executing an instruction in the computer processor.

4. Outline the main functions of the control unit in a processor.

5. Explain how negative numbers can be stored in a central processor. Using a 12-bit word, illustrate the storage of (a) a positive number and (b) a negative number.

6. With the aid of a simple sketch, describe the basic working of a core store. In a commercial application, what type of information is likely to be found in the store during a processing run?

7. What do you think are the main characteristics that distinguish a computer from other forms of calculating device?

8. What do you understand by a *machine code*? Explain how machine codes are stored in the processor and state the purpose they are intended to accomplish.

9. Describe how the storage of data is organized in the store of the central processor.

10. Explain the functions of

    (a) the accumulator, and

    (b) the arithmetic unit

showing the relationship between these.

7

Computer storage

It has already been shown that one of the fundamental characteristics of a computer is its capacity to store large quantities of information, including not only the data involved in a procedure, but also the program necessary to carry it out.

In large scale data processing, the volume of facts and figures is often so great that it would be impractical to have a central processor capable of storing all of them. Take, for example, a simple Sales Ledger system with five thousand customer accounts. Each account would record initially the customer name and address, the account number and an opening balance. Postings would then be made to these accounts from invoices for goods sold, credit notes for goods returned, and for cash received. The data on each account could well comprise upwards of 200 characters, making over 1 000 000 characters on the file as a whole. It would need a large and expensive processor to store this quantity of data in addition to the program for processing it. Indeed, it would be unnecessary, since the processor will only be concerned with that section of the data on which it is currently working. Provided all the data is quickly accessible, there is no need for the whole to be stored in the processor itself.

This is much the same situation we would find in, say, an accounting procedure using keyboard accounting machines. For example, in a sales ledger system we would have a file of sales ledger cards, probably in numerical or alphabetical order, and a file of sales invoices, in the same order, to be posted to the ledger cards. The card with the same reference number or name corresponding with the top invoice would be selected and inserted into the machine. The data would then be read from the invoice and posted to the card through the machine keyboard, the machine automatically calculating and printing a revised balance on the card. The whole operation would be guided by a program built into the machine. The posting to one card having been completed, it would be returned to the file and the operation repeated for the next card until, finally, the whole file had been dealt with (see Figure 7.1).

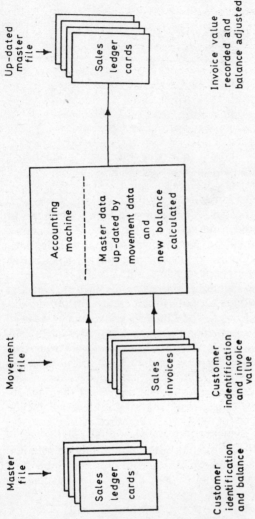

Figure 7.1   Updating sales ledger cards by sales invoices

During the processing run the machine only contains data relating to the account it is immediately processing. It accepts data for that one account from the two files, processes it and returns the up-dated card to the file before accepting further data for the next account.

Similarly, in the case of a computer, files of data can be kept external to the processor. Information is read in from these files as it is required, processed, the results returned to the file and the process repeated for the next section of data. When the posting run is completed the up-dated data is now stored in a file external to the processor and the processor's store is now empty, ready to accept data for another system.

The kinds of storage can, therefore, be divided into (1) *internal storage,* i.e. storage within the central processor, and (2) *external storage* or *backing storage* which exists outside the processor but is accessible by the processor when required.

Internal storage

This is the storage that forms an integral part of the central processing unit. Often referred to as the computer's *memory* but, as a type of storage it is known as an *immediate access store.* As we shall see, the most significant feature that distinguishes this type of storage from external or backing storage is that it is purely electronic with no mechanical moving parts. It is this that gives the processor immediate access to any part of the store, irrespective of where the information is held in it.

As we saw in Chapter 6, the basic indivisible unit of store is a binary bit. A store must, therefore, consist of an array of devices each of which is capable of representing a binary 1 or a binary 0. In principle rather like an electric lamp that could represent 0 when switched off and 1 when switched on. The two most commonly used devices in computers today are the ferrite core and the semiconductor store.

Ferrite core store

This makes use of the elementary electrical principle that when an electric current is passed through a wire a magnetic field will be set up around it in a clockwise direction in relation to the direction of the

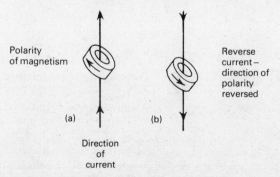

Figure 7.2   Principle of ferrite core storage (a) 0 stored (b) 1 stored

current. Reverse the direction of the current and the direction of the magnetic field will be reversed. If we thread a wire through the centre of a small ferrite ring capable of being magnetized, then on passing a current through the wire the north-seeking ends of the particles of ferrite will point in a clockwise direction following the force lines of the magnetic field and will remain in this state even when the current is switched off. However, if we pass sufficient current in the opposite direction along the wire then the polarity of the magnetism will be reversed. This gives us a convenient and relatively easily operated two-state device (Figure 7.2).

A ferrite core is a small ferrite ring, 0.3–1.3 mm (0.012–0.05 inch) outside diameter, which by virtue of the direction of its magnetism

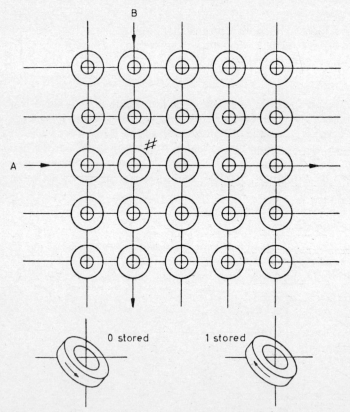

Figure 7.3 Section of a magnetic core store matrix. To change the state of core currents of equal strength are sent simultaneously through wires A and B. The amplitude of a single pulse is insufficient to change the state of any core but at the point of coincidence the sum currents A and B is sufficient to change that core's magnetic state

can be made to represent one binary 0 or 1. However, we need many thousands of these rings to store all of the information required in the processor and in turn these rings must be assembled into groups representing computer words as we discussed in Chapter 6. The storage capacity of the processor is defined by the number of words it contains. This is expressed in terms of K, 1K representing 1024 words. Stores are usually constructed in multiples of 4K, thus we could have a 4K, 8K, 16K, 32K etc. store. This means, assuming a word size of 24 bits, a 4K store would be made of, ignoring for the moment any other factors, over 24 000 ferrite rings.

Within the store, a number of these ferrite cores are arranged in a square, or *matrix*, each line of cores being threaded by wires in two

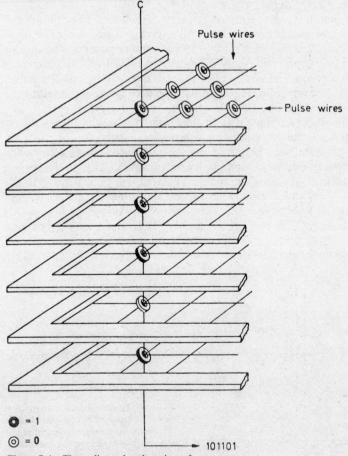

Figure 7.4   Three-dimensional section of a core store

directions at right angles to each other (Figure 7.3). We then have the situation that only one core lies at the intersection of any two wires. The current required to alter the direction of the magnestism in a core must be of a minimum critical value, thus if currents of one half of this value are passed through two wires at right angles to each other this critical minimum will only be located where the two wires intersect. That is, at this point, the sum of the two half pulses is sufficient to change the condition of the core, but at this point only. This means that any individual core in the matrix can be selected according to its unique reference on the grid of wires.

However, in one matrix, or plane, only one core can be accessed at a time. If, for example, an attempt was made to access two cores through two wires in each direction, since these intersect at four points, four, not two, cores would be effected.

To enable access to a number of cores simultaneously a number of planes are assembled vertically thus giving a number of vertical columns of cores. Each core in the column represents a binary bit and the column represents a binary word. All of the cores in a selected column can be accessed simultaneously by passing pulses through the appropriate pair of wires in each plane at the same time (see Figure 7.4).

While this technique will set the cores to represent binary digits, we must, of course, provide the capacity to interpret, or read, the state of each core. This function is again based on an elementary electrical principle: if the polarity of a magnetic field is changed in conjunction to a wire, an induced current will be generated in the wire. To pick up this induced current we thread a third wire S (see Figure 7.5) through each core. Now if half-pulses are passed simultaneously through A′–A and B′–B, then in core (a) the direction of magnetism, clockwise to the direction of the current, will remain unchanged and no pulse will be set up in S, but in core (b) the

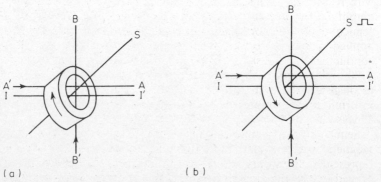

(a)   (b)

Figure 7.5   Reading from ferrite core

effect will be to reverse the direction of the field and this reversal will cause an induced pulse in S.

We now have in the sense wire S a representation of the binary state of the two cores (a) and (b)—no pulse = zero, a pulse = one—but in doing so we have destroyed the information originally held since both cores now read zero. It now becomes necessary to regenerate the original state of the cores.

Normally it will be required to retain the information originally represented which means it must now be written back to the original positions. This is known as a *regeneration cycle.* It is done immediately and automatically by copying back from a special register that accepted the information when it was originally read from store.

One major disadvantage of ferrite core memories is that they are expensive to produce. Their construction is time consuming because of the need to assemble the cores by threading through each one the read/write and sense wires.

Technical advances over the past few years in the fields of integrated circuitry and microelectronics have opened the way for the use of semiconductors as a basic memory element.

Semiconductor storage

It is usual in bulk storage memories to use *metal oxide semiconductors* (*MOS*) devices. These devices consist of a sandwich of metal oxide between a metal plate and a strip of silicon. The resistance and thus the conductivity of the silicon can be changed by applying a charge to the metal plate. We then have a situation in which a low degree of conductivity could be made to represent a binary 1 and a high degree of conductivity a binary 0. With, in effect, wires attached to either end of the silicon chip—a source and a drain wire respectively—the source wire can be tested through a sense amplifier for current flow. One problem with this type of semiconductor memory is that it is *volatile.* This means that, having applied a charge to the metal plate—the gate—the increased conductivity of the silicon chip is of short duration only, around 2-20 milliseconds. It is therefore necessary continually to reconstitute the state of the semiconductors by recycling the information they represent back to them every few milliseconds. This is known as a *refresh cycle.*

Semiconductor memories of this type, in contrast to the ferro-magnetic core memory, aré current dependent—the information represented disappears as soon as the current is disconnected. It is argued that in the modern computer this is no great disadvantage since very fast peripheral transfers obviate the need to store data or programs in the memory for any significant period of time.

Techniques in microelectronic technology now permit the assembly of a very large number of MOS memory cells on a very small silicon chip and to produce them relatively cheaply. For example, a chip no more than a quarter of an inch square can hold over 64K of memory. The layout of a MOS memory is shown in Figure 7.6.

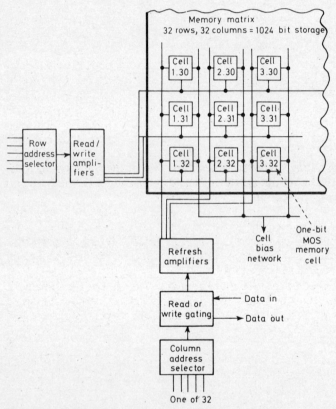

Figure 7.6   Example of semiconductor random access memory

Read only memories

Some of the information held in the central processor is unchanging and permanent, for example control information such as the machine function code.

To hold this static data, memory devices are required to hold a binary representation which is incapable of being changed once the registers have been constructed. These are known as *read only memories* (ROM). The state of these registers in binary terms is constant and their output will always be the same whenever input pulses are submitted to them.

External storage

As was indicated earlier, it is unnecessary for the internal store of a computer to store all of the information required in processing an average business system. Only a small proportion of the information is required at any one time and the mass of data relating to the system can be stored on devices external to the processor. This form of storage is known as *backing storage*.

Current computer technology has produced a mass of different models of backing storage devices and it is beyond the province of this book to give a comprehensive review of all of them. Basically we can divide them into two types of store, one known as *serial access* and the other as *direct* or *random access*. The difference between these two hinges on the way in which data can be located when required. To illustrate this, if we had half-a-dozen table tennis balls stored in a long square sectioned box, two of the ways in which the balls could be got out are through a lid at the end, or through a lid on one side down the full length of the box.

In the first case, if we wanted to get at the third ball it would be necessary to remove the first two before it became accessible. This is an example of serial access storage. In order to reach one particular item of data in serial access storage it is necessary to run through all the items of data preceding it.

In the second case we could gain access to the third ball without disturbing the others since they appear all laid out in a row. This is an example of direct access storage. Data in direct access storage is laid out in such a way that any item can be selected without reference to the others.

Some early computers used punched cards and/or punched paper tape as backing storage, holding files of data on these and reading them into the computer as and when required. This is rarely the case nowadays, magnetic recording being the basis of the most extensively used forms of backing storage.

Serial access storage

Magnetic tape

Magnetic tape is a very convenient way of storing large volumes of data in a comparatively small space. Magnetic tape decks are linked permanently to the computer but the reels of tape are interchangeable. This means that a library of tapes can be built up containing stored data and programs, tapes being selected at will and loaded on to a deck for processing as and when required. Data items recorded on magnetic tape can only be serially accessed by the computer. It is impractical for the computer to jump from one location to another on the tape in order to find the required item, so it must progress serially through the tape, rejecting irrelevant data, until it finds the item required. This form of storage then is used for data which is to be processed in the same sequence as it appears on the tape.

Characteristics of magnetic tape   Most magnetic tape used in computer storage is $\frac{1}{2}$ inch wide and made of a tough plastic such as Mylar. It is coated with a material that can be magnetized and is held on spools of varying lengths, up to 2400 ft.

Tape is processed on an 'on-line' peripheral known as a *tape deck*. A number of such tape decks can be linked to the processor at the same time. In some ways it is similar to a domestic tape recorder having three main elements: (Figure 7.7)

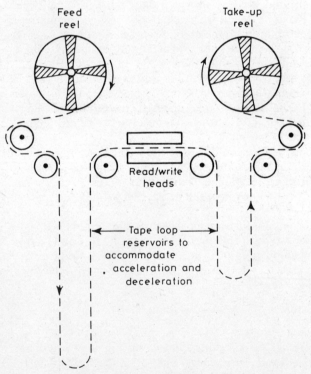

Figure 7.7   Magnetic tape deck (schematic)

(1) A recording, reading and erasing device.
(2) A driving mechanism to move the tape past the read/write head
(3) Two reels, one holding the unprocessed tape and the other to take up the processed tape.

On either side of the read/write head are loops or reservoirs of tape which help to ensure that the tape passes the head at a constant speed.

Individual characters are recorded as a row of small areas or dots across the width of the tape representing binary bits, magnetized in

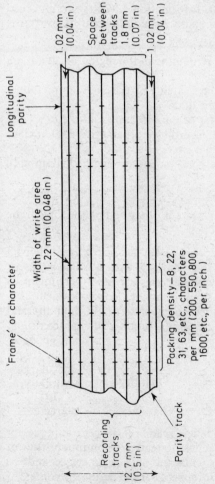

Figure 7.8   Example of section of magnetic tape

the opposite direction to the permanent field of the tape. This row of bits is known as a *frame* while the positioning of bits longitudinally on the tape are on what are known as *tracks* (see Figure 7.8). Each character is represented by a unique pattern of bits, often using the same binary code as that used in the internal store of the processor. One track is used for parity checking purposes in the same way as on paper tape.

The number of characters recorded on a given length of tape is known as the *packing density* and varies from system to system. It is expressed in terms of characters per inch common packing densities being 200, 550, 800 and 1600. Information is written to and read from the tape on program command through the central processor.

Other important characteristics are

(1) Capacity of a 2400 ft tape could be in the region of 20 million characters.
(2) Reels of tape can be used repeatedly by erasing data no longer required and recording new data.
(3) While the speed of transfer of data to and from the tapes will vary with the way in which recording is organized it could well be in the region of 300 000 characters a second.
(4) Data may be preserved for an indefinite length of time until deliberately erased.

Organization of data on tape   Data is organized on the tape in the following way:

First, a number of characters are assembled into what is called a *field*. A number of fields together comprise what is called a *record*. As a practical example of how these terms are used there might be one record for each item of stock in a stock control system each consisting of four fields—part number, description, quantity and unit price—and each field made up of a number of characters.

	RECORD		
FIELD	FIELD	FIELD	FIELD
Part Number	Description	Quantity	Unit Price
4	15	3	10
characters	characters	characters	characters

We have already seen that data is read into the central processor when it is required. It is impractical to read in a continuous flow of data as there must be pauses while the data is processed and the results written out. It is, therefore, necessary to define the volume of data that can be transferred at any one time. This may be just one single record or will more likely be a multiple number of records and is known as a *block* of data.

A number of characters = a field
A number of fields   = a record
A number of records   = a block.

Bearing in mind that each character is represented by a row of magnetized dots across the tape, it will be appreciated that a continuous succession of such rows representing characters would, in itself, be completely meaningless. Some method must be devised of defining the limits of each data field, each data record and indeed each data block. Two ways of doing this suggest themselves.

One way is to use *fixed length records,* which means that the number of frames allocated to each field and the number of fields allocated to each record are always constant. If we then write into the program a definition of these field and records lengths the processor will be able to tell when each ends by counting the number of characters as they are transferred.

Such a method, however, has one obvious disadvantage. When setting sizes, they must be large enough to accommodate the longest data item that is likely to occur which means a great deal of space is likely to be unused. One way of getting around this problem is to use what are known as *variable length records.*

The use of a variable length recording mode means that only the precise number of frames required to record a data item are used. This still leaves the problem of defining the limits of each field, record etc, and this is done by inserting *markers*, i.e. a special pattern of bits the computer will recognize as such, at the end of each data element. At the end of each field an *End of Field Marker* (EFM) and at the end of each record an *End of Record Marker* (ERM). Furthermore, as we saw earlier it is necessary to move data to and from the tape in blocks, an additional marker known as an *End of Block Marker* (EBM) is used to define the limits of a block (Figure 7.9).

Given then this principle of transferring data in blocks, the tape itself, instead of moving at a continuous even speed will be required to move in short bursts, starting at the beginning and stopping at the end of each block. Since reading and writing takes place at a critical speed of tape movement, an unrecorded length of tape must be left between blocks to enable the tape to decelerate to a stop and then to accelerate again to reach the required transfer speed. This space is known as an *inter-block gap* (see Figure 7.9).

Data blocks need not be of a fixed length or indeed contain a standard number of records. Systems considerations will determine

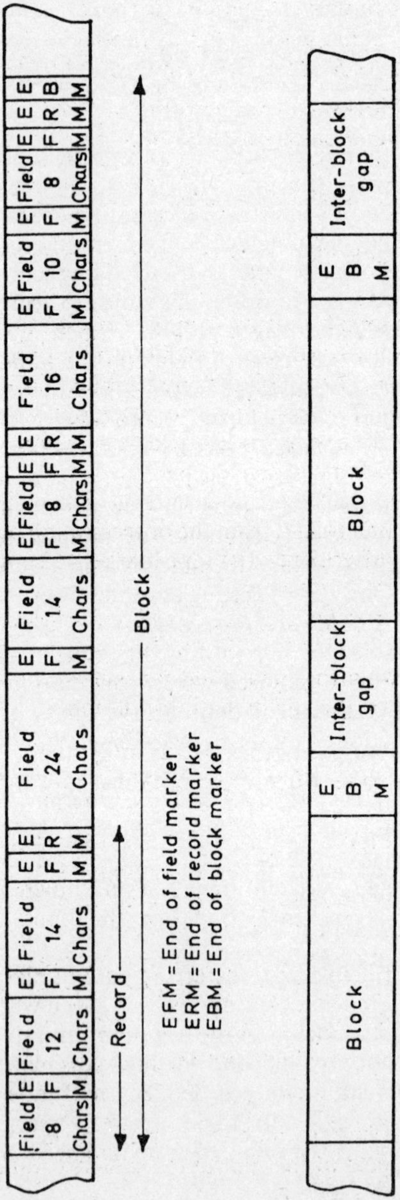

Figure 7.9 Organization of data on magnetic tape

whether a variable or fixed length block recording mode is used, bearing in mind, however, that blocks will have both a critical minimum and maximum length determined by hardware considerations. Records may be assembled in blocks as

(1) Fixed-fixed blocks—a fixed number of fixed length records.
(2) Fixed-variable blocks—a fixed number of variable length records.
(3) Variable-fixed blocks—a variable number of fixed length records.
(4) Variable-variable blocks—a variable number of variable length records.

On a magnetic tape provision is made for indicating the point at which recording may start and, to avoid over-running the end of the tape, where it must finish. This is done by siting markers on the tape known as *load point marker* and *end of tape marker* respectively. These are light reflective strips mounted on the reverse side of the tape that are detected by the mechanism of the tape deck. It is between these two markers that recording takes place. However, since the transfer unit to and from the processor is a block, sufficient space must be left after the end of tape marker to complete writing a block of data.

Another factor incorporated into the tape are *labels* occupying the first and the last recording blocks. The first of these at the beginning of the tape following the load point marker is known as a *header label*. It will contain the following information:

(1) A code identifying the block as a header label.
(2) Tape serial number (identification of the tape itself rather than its contents).
(3) File identification by name and the reel number within the file (should the file consist of two or more reels).
(4) The generation or version reference of the file.
(5) The date on which the file was written.
(6) The purge data. This, for security purposes, indicates the earliest date on which the data can be destroyed by over-writing.
(7) Control software.

The other label, occupying the final block on the tape—known as a *trailer label*—will contain:

(1) A code identifying the block as a trailer label.
(2) Probably a repeat of the file name, sequence number within the file and version reference.
(3) File control information specifying whether end of file or referring to file continuation tape.

(4) Data block count (statement of number of blocks contained on tape).

These two labels provide a means for security checks to take place when the tape is loaded and run. File identification data is communicated to the computer by the operator through supervisory software and a check made against the detail in the header label to ensure the correct file has been loaded. While processing, a block count is made for checking against the count in the trailer label and a report made of any discrepancy. A check is also made of the purge date and should this be after the current run date the computer will now allow overwriting to take place.

Read and write checks are incorporated into tape systems although the mechanics of the checks tend to vary system to system. However, it is usual to make parity checks and many systems have an *echo check*. This latter is a second reading of each character, or a read after write check, the two being compared for discrepancies.

Other read and write functions include a rewind facility to wind the tape back on to the original feed reel, and the ability to back space one block at a time. This enables a second attempt to be made should a fault have been signalled in the initial read or write operation. Some tape systems incorporate a read-reverse function, which simply means that data can be read when the tape is moving from the take-up reel to the feed-reel.

Tape operation speeds and capacity   Two main factors will govern the transfer rate of data to and from magnetic tape. These are (a) the packing density and (b) the speed of tape movement over the read/write heads.

This transfer rate is expressed in thousands of characters per second abbreviated as k ch/s. For example, the theoretical transfer rate of a tape moving at 120 ins a second with a packing density of 800 cpi is 96 k ch/s, but, of course, the average transfer rate for the whole tape will be considerably less because of the time spent in stop/start operations at inter-block gaps. Probably a fair average for the bulk of the systems used in commercial data processing is about 150–200 k ch/s.

The criteria which determine the total recording capacity of a given length reel of tape are the packing density, file design considerations such as the use of fixed or variable record lengths, the size of data blocks and the frequency of inter-block gaps. To quote a standard for, say, a 2400 ft tape is impractical but, with a packing density of 800 cpi it could well be in the region of 200 million characters.

Example of processing using magnetic tape We will consider the example quoted earlier in this chapter of a Sales Ledger system where movement data, sales, returns, cash etc, have to be posted to Sales Ledger accounts.

Initially a master tape would be prepared containing customer name and address, account reference and opening balance. Movement data would then be written to a second tape from, say, punched cards prepared from source documentation.

The two tapes are then linked on-line to the central processor. Data is read into the processor store from the master tape for the first account and also the movement data relating to the same account from the movements tape. The master data and the movement data are merged, at the same time calculating a new balance, and then the whole of the up-dated data written to a third tape. This third tape now becomes the master tape for the next up-dating run (Figure 7.10).

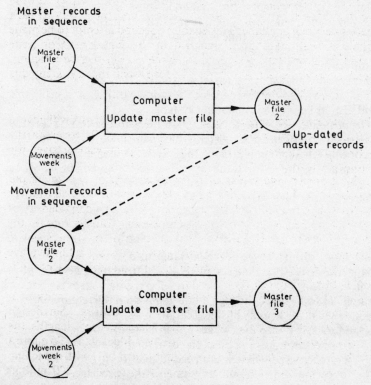

Figure 7.10 Processing data held on magnetic tape

The product of this kind of processing is a series of versions or *generations* of master tape each one more up to date than its predecessor. It is customary to keep on file at least three consecutive versions together with the movement tapes used for up-dating so that in the event of destruction or corruption of a file the means exist to reconstitute it. This practice is often referred to as a 'grandfather-father-son' technique.

Since records on tape are processed serially, i.e. one after another throughout the length of the tape, it is important that the records on both the master and movement tapes are stored in the same order. This is usually achieved by giving each data element e.g. each Sales Ledger account a unique reference number, known as a *key*, and sorting and storing both master and movement records in key sequence.

Magnetic tape cassettes

The above comments on magnetic tape centre around the conventional open spool system found in most mainframe computer installations. A cassette tape is one stored in a container—a cassette—in many cases virtually identical with the tape cassette used in audio systems. They have the virtue that they are easy to store and can be easily loaded into a cassette handler. They are widely used in small microcomputer systems for the storage of files and programs and also in key-to-tape encoding systems.

In principle, their use follows much the same pattern as already described for open-spool systems the main difference being that recording is by bits serially along the length of the tape rather than in frames across the width of the tape. A cassette tape will probably be between 200 and 300 feet in length and will record up to 100 characters per inch.

Direct or random access stores

One major disadvantage in the backing store so far considered, viz magnetic tape, is that data can only be read from it in the same order as it was recorded. If it is required to select a data item at random, a search has to be made through all the items until the required data is found, which is a lengthy business entailing transferring every record to the processor until the correct one is located.

Direct access storage enables the computer to select any item of data irrespective of where it is stored in relation to the other items. The following is an account of some of the direct access storage devices available.

Magnetic discs

There is today on the market a very wide range of types of disc storage unit from large high capacity *fixed disc stores* to small *minifloppy discs* developed for use with microcomputers. This section will deal in detail with one of these only: the most widely used type of disc unit with mainframe machines known as an *exchangeable disc store.* A brief summary of other types of disc store is given at the end.

Physical characteristics   A disc has, on either side, a recording surface on which small areas, or dots, can be magnetized to represent binary bits. The disc surface is divided into a number of concentric circles, known as *tracks,* along which recording takes place. The surface is also divided into *sectors* by a number of non-recording lines set as radii from the centre of the disc to its circumference (Figure 7.11). Each sector of each track can record a fixed maximum number of characters.

In an exchangeable disc system, a number of discs are mounted parallel to each other on a central spindle so providing a multiple number of recording surfaces. These sets of discs, known as *disc cartridges* or *disc packs,* can be mounted or removed at will from the transport. The transport is kept permanently on-line to the processor while the disc packs themselves, holding data files or programs, can be stored in plastic containers remote from the computer for use as required.

The discs themselves are around 14 inch diameter and while the number of discs in a pack vary with the manufacturer, the most popular is a pack containing six discs. Of the twelve surfaces available only ten are used for recording purposes, the exposed top and bottom surfaces not being used.

The disc transport contains a number of read/write heads, one for each recording surface. These are fixed on the ends of a number of retractable arms, two per arm, so they can be moved within the spaces between the discs, one head scanning each surface. These arms are in turn fixed to a retractable assembly known as a *tracking arm.* Individual read/write heads are unable to move independently, all moving at the same time with the tracking arm. This means that at any one time all tracks in the same relative position on the discs are accessed simultaneously. The disc pack rotates at high speed in relation to the read/write heads conveying every sector of the track to its head in turn (Figure 7.12).

Mode of recording   As is the case with other forms of magnetic storage media, the basic recording unit is a binary digit (a bit). In the

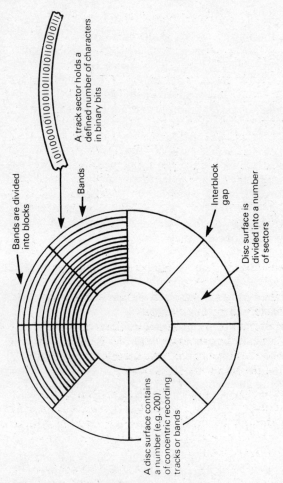

Bands are divided into blocks

Bands

A track sector holds a defined number of characters in binary bits

Interblock gap

Disc surface is divided into a number of sectors

A disc surface contains a number (e.g. 200) of concentric recording tracks or bands

Figure 7.11   A disc surface

case of a disc, these bits are recorded in succession along the length of the track, and, in order to distinguish character from character, may well be organized in groups of six. We have then a number of surfaces, each containing a number of circular tracks, say 200, each track divided into a number of sectors, usually known as *blocks*, say 8 per track, and each block capable of holding a number of characters in 6-bit groupings, say 512. In order to locate any item of stored data each block must have a unique address. This is constructed by reference to the disc surface, the number of the track

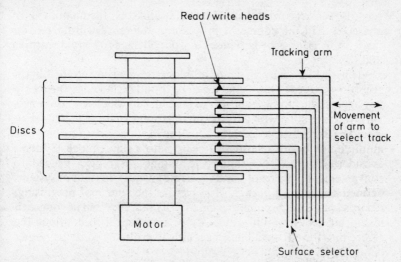

Figure 7.12   Exchangeable disc unit showing track and surface selection

on the surface and the number of the block within the track. A block, then, is an addressable unit of disc storage.

Read/write operations are by program command, transferring data between the disc and the processor store. Such commands will specify the address on the disc that has to be accessed. On initiating a read/write operation the following takes place:

(1) The tracking arm moves all the read/write heads together until they are positioned over the track that has been addressed. The time taken for this operation is known as *seek time* and will, of course, depend on the distance the heads have to travel. A typical average time is about 30 milliseconds.

(2) An electronic surface selector switch (see Figure 7.12) activates the read/write head in conjunction with the surface addressed. The time taken for this is negligible.

(3) The disc, which is continuously revolving, turns until the addressed block is under the read/write head. The time taken for this operation is known as *rotational delay* a typical average time being around 10 milliseconds.

(4) The contents of the addressed block are then transferred to store at between 300 and 600 k cps depending on the system.

Organization of data on disc   Let us remind ourselves that when storing data on discs it is in the forms of files, for example a stock control file, a sales ledger file etc. Each file is made up of a number of records, each record a number of fields and each field a number of characters. In the course of processing, reference will have to be made to specific records. These records will have to be (a) identified and (b) located.

Identification is by virtue of a unique reference contained in the record—the record key—and it can be found by indexing the record key against the physical address of the block in which it is contained.

If we are dealing with a fixed unit of storage space, e.g. a block, it would be unrealistic to expect a situation in which a data record, or a multiple number of records, fit neatly into a single block. Systems considerations will determine the number of blocks needed to conveniently hold a record and the name given to this unit of systems defined storage is a *bucket*. However, in the course of processing, records could well become expanded to a point they will no longer fit into a bucket. It would obviously be impractical to continue the record into the adjacent bucket as this will probably contain another data record.

This problem is resolved by reserving on the disc a number of tracks known as *overflow tracks*. Should a record become too large for its original location it is moved to an overflow track and a re-directing notice inserted in its original home track. This redirecting reference, usually known as a *tag* or a *pointer* quotes the new address of the re-located record (Figure 7.13).

When a file is first written to disc, it may appear that the best way would be to start recording on the outermost track of a selected disc, when that was full proceed to the next track inwards and so on. Further consideration would reveal that in this situation, every time we wished to refer to a record on another track the read/write head would have to be moved taking around 40–80 milliseconds. If, however, we used the same relative track on each of the ten recording surfaces giving a vertical rather than a horizontal array of tracks (Figure 7.14), we have a situation where ten times the number of records are accessible without any movement of the read/write heads. The name given to a set of tracks used in this way is a *cylinder*. Of course, a number of adjacent cylinders may be required to accommodate a data file, involving a degree of head movement to access different cylinders, but this technique has the effect of minimizing the seek time.

Disc operation speeds and capacity   In view of the wide range of different disc systems in use, it is impractical to quote firm recording capacities and read/write speeds. The number of recording tracks per disc will vary between 100 and 200 from model to model. Packing density tends to vary from system to system. It may be as

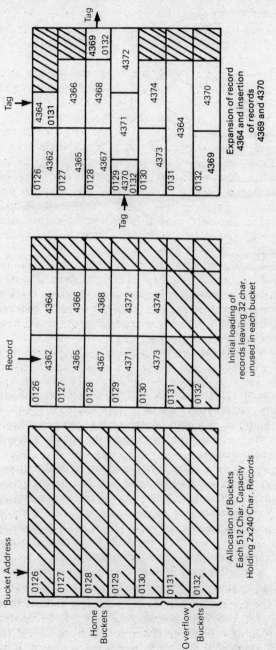

Figure 7.13 Storage of records on disc

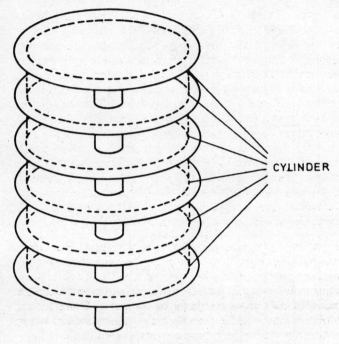

CYLINDER

Figure 7.14   Schematic storage cylinder

low as 250 bpi or as high as 3000. A fair average in an exchangeable disc system is around 1000. It will be appreciated that for any one disc, since the physical length of the track at the perimeter will be greater than the one at the centre, the packing density will vary with the position of the track.

The following is an example of an exchangeable disc store: Each disc transport carries one pack of six 14 inch discs giving a total of 10 recording surfaces. There are 200 recording tracks per surface, each divided into eight blocks. A block has a capacity to record 512 characters, giving 4096 characters per track, 819 200 characters per surface and 8 192 000 characters per unit. Each character is held in six bits, four characters making up the basic unit of storage, viz. a 24 bit word. It is possible to link 8 transports simultaneously on-line giving a total storage capacity of 65·536 million characters.

The discs revolve at 2400 rev/min, each surface having one read/write head. Transfer rate is 208 k chs and average access time is 97.6 ms made up of average latency 12.5 ms and average seek time 85 ms. Cylinder capacity is 40 960 characters.

Fixed disc stores   This usually consists of one or more large discs permanently mounted vertically on a horizontal spindle rotating at high speed, say 1800 rev/min under read/write heads. Different size discs are available ranging from 25 to 39 inches diameter. Due to the size of the disc the time taken for the head to move through the distance necessary to locate a specific track, the seek time, is quite high. To reduce this, many systems incorporate a multiple number of heads on each arm, each head servicing only a small number of tracks, while others use one head per track, so eliminating the seek time completely. Fixed disc stores can provide a massive on-line storage capacity. Units are available that will hold up to 600 million characters and a number of such units can be linked simultaneously on-line to the processor. Due to the use of a multiple number of read/write heads, access time is likely to be faster than with exchangeable disc stores, in the region of 20–25 ms.

Small disc systems   Often known as *diskettes*, a range of these small disc systems has been introduced over the recent past for use with microcomputer systems. They also have an application in key-to-disc encoding techniques and further provide a convenient means of mailing recorded data from computer to computer. Diskettes are made of a pliable plastic rather than the rigid construction of larger discs and this gives rise to their popular name *floppy discs*.

A diskette is a single disc, around 8 inch diameter, housed in a square sleeve. It is not removed from the sleeve when loaded on to the disc unit. In principle, diskettes are used for much the same purpose as larger discs, storage of master files, programs etc. Each side has a recording capacity of around 240 000 characters.

A smaller version, approx $5\frac{1}{4}$ inch diameter known as a *mini-diskette* or more popularly as a *mini-floppy disc* is also available for use with small microcomputers. In principle, they operate in the same way as diskettes but, of course, have a smaller capacity, in the region of about 90 000 characters.

Magnetic drums

This device consists essentially of a cylinder coated with magnetizable material. The surface is divided into a number of circular tracks, each in turn divided into a number of recording sectors each uniquely addressable through the track and sector reference. The drum is permanently mounted in a device where it rotates at high speed.

In early days of computers they were used as a central processor store either in their own right or as a back-up to mercury delay line

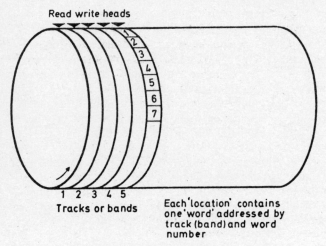

Figure 7.15   Diagrammatic representation of drum storage

stores or small core stores. With the introduction of the much faster ferrite core stores, they were no longer used for this purpose although more recently have been reintroduced as a high speed direct access backing store (Figure 7.15).

Reading and writing to drums is through heads aerodynamically floated over the drum surface. In most drum systems there is one head per track. This provides very fast access by eliminating seek time, and with the drum rotating at over 7000 rev/min, the rotational delay time is very small. Among the faster drum systems, a $10\frac{1}{2}$ inch diameter drum, revolving at over 7000 rev/min will give an average access time of 4.25 ms and data transfer rates of nearly 1500 k cps.

The storage capacity of drums varies widely for different designs from say 1.5 million to 130 million characters. A number of drum units can be linked on-line to the processor simultaneously, giving a massive backing store facility. The fast access time offered by some drum systems compared with discs, lend them for use in time-sharing and real time systems where fast access times and transfer rates are called for.

Exercises

1. Compare and contrast magnetic tape and disc files and indicate the most appropriate method of arranging files on these media.

2. Define and illustrate the difference between direct and serial access stores.

3. What is a *backing store*? Suggest types of backing store available and explain how these work in relation to the central processor.

4. Distinguish between an *immediate access store* and a *backing store*, giving a brief account of the relationship between the two.

5. Explain how data is organized on magnetic tape and how data items may be accessed.

6. Draw a diagram to show how data is recorded on magnetic tape. What is the difference between fixed and variable length fields? Give examples of the use of each.

7. What do you understand by the term *up-dating*? Draw a diagram to show how a Master Stock Ledger File would be up-dated by issues and receipts from stock.

8. Explain the following terms in relation to magnetic tape:

   (a) A Block
   (b) A Field
   (c) A Record

9. Explain how data is recorded on a magnetic disc and suggest how data items may be located.

10. Compare and contrast a *fixed disc store* with an *exchangeable disc store*.

11. Explain the *cylinder* concept of holding records on disc mentioning any advantages you feel accrue to this technique.

12. What do you understand by the terms *seek-time* and *rotational-delay* in connection with disc storage?

13. What is the purpose of (a) a header label and (b) a trailer label? Give some indication of the contents of these two labels.

14. Explain how the recording of data is organized on disc specifically explaining in your answer the meaning of the following terms:

   (a) Track
   (b) Block
   (c) Bucket

15. Explain how the computer deals with the situation when a record held on disc has grown too large for its location to accommodate it.

8

Digital computers and processing modes

We have, so far, been thinking about digital computers in a rather general sense, as a machine with these five basic functions:

INPUT   STORAGE   PROCESSING   CONTROL   OUTPUT

consisting of hardware to perform these functions:

CENTRAL PROCESSOR   INPUT DEVICES   STORAGE DEVICES   OUTPUT DEVICES

with software to define the operations

PROGRAM INSTRUCTIONS

and the throughput as one main stream of data

READ IN   PROCESS   WRITE OUT

The purpose of this chapter is to extend our thinking a little in terms of two factors (a) different categories of digital computer and (b) different computer operating modes. We will look in a little more detail at computer software in a later chapter.

Types of digital computer

Three terms often encountered in computer descriptions and specifications are *main frame computers, minicomputers,* and *microcomputers.*

While the demarcation lines between these tend to be a little hazy, the following tries to put them within a meaningful framework although at best, bearing in mind the wide range of machines currently on the market, it is possible to make only a number of generalizations.

Main frame computers

This term generally refers to medium or large machines designed for large scale data processing coping with a wide spectrum of commercial systems such as sales and purchase accounting, stock inventory and control systems, wages systems etc.

The main features of this type of machine include:

(1) Range of peripheral input, output and storage devices.
(2) Large, fast central processor store.
(3) Support services for data preparation, data control, programming system design and operating.
(4) Usually a centralized service department in its own right.
(5) Subject to environmental control, e.g. airconditioning, temperature control.
(6) Often supports remote input/output terminals.

Main frame computer installations are very expensive to install and are justified only in very high volume data processing situations.

Minicomputers

As the name suggests this is a smaller version of a digital computer with both the central processor and the peripherals being on a smaller scale. Features of this type of machine include:

(1) Physically smaller hardware units.
(2) Central processor store tends to be small although, with the introduction of semiconductor memories, recent models have tended to substantially increase memory capacity.
(3) Backing storage peripherals, if used at all, tend to be smaller, e.g. small flexible disc units rather than the standard exchangeable disc pack unit and smaller magnetic tapes of perhaps 600 ft instead of the standard main frame 2400 ft tape.
(4) Range of input/output peripherals tends to be limited. Punched card, paper tape and keyboard inputs are fairly common while printed output is usually by serial printer, matrix printer and/or VDU.
(5) Minicomputers will probably have a shorter central processor word length than main frame computers, up to 16 bits, and the range of machine functions, machine code, tends to be smaller. These two factors may result in a slower operation time.
(6) The controlled environment necessary for main frame machines is not needed for a minicomputer.

Minicomputers are far less expensive than main frame machines but are capable of coping with most of the data processing jobs done on the larger machines.

Software for these machines has reached a high state of development, some machines offer multiprogramming operating systems and a range of utility programs and compilers are available.

Microcomputers

The microcomputer is one of the products of the development of microelectronics over the past few years. Its construction is based on silicon integrated circuits (silicon chips). A silicon chip only 5 mm² by 0.1 mm thick is capable of holding many thousands of semi-conductor circuits. Indeed, such a chip may hold 64 K of memory.

The main features of microcomputers are:

(1) Very small since they are based on silicon chip technology.
(2) Very cheap, a small fraction of the cost of a main frame computer.
(3) Backing storage peripherals usually small floppy discs or cassette magnetic tape.
(4) Input/output peripherals limited. In many machines program and data entered through keyboard while output through display unit and/or serial printer.
(5) Software development has tended to lag behind technical advances. However, some standard package application programs are available from manufacturers for use on their own machines but the cost of these is relatively high compared with hardware costs.
(6) Some machines offer one language only, often BASIC, the compiler or interpreter being permanently stored in the hardware in the form of read only memory chips. Other machines are able to cope with modified forms of COBOL and FORTRAN.
(7) Compared with main frame machines, the operating time of micros is slow.
(8) The use of microelectronics mounted on plug-in modules enables microcomputers to be up-dated fairly readily e.g. to increase memory capacity.

All in all, the future of the microcomputer in commercial data processing may lie in their use as dedicated machines programmed for particular applications in specific departments in contrast to the main frame centralized machine catering for all processing jobs within an organization. This would appear to be economically viable in terms both of hardware and operating costs.

Two major current applications for the use of microcomputers in commerce are in *word processing* for which software packages are available and *visible record computers*.

Visible record computers

One important feature of a computer system that holds its files in an electronic or magnetic storage medium is that these records are unreadable by sight. To retrieve the records in a readable form we have to ask the computer to print them out or display them. This is in contrast to the old accounting machine in which a ledger card holding a printed record was available for immediate inspection. This card not only gave up-to-date balances, but also contained the history of transactions over a period of time. It was a very convenient and ready 'look-up' medium which many firms have been reluctant to dispense with.

Another factor, particular for the small or medium sized company, is that small processing volumes do not justify the capital and running costs of a conventional computer.

Over the past few years there has been a growing demand for small computers that will satisfy these two conditions: machines that are relatively cheap to install and operate and that will provide a visible record of transactions, the visible record computer. While this type of machine was on the market before the advent of microtechnology, the use of microcomputers as the base for these machines has increased their versatility and reduced their cost.

From a systems point of view these computers have not departed in principle from the old mechanical accounting machines where a file of ledger cards was held, each card containing a printed record of past transactions. As new transactions were made, having first been recorded on source documents—invoices, stock requisitions etc.— they were entered through the keyboard bringing the ledger card up to date and automatically calculating current balances.

One important change from a hardware point of view has been to provide a means for the automatic entry of master data relating to each ledger card. This is usually done by storing the data magnetically on a magnetic stripe running down the length of the card. For example, in a sales ledger system the following information would be stored:

Customer name and address
Customer account number
Credit limit
Current balance
Age analysis of outstanding balance, i.e. 1 month, 2 months etc.

On inserting the card into the machine this data is automatically written to the computer's memory.

Primary input of movement data is through a normally operated keyboard. Identifying data, e.g. account number, is checked on keyboard entry against the version stored in the magnetic stripe and the card rejected if the two do not coincide. Movement data is then entered, accepted into the machine's memory and also printed as a hard copy on the ledger card. New balances are calculated in the machine's arithmetic unit and written out, with relevant movement data, to the card's magnetic stripe. Many machines incorporate an alpha/numeric visual line display to provide a visual verification of data as it is entered through the keyboard. There is provision on some machines for backing storage additional to the magnetic stripes on the ledger card. The form this takes varies from machine to machine but the convenience of floppy discs and magnetic tape cassettes make these popular.

In this type of system, programs for specific applications are usually obtained direct from the manufacturer although it is possible for the user, using the instruction code list applicable to his machine, to write programs and enter them manually through the keyboard.

Among the advantages claimed for VRCs are

(1) They will fit into a normal office situation, the machine becoming part of the department rather than the department becoming part of the machine.
(2) Will do many commercial applications just as adequately and efficiently as a large computer, although more slowly.
(3) No need for environmental control.
(4) Machine operation relatively easy and requires only a short period of training.
(5) No need for working in shifts. It is probably cheaper to buy a second machine than run an existing one for double the hours.
(6) Skilled systems and programming staff not required.
(7) The VRC tends to be a very reliable piece of equipment. Maintenance costs are low and time losses from 'down' periods tend to be small.

Processing modes

Batch processing

As the name suggests, this processing mode is designed to process a number, a batch, of records at the same time rather than each individual record as it arises. Source documents recording movement data are collected together over a period of time such as a day, a week or a month. Should these documents be in a non-machine-acceptable form, e.g. hand-written records, they are first converted into machine-acceptable medium such as punched cards or punched paper tape.

These batches of movement data are then transferred periodically through the computer to backing storage—say magnetic tape—and so progressively over a period of time all of the movement records are concentrated on to one file, a 'movements file'. At the end of an accounting period this movements file is run against master files, for example sales ledger, purchase ledger or stock inventory, and the master records are updated to produce the required end product, e.g. sales statements, invoices, stock movement lists etc. An example of a batch processing application is given in Chaper 14.

Multi-programming

A limiting factor in the degree of efficiency at which a processor will work is the comparatively slow operational speeds of input and output devices. One most significant feature of a computer is the incredibly fast speed at which its central processor will work. As we saw earlier, in modern machines, the operation cycle time is measured in thousandths of millionths of a second. While however it is capable of these speeds, one inhibiting factor from a practical point of view centres around the problem of supplying it with input data fast enough to keep it occupied and, indeed, extracting processed results fast enough to let it get on with the next problem. A popular title given to this situation when the central processor is kept waiting for new data to get on with is *peripheral bound*.

It is rather like working on a production line where the objects on which you are working arrive at one minute intervals, but it takes you only six seconds to do the work. In these circumstances we may argue that the sensible thing to do would be to start a second production line so that you could alternate between the two instead of waiting for 54 seconds in each minute. This would at any rate have the effect of doubling your efficiency from a resource usage point of view, from 10% to 20%. We may further argue that by providing ten production lines your efficiency rating could be maximized at 100%. Theoretically, but hardly possible in practice.

Similarly with a central processor. If while processing one job there are lengthy idle intervals while waiting for input/output operations to be completed, why not provide another job it can be getting on with during these intervals? This can be done by holding two or more programs in the processor at the same time so that when unable to work on one of them due to slow peripheral activity it can switch to another that is demanding processing time. This mode of operating is known as *multi-programming*.

Multi-programming can only be carried out on a configuration designed to provide this facility. A sophisticated operating system is necessary and also a sufficient range of on-line peripherals to support the concurrent running of a number of jobs.

As a simple example, let us assume that two programs A and B are held in the processor. Program A calls for reading in a block of records from magnetic tape on each of which a simple calculation is to be carried out while program B calls for a lengthy calculation taking up to 200 milliseconds of processing time. Now if it takes say 50 milliseconds to read in the block of records but only 5 milliseconds to perform the calculations, the processor will be sitting idle for 45 milliseconds waiting for the next block to arrive. On completion of the 5 milliseconds processing time the operating system will communicate with the magnetic tape deck only to find it is still reading. It will at this point stop operating on program A, although its read instruction will continue autonomously until completed, and look around for something else to keep the processor busy. This operation is known as *program suspend*. Program B is queued up waiting for time and so the operating system switches control to that and the processor gets on with the 200 milliseconds calculation called for. After 45 milliseconds the tape reading for program A will have been completed and the operating system informed to that effect. We now have two programs demanding processing time and the system will have to decide which of the two is going to be operated. This decision is made in the light of priorities previously determined by the programmer and written in to the operating system. This is known as *work scheduling*. If we assume that A has precedence over B then control is switched back to A at this point interrupting the work being done on B even though this may not have been completed. This is known as a *program interrupt*. Control will be switched back to B again when there is next a spell of idle time arising from A. Perhaps it should be noted that, when interrupted, the processor will dump the intermediate results of its processing in special registers so that it can automatically take up the point at which it left off when more time is available.

This example is based on two programs only, a situation referred to as *dual programming*. Multi-programming is when several programs are operating simultaneously, each with its own level of priority. In practice, time is taken up by the operating system switching and searching activities, and also the sequence of processing activities between programs is highly unlikely to be continuous, the central processor utilization is still therefore less than full. Nevertheless, this operating mode does provide a very marked increase in processor efficiency.

Time sharing

As we saw in Chapter 4 when discussing input devices, data for computer entry does not always originate in close proximity to the computer but it may originate in a number of scattered points remote from the machine. This situation gives rise to two alternative approaches: either to site a number of small machines at the remote points processing the data locally or to transmit the data by one means or another to a larger centralized machine.

While the second alternative has the inherent disadvantage of having to move data over long distances, it has in many cases the overriding advantages of economy in hardware, a centralized source of information and a closer control of the organization as a whole. In fact, there has been a tendency over the past few years towards the establishment of large powerful central computers capable of dealing with data originating over a very wide area. We further saw in Chapter 4 that it is usual to transmit this data over communication links and that a number of types of terminal are available for this purpose.

A *time-sharing system* provides a situation where a number of users have access to the computer virtually simultaneously via say, teletype or visual display terminals, linked by transmission line to the computer. Each terminal is provided with its own small data store, known as a buffer, in which data is held while being entered through the terminal. The reason for this is that if data was transmitted character by character as entered through a terminal keyboard it would be a far too slow process for the computer at the other end. When entry is completed, the contents of the buffer is transferred at high speed in bulk. By the same token, computer output is similarly transferred to the buffer where the terminal can take its time printing it out. While this input/output process is going on at one terminal, the processor can carry on with work submitted by other terminals.

In practice what happens is that each user terminal is allocated a period of time during which the program it requires is made available in the processor and it has, in effect, exclusive use of the processor during this period. This time period, known as a *time slice* is quite small, around 10 ms.

The operating system in a time sharing situation will circulate all terminals allocating a time slice to each in rotation (Figure 8.1). In one second, a modern time sharing system can service many terminals. With a large number of users linked to one machine, all demanding processing facilities, a correspondingly large number of programs may have to be available to meet these needs. A processor can work on one program only at a time, so it becomes necessary to store all users' programs on some form of direct access storage device from which they can be transferred to the processor on demand as required although there is no reason why more than one program should not be stored in the processor at any one time.

For example, let us assume that programs for users A and B are

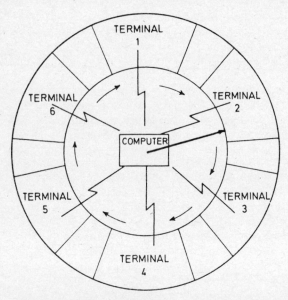

Figure 8.1 Time-sharing system

concurrently stored. As the time slice allocated to A expires, control immediately is switched to program B. While B is being operated A is moved out of memory back to backing storage and C is transferred in to take its place. When time has expired for B then C is operated, B moved out and D moved in. This process continues until all users have been given a slice of processing time and then the cycle starts all over again.

Real time systems

The essence of a *real-time system* is that it is designed to accept data relating to an activity immediately it occurs, to process the data and to output the results quickly enough to have an effect on the activity. This means that

(1) The files containing records and programs relating to a procedure must be held in a direct access storage, usually magnetic disc, permanently on-line to the computer.
(2) Facilities must exist, also permanently on-line, for the input and output of data, usually teletype or VDU terminals.
(3) While the computer may not be dedicated to real-time processing, i.e. it may work in batch mode as well, there must be an operating system that will instantly interrupt other work in favour of a real-time demand emanating from a terminal.

Features of a real-time system include

(a) Transactions or enquiries may be entered into the system on demand at any time.
(2) A response is received from the computer in a very short time. This *response time* must be short enough to enable any modification to take place to the activity giving rise to the enquiry.
(3) Master files are up-dated immediately movement data is received and so always show a completely up-to-date situation.

Because of this facility for receiving an enquiry on demand and providing an immediate up-to-date reply, on-line systems are frequently described as *conversational, interrogative* and *interactive* system (Figure 8.2).

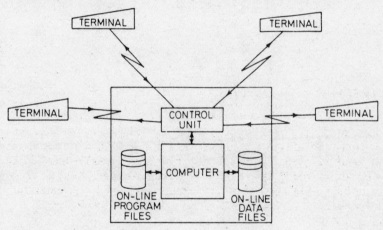

Figure 8.2   Real-time working

The classic example of a real-time system is airline seat reservations. In this, a request for a seat being entered through a terminal will result in a display of the seats available on a flight. On the seat being booked this must be immediately recorded, i.e. the files held in backing storage updated, otherwise incorrect information will be shown when the next customer comes along.

Another example is in banking when it may be required to check the balance on a customer's account at very short notice as, for example, when a cheque for withdrawal of cash is presented.

There are, however, problems associated with the use of real-time systems:

(1) Real-time systems are expensive both for hardware and software. In addition to a central processor with a large

immediate access store, hardware costs will include high volume direct access backing storage, terminals, and data transmission links between the computer and terminals. On the software side, an operating system is needed to cope with transactions and enquiries from remote points.

(2) Checks on data accuracy may be less stringent than those imposed in a batch processing situation.

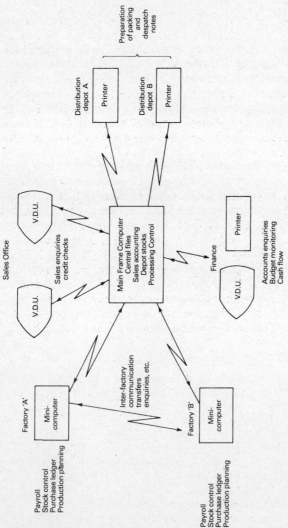

Figure 8.3   Distributed processing

(3) Since a large number of users may have access to master files, data on these may be less secure.
(4) The system is vulnerable in the event of a breakdown. It may be necessary to provide standby systems for use in the event of a major hardware or software failure.

Distributed processing

As we saw earlier, when data originates at a number of scattered remote points, one way of dealing with the situation is to site a small computer at each of these points. When these machines work in a 'stand-alone' capacity, i.e. not connected to or reliant on each other, the term *de-centralized processing* is often used. However, this situation is not common, the tendency being either to have terminals at the remote points transmitting data for centralized processing, as we have already seen, or to site small 'satellite' computers at each point and have them not only linked to a central machine but also interlinked with each other known as *distributed processing*. It is a system that has become more viable with the advent of mini and microcomputers.

Such a system means that hardware applicable to local needs is sited in remote departments, factories etc. This hardware may range from interrogating terminals in sales offices for ascertaining stock availability, customer credit limits, to machines capable of coping with production planning, stock control, payroll etc, in individual factories. Access is available where necessary to the centralized files on the main computer on a database principle. Also, when desirable, machines are linked with each other as could be the case with factory site computers in order for example to co-ordinate production scheduling, maintenance of optimum stock levels etc (see Figure 8.3).

Database systems

Traditionally, clerical procedures and systems within an organization tended to be departmentalized. An organization would have its wages office, invoicing office, personnel department, cost office, accounts office etc, with each unit being responsible for keeping its own files, maintaining its own records, processing its own data, producing its own reports and so on.

While the introduction of computer systems resulted in the centralization of many of these procedures there remained, and still remains, a tendency even within the computer function to treat systems in isolation. A sales ledger system with its own master and movements files, a wages system with its own set of files, personnel records with another set etc. Indeed, in some situations, for example batch processing, this may well be the most effective and economic file structure to use.

A *database system*, however, seeks to break down this compartmentalization of records relating to specific systems in favour of one large consolidated file containing all the records necessary to support all systems.

Perhaps the concept of a database system can best be explained by using a simple illustration. An organization purchases goods from a supplier, L. Smith & Co. Now data relating to Smith's must be available to support at least two business functions: (Figure 8.4)

(1) the accounting function. Data on a purchase ledger system will contain name, address, account number, invoice and payment details, cash settlement terms etc.
(2) the stock inventory/purchasing function. Data will include name, address, account number, product identification, unit price, quantity discount terms, delivery periods etc.

Now some disadvantages are evident if this data is held on systems-based files, i.e. both a purchase ledger system and a stock inventory system:

(1) Some data is duplicated, e.g. name, address and account number.
(2) Different aspects of the same supplier appear on different files, i.e. no one file contains the whole of the information.
(3) Processing is duplicated if two or more files have to be referred to in order to obtain a complete picture.
(4) Management information may be incomplete or misleading if one file only is relied upon for information.

The above example is a very simple one. In practice, aspects of one data element may be required over a range of systems. Different aspects of data relating to the same employee would be used in wages records, personnel and pension records. Data relating to a product used in a manufacturing process may well involve production scheduling, stock control, purchase accounting and costing systems.

A database seeks to obviate the disadvantages listed above by bringing together all of the data common to each element held on the system files, and holding these records on one large file which will then contain the whole of the data requirements for all systems. This total assembly of data is known as a *data bank*.

The operation of a database system is dependent upon the bank of

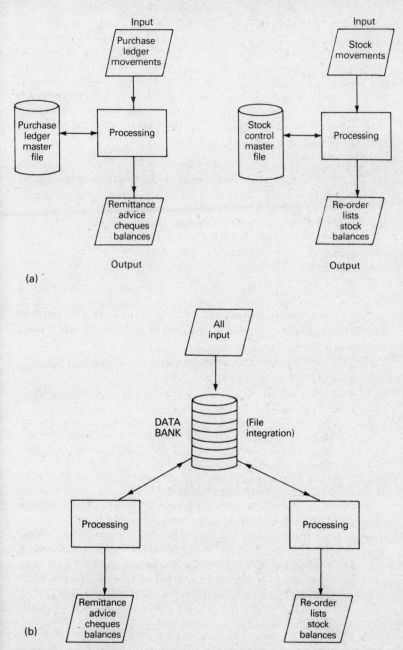

Figure 8.4   (a) Systems approach (b) Data base approach

data being available in on-line direct access storage media, the accessibility of this data by every system as and when required and a multiprogramming facility.

Looked at realistically, while a great deal of research has gone into the development of database systems, such as CODASYL set up in the late 1960s, and while software packages have been introduced, such as IDS Integrated Data Store (Honeywell), ADABAS (Adaptable Data Base Management System), there are problems associated with the introduction of data base systems. These include:

(1) Very high hardware and software costs.
(2) Problems in allocating 'key' fields to identify data elements that will meet needs of all users.
(3) Data security problems. Who has access to what?
(4) Complexity of designing file and record structures that will adequately meet the needs of all systems at all levels.
(5) Since this is an on-line system, back up facilities may be necessary.

All in all, while a database system may seem attractive in theory, it is, in practice, an extremely costly and complex structure to introduce, and its anticipated benefits must be carefully weighed against the economic and other problems associated with it. This is particularly so in the light of current developments in relatively cheap, but powerful, microcomputers with a possible economically attractive alternative in distributed processing.

Integrated systems

The principle of an integrated system within a business context seeks to recognize the inter-relation and inter-dependence of all activities and procedures within the business. It looks at all such activities as making up one whole system rather than viewing them as a number of isolated sub-systems and procedures.

The implication from a data processing viewpoint lies in the integration of all data records on to one central file available for all systems applications within an organization. It is somewhat similar in concept to a databank but may imply a wider spectrum of record consolidation, indeed a total consolidation, in contrast to a data bank which may be designed around functional areas of activity rather than a total activity principle.

Exercises

1. Present arguments for and against the use of microcomputers based departmentally and dedicated to specific systems compared

with the use of centralized main-frame computer coping with all systems.

2. Differentiate between (a) a mainframe computer, (b) a minicomputer, (c) a microcomputer.
3. What do you understand by a visible record computer? Suggest any advantages that may accrue through the use of these.
4. Give an explanation of what is meant by multi-programming. Describe how the computer deals with the situation when two systems are being processed concurrently.
4. Explain how a time-sharing system is able to provide processing facilities for a number of users virtually simultaneously.
5. What is the object of a real-time system? Suggest the hardware and software you feel essential for operating such a system.
6. Under what circumstances do you think a multi-programming facility in a computer processor is essential.
7. Give an account of a database system and mention any advantages or disadvantages such a system may have.
8. Write a short essay on *The future of microcomputers.*

9

Flowcharts and decision tables

Flowcharting is a convenient way of expressing on paper in diagrammatic form the activities involved in attaining a required objective, and the sequence in which these activities must be performed. As a recording technique it serves three useful purposes. As an aid to working out how a problem can best be solved, as a means of illustrating a proposed system for management consideration and as a permanent record of procedures and activities, to be used as a standard for operating purposes.

Flowcharts

Preparing flowcharts

The basic factors with which we are concerned when constructing a flowchart are

(a) An objective
In other words we start with an aim in mind—the flowchart is the process of working out how this aim can be achieved.

(b) A starting point
This is some circumstance or event that triggers off the series of activities necessary to achieve the aim. For example, if the aim is to dig the garden the starting point might just be 'arrive home', or if to supply a customer with goods 'receive order'.

(c) The activities that are necessary and the sequence in which these must be performed
Now if the circumstances of a situation were always constant then the activities resulting would always be the same and it would just be a case of putting them into a logical sequence, a to b, b to c, c to d and so on. However this is rarely the case. Circumstances tend to vary within a situation giving rise to the need for alternative activities, thus instead of progressing from (a) to (b) we find that (a) will lead to

(b) or (c) depending on the circumstances. In flow-charting we are concerned with taking into account all of the circumstances that could arise and defining all of the activities that these give rise to.

(d) Decisions

This is the process of deciding which alternative activities must be performed in order to reach our aim when faced with differing circumstances. For example, if our starting point is 'receive order from customer', then we are faced with the position that the order may have been received from a cash customer or from a credit customer. The aim is the same in each case, the execution of the order, but the activities leading up to this could well be different.

As a simple example to illustrate these four points let us take as an aim 'make a cup of tea'. The starting point might be 'get out of bed', and the activities include 'dress', 'go down stairs', 'fill kettle', 'put kettle on gas', 'get milk, sugar and tea' etc. This is all very well but what happens if there is no tea? In other words we are faced with one of two situations 'there is some tea' or 'there is no tea'. In the first case the next activity might be 'put tea in teapot' and in the second case 'go next door and borrow some tea'. If we trace this second series of activities the next thing to ask is 'get any tea from next door?', if the answer is yes we can go back to the first series and 'put tea in teapot', if it is no, then we must consider what further activities are necessary to achieve our aim.

With these four factors in mind, the following is suggested as an approach to the construction of a flowchart:

(1) Make a note of the aim of the chart.
(2) Decide at what point the series of activities are going to start.
(3) Make a note of the main activities that are likely to be involved trying to put them in a logical order, although the best order may not become apparent until the chart is under way.
(4) Start with the first activity and decide what different actions this could give rise to.
(5) One at a time, trace these actions arising out of a decision, going as far as possible with one before going back to the alternatives.
(6) Show each action once only on the flowchart, using flowlines and connectors to go back to it whenever necessary.

The flowchart will be constructed by the use of symbols connected with flow lines with arrows indicating the direction of flow. The activities should be briefly described either in the symbols themselves or as notes appended to the flowchart and cross referenced to the symbols. A flowchart symbols template should be used for drawing the symbols, and the connecting lines should be straight, either

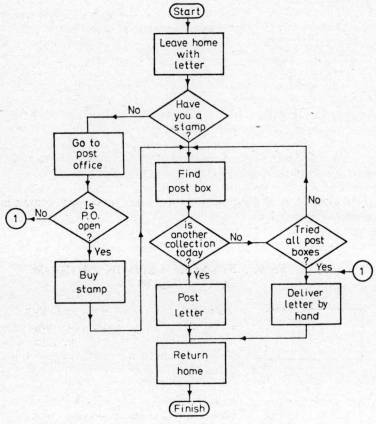

Figure 9.1   Flowchart illustrating the use of four basic symbols

vertical or horizontal. While there are recognized methods of drawing flowcharts horizontally, that is starting at the left and proceeding to the right-hand side of the paper, it is more usual in systems and program flowcharting to construct them vertically, from top to bottom of the paper. Attention should be paid to the layout of the chart in the sense that it should be well balanced, symbol sizes should be consistent within the one chart and evenly spaced as far as possible. It is important that final flowcharts should be neat, with legible writing so that no difficulty in interpretation will arise when it is used by people other than the compiler.

The four most commonly used symbols in flowcharting are illustrated below, but for charting systems and programs a wide range of symbols are available. These are shown in Fig 9.2.

Used for any form of action. The action is usually described in the box.

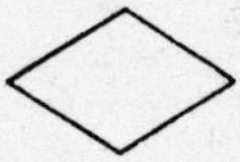

Decision box. Used to lead to different actions.

Terminal box. Showing the start or finish of a procedure.

Connecting box. Connects one section of a flowchart with another.

An illustration of a simple flowchart using these four symbols is given in Figure 9.1.

Fig 9.2: **SYMBOLS USED IN PROGRAM FLOW CHARTS**

GENERAL OPERATIONAL SYMBOL. Representing any kind of processing function, or used for any operation for which no particular symbol has been defined.

PRE-DEFINED PROCESS SYMBOL. Representing a named process consisting of one or more operations or program steps, e.g. a program segment or a subroutine.

INPUT/OUTPUT. Indicating making available information for processing, or recording processed information.

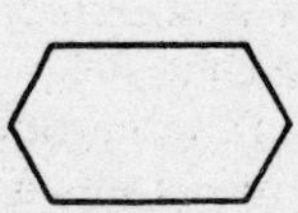

PREPARATION SYMBOL. Represents the modification of an instruction or group of instructions which change the program itself. e.g. Initialize a routine, set a switch, or modify an index register.

Fig 9.2 (*cont.*)

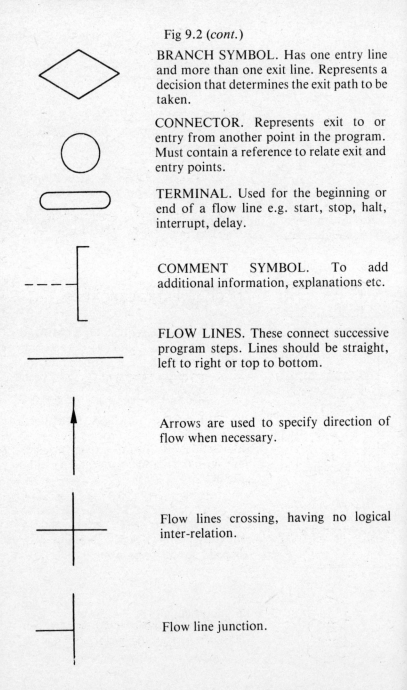

BRANCH SYMBOL. Has one entry line and more than one exit line. Represents a decision that determines the exit path to be taken.

CONNECTOR. Represents exit to or entry from another point in the program. Must contain a reference to relate exit and entry points.

TERMINAL. Used for the beginning or end of a flow line e.g. start, stop, halt, interrupt, delay.

COMMENT SYMBOL. To add additional information, explanations etc.

FLOW LINES. These connect successive program steps. Lines should be straight, left to right or top to bottom.

Arrows are used to specify direction of flow when necessary.

Flow lines crossing, having no logical inter-relation.

Flow line junction.

Fig 9.2 (*cont.*)

In addition to the above symbols, the following are used in systems flow charts.

DOCUMENT. Used to represent a document input to or output from a system or computer.

PUNCHED CARD. Representing the use of punched cards in a system.

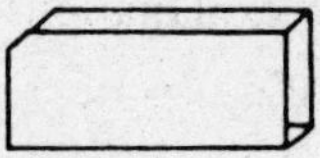

DECK OF PUNCHED CARDS.

PUNCHED PAPER TAPE.

MAGNETIC TAPE. Representing magnetic tape input or output.

MAGNETIC DRUM. Representing magnetic drum storage.

MAGNETIC DISC. Used to represent either fixed or exchangeable disc stores.

Fig 9.2 (*cont.*)

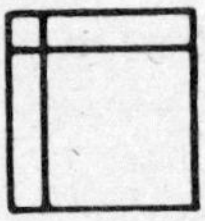

CORE SYMBOL. Representing internal central processor storage.

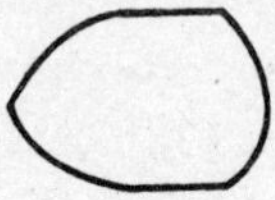

VISUAL DISPLAY. Representing the use of a visual display unit in conjunction with a computer.

GRAPH PLOTTER. Representing use of graph plotter with a computer.

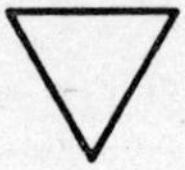

MERGING SYMBOL. Represents combining two or more sets of items in sequence according to a common key, into one set of items.

EXTRACT SYMBOL. To represent an operation which removes one or more sets of items from a single set.

COLLATING SYMBOL. Represents a combination of merging and extracting procedures.

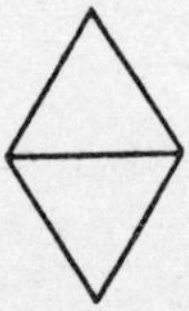

SORT SYMBOL. Any operation to arrange a set of items in sequence according to a certain key.

Fig 9.2 (*cont.*)

MANUAL INTERVENTION SYMBOL. Used to indicate input or output to the computer performed manually. e.g. operating a keyboard or a console.

MANUAL OPERATION. To indicate a manual off-line process.

COMMUNICATION LINK. Representing the transmission of data by tele-communication link.

ON-LINE STORAGE. Use of on-line storage when storage medium cannot be defined.

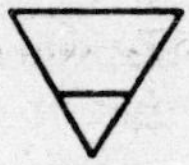

OFF-LINE STORAGE. The storage or filing of information external to the computer.

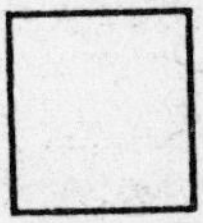

AUXILIARY OPERATION. A mechanical operation, not under computer control, having no specific symbol. e.g. punching and verifying cards.

So far we have used the term flowchart in a general sense as a chart showing a sequence of activities. In computer work different forms of chart are used at different stages in the development and definition of a system, showing different degrees of detail. While there appears to be no generally accepted terminology for these, they can be classified as follows:

(1) *Block charts.*
   Showing in broad outline the sequence of activities in a system.

(2) *Systems flow charts.*
Showing the sequence of activities and procedures in more detail.

(3) *Program flow charts.*
These are concerned with those parts of the system that are computer processed and show the operations, in sequence, that the computer will perform.

Block chart

Perhaps this could be called the simplest form of flowchart. It shows the sequence of the main procedures within a system without showing in detail how these are carried out. It is usual to use only one symbol, a rectangle, to indicate each procedure and into this is written a short narrative explanation. These rectangles are joined by flow lines to indicate direction of flow. The chart is often supported by more detailed notes, the notes being cross-referenced to the number contained in the rectangle. An example of a section of a block chart is shown in Figure 9.3. This shows the main procedures in a routine for dealing with orders received from credit customers.

Systems flowchart

This expands the block chart, breaking each procedure down into more detailed operations and again showing the sequence in which these operations are performed. It is constructed using standard flowchart symbols. As with a blockchart it should be accompanied by a narrative description either written into the boxes or appended separately and referenced to the boxes.

Unlike the blockchart where it is usually possible to show a whole routine in broad outline in one chart, the additional detail in a systems flowchart often makes this impractical, and a series of charts are made for different sections of the routine. These are inter-related by the use of connector symbols. In contrast to a program flowchart, a systems flowchart does not just specify the procedures that are computer processed, but is concerned with the system as a whole. The flowchart can often be conveniently sectionalized. For example, one section may deal with the manual procedures up to the time source documents are received by the computer department, another with the procedures involved in the data preparation stage, a third for the computer processing operations and a fourth showing the routine for dealing with output reports. Figure 9.4 illustrates a systems flowchart, showing the procedures for dealing with orders up to the time the documents are passed to the computer department

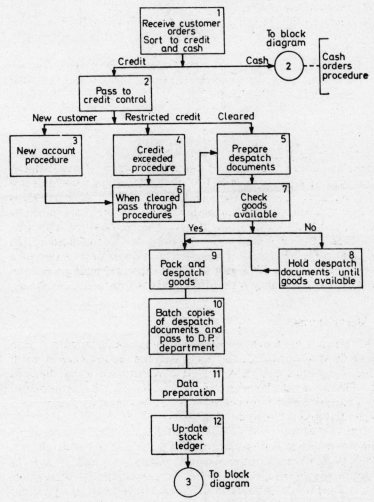

Figure 9.3   Example of a blockchart

for processing. Further examples of flowcharts will be found in Chapter 14 dealing with applications.

Program flowchart

From the systems flowchart we now move to a more detailed definition of that part of the system to be computer processed, i.e. a

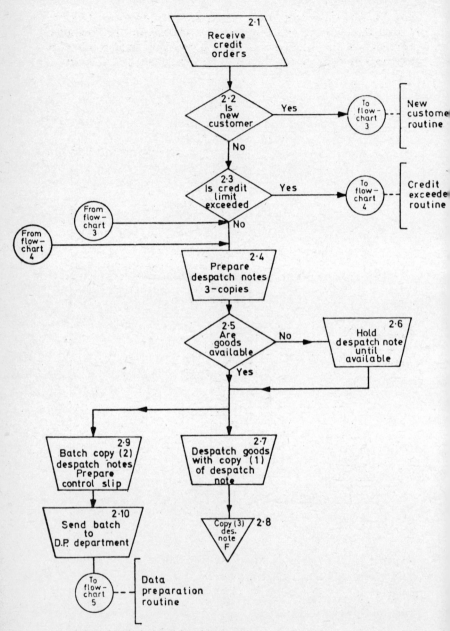

Figure 9.4   Example of a systems flowchart

program flowchart specifying the computer operations. Since it is from this that the list of instructions making up the computer program will be encoded, it will be appreciated that a program flowchart must be constructed in a very detailed form. However,

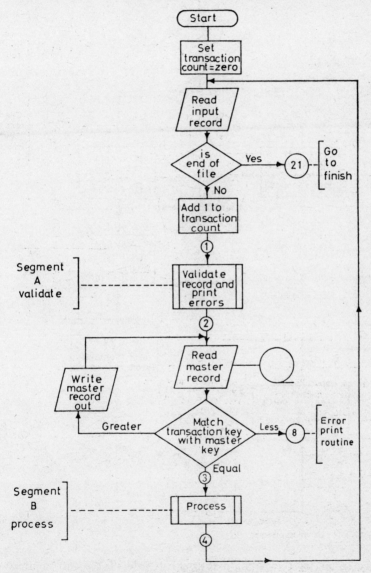

Figure 9.5   Example of an outline program flowchart

with a lengthy and complex system, it is not always possible to convert the systems flowchart to a program flowchart giving the required amount of detail, in one stage. For this reason program flowcharts are often constructed at a series of 'levels' each

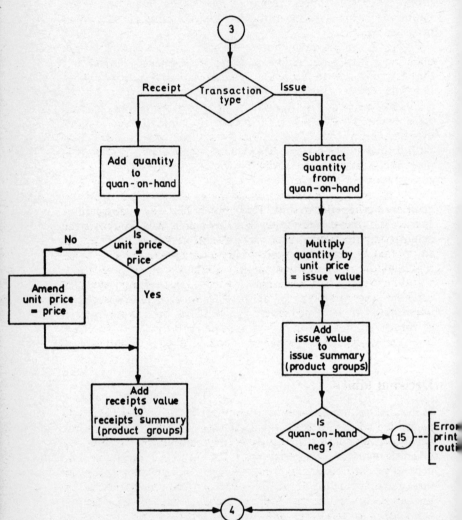

Figure 9.6   Detailed program flowchart

succeeding level expanding into greater detail the information contained in the chart at the previous level. The terms *outline program flowchart* and *detailed program flowchart* are often used in this context. The outline chart records the main run of the program, showing the various procedures involved, and then detailed charts constructed for each of the procedures showing in detail the operations necessary to accomplish the procedure. These outline procedures shown in the first chart are usually known as program Segments.

Figure 9.5 illustrates a simple outline program flowchart for updating a Stock Ledger. This contains two segments, 'A' and 'B', the latter being the subject of the detailed program flowchart, shown in Figure 9.6.

Finally, one or two general points. Constructing flowcharts is to a great extent a matter of trial and error. It is initially a process of experimentation involving repeated attempts and modifications until a final solution is reached. Having completed a flowchart it must not be taken as necessarily the best, or even a correct solution. It must be thoroughly checked for both the accuracy of its logic and for its adequacy to deal with all of the possible variations of the problem it is intended to solve. Probably the best way of doing this is to trace the course of test input data through it, thus simulating the actual computer operations. Care should be taken however, to ensure that sufficient variations of input data are tested so as to be representative of all of the situations catered for in the program.

It should be borne in mind that different people will be involved at different stages in the preparation of flowcharts. It is, therefore, important that the chart should be clear, not only to the person constructing it but to others who will work from it. A good flowchart has clear writing, a neat presentation and uses agreed symbols.

Decision tables

In the analysis and design of computer systems it is often difficult to appreciate all of the aspects of a problem and all of the possible situations that might arise from a set of circumstances. The purpose of a decision table is to set out in a formal way all of the factors that need to be considered and the procedure that any combination of these factors will give rise to. The factors taken into consideration are called *conditions,* the different combinations of these factors are known as *condition rules* and the procedure the condition rules give rise to are known as *action rules.*

For example, when servicing a car we might say 'If the petrol is low and if the oil is low I will get some petrol and some oil'. Now within this situation there are two conditions. Is the petrol low? and is the oil low? This in turn leads us to four different combinations of conditions, or condition rules. Both petrol and oil are low, only petrol is low, only oil is low and neither are low. The four alternative courses of action, or action rules, arising from these condition rules are: get petrol and oil, get petrol, get oil and get neither. This problem is set out in the form of a decision table in Figure 9.7.

Decision table

Conditions	Rule number			
	1	2	3	4
Is petrol low ?	Y	Y	N	N
Is oil low ?	Y	N	Y	N
Actions	Action rules			
Get petrol	X	X		
Get oil	X		X	
Get neither			•	X

Figure 9.7   Example of a simple decision table

The top half of the table contains a list of conditions on the left hand side with a number of vertical columns on the right headed Rule Number. These contain the different combinations of conditions. If the condition is present it is indicated by inserting a 'Y' for Yes, otherwise an 'N' for No. The lower half of the table lists the possible actions that could arise, showing those resulting from any given combination of conditions by inserting 'X's in the appropriate columns.

In order to ensure that every possible combination of conditions is taken into account, the number of condition rules can be determined as being equal to 2^n where n is the number of conditions. Having found the possible number of combinations, to ensure that each combination is unique the following rule, known as the *Halve Rule* is applied.

In the first row Y's are repeated for one half of the number of condition rules, that is 2^{n-1} times, followed by the same number of

N's. In the second row, groups of Y's and N's alternate, the size of the groups being one half of those in the first row. This means Y's and N's are repeated 2^{n-2} times. This process of halving the group

Decision table

Table number 146	Table name: Course entry	Date 30th Sept	Author B.Smith	Conditions		Rule number															
						1	2	3	4	5	6	7	8	9	10	11	12	13	14	15	16
				C1	3 G.C.E passes	Y	Y	Y	Y	N	N	N	N								
				C2	Good school report	Y	Y	N	N	Y	Y	N	N								
				C3	Satisfactory interview	Y	N	Y	N	Y	N	Y	N								
				Actions.																	
				A1	Accept applicant	X	X	X		X											
				A2	Reject applicant				X		X	X	X								

Figure 9.8   A decision table showing rules for the admission to college of applicants who must satisfy two of the three conditions.

size is repeated for successive rows until the final row contains single Y's and N's. Figure 9.8 illustrates this process in a table containing three conditions. In this case n being equal to three, the number of condition rules is 2^3 equals 8. The first row contains a block of Y's equal to one half of this number, i.e. four, followed by a similar block of N's. The second row blocks of Y's and N's one half the size of those in the first row, the size of these blocks being in turn halved for the third row.

To simplify the table by reducing the number of condition rules, if two rules, different in one row only, result in the same action, then these two rules can be combined. This is done by placing a dash '—' in the appropriate row. An example of this is shown in Figure 9.9 where rules 1 and 2, the same except for row three, result in the same action. That is, the performance of condition three is immaterial to the action taken. The same situation occurs in rules 7 and 8. By combining these two pairs of rules the number of rules is reduced to six. This principle is known as the *Dash Rule*.

This now means that the number of rules is no longer equal to 2^n.

In order to prove that all rules have been considered a Dash Count column is added to the right of the condition rules in which the number of rules absorbed is entered. This dash count plus the number of rules will now reconcile with 2^n.

When considering the combinations of conditions in a decision table it is sometimes found that some rules represent either an impossible situation or that the occurrence is highly unlikely. In order to save specifying these rules use may be made of what is known as the *Else Rule*. This requires the insertion of the word 'else' after the entry of all the rules from which anticipated action will result. This means it denotes an exceptional or unanticipated condition that requires special treatment. However this rule should be used with great care as it introduces the possibility of a relevant set of conditions being missed.

Advantages claimed for the decision table method over other forms of charting are:

(1) The problem is more easily defined. It helps to identify the problem and the rules associated with it.
(2) Provides an element of control over analysis and design. That is it positively determines the number of different conditions and the action arising from each.
(3) It provides a uniform method of describing the logic of a system.
(4) It is a means of communicating the logic of a situation to programmers.
(5) Since the logic can be broken down into small natural modules it

DECISION TABLE

Table number 146	Table name. Course entry	Date 30th Sept	Author B.Smith	Rule number.																D/C
				1	2	3	4	5	6	7	8	9	10	11	12	13	14	15	16	
Conditions																				
C1	3 GCE passes			Y	Y	Y	N	N	N											
C2	Good school report			Y	N	N	Y	Y	N											
C3	Satisfactory interview			–	Y	N	Y	N	–											2
Actions																				
A1	Accept applicant			X	X		X													
A2	Reject applicant				X	X		X	X											

Figure 9.9   A decision table showing the 'dash' rule

facilitates the amendment of a system. It eases the problem of keeping a system up to date with changing conditions.

Finally it is not suggested that decision tables can take the place of flowcharts, but rather that they supplement these by ensuring that all circumstances are taken into consideration.

Exercises

1. Draw a flowchart to illustrate the activities involved in borrowing a specific book from a library.
2. On 10 separate occasions an observer records the numbers of men, women and children using an escalator. Each set of observations is punched into a card or to paper tape in this order:
   (a) Men
   (b) Women
   (c) Children.
   Draw a flow diagram to read in this data, process it and provide the following output:
   (a) The separate totals of men, women and children.
   (b) The average number of children per observation.
3. A Credit Control Department rates customers accounts as A, B or C. When accounts are 30 days overdue a reminder is sent to B and C accounts if the amount outstanding is more than £10, and to A accounts if the amount is more than £25. For amounts of £10 or less no action is taken until the accounts are 60 days overdue when a reminder is sent to all customers concerned. For B and C accounts, if more than £10 is still outstanding after 60 days a warning is sent to the customer and also, in the case of C accounts a 'stop supply' notice is sent to the sales office. Accounts rated A are sent a reminder when 60 days overdue if the amount is £25 or less otherwise a warning is sent.
   Show the above procedure in flowchart form.
4. Draw a flowchart to read 1000 cards each containing a number. The numbers are to be added and the result printed.
5. ABC Co. allow discounts when invoicing customers with goods. A bulk order discount of 5 per cent is given on *all* orders in excess of £100. Trade customers receive a trade discount of 10 per cent irrespective of the value of the order, and trade customers who are also members of the ABC Product Group qualify for an additional 5 per cent discount.
   Construct a decision table showing the actions to be taken in respect of each type of customer.
6. Draw a flowchart to read 100 cards each containing a positive number and to print out the highest.

7. Draw a flowchart illustrating the activities involved in making a telephone call from a public call box.

8. Passes in an examination at the end of a course are assessed on the following factors:

   (1) 45 per cent or more marks must be gained in each paper.
   (2) An average of 50 per cent marks must be obtained over all papers.
   (3) There must be an attendance record of at least 60 per cent at lectures.
   (4) Assessment of in-course work must be at least 60 per cent.

   A pass is automatically given if all four of the above conditions are met. In the event of the in-course assessment being less than 60 per cent the case is submitted to a moderator for decision providing the other three conditions are met. If the average examination mark is 50 per cent or more but the mark in any of the individual papers is less than 45 per cent, the candidate is referred in these subjects providing the last two conditions are met. In all other cases the candidate is failed.

   (a) Draw up a decision table.
   (b) Construct a flowchart to illustrate these procedures.

9. A stores control clerk performs the following routine in respect of each requisition for materials issued from store.

   (1) Checks job number on requisition against current job number list. If not on the list the requisition is referred back for correction.
   (2) Looks up the appropriate stock record sheet for each item on the requisition and deducts the requisitioned quantity from the stock balance.
   (3) Compares revised stock balance with the re-order level stated on the stock control sheet. If the stock balance is lower he prepares a re-order request after he has checked the physical stock to ensure that this conforms with the amount on the record sheet.
   (4) If the physical stock does not agree with the balance on the record sheet he prepares a stores discrepancy note and hands this to the chief store-keeper. If the physical stock is less than the re-order level he still prepares a re-order request.

   Show the above procedure in flowchart form.

10. Draw a block chart that shows the procedures involved in dealing with purchase invoices that have to be:

   (1) Sorted into net and cash discount settlement terms, and the latter given priority in clearance for payment.
   (2) Checked to ensure that the goods charged have been received.

(3) Checked for prices, extensions, calculations and discounts. In the event of error the invoice is referred back to the supplier.
(4) Authorized for payment by the chief buyer.
(5) Remittance advice prepared.
(6) Cheque drawn.
(7) (5) and (6) posted to the supplier.

11. Each card of a deck is punched with a separate record. Draw two flowcharts that will cause the contents of each card to be read into the core store of the computer subject to the following conditions.
Flowchart 1—where the number of cards is known to be 500.
Flowchart 2—where the number of cards is unknown.
Explain the peculiarities of each method by reference to your flowcharts.
Assume that a card may be read by the use of one instruction.

12. Consider the following statement:
'Service will be provided on model A once a year during the first two years of use and subsequently twice a year until five years of use have elapsed. Thereafter frequency of service will become the subject of special agreement.
The service agreement for model B is identical except that twice yearly service will be provided during the first two years of use'.
(a) Derive a decision table to satisfy these conditions.
(b) Draw a conventional flowchart to illustrate the same logic.
(c) Indicate briefly what advantage is to be gained by the use of decision tables in expressing logical requirements.

13. A farmer hopes to carry out the following tasks using a computer:
(a) provide up-to-date records of milk yield for each cow;
(b) breeding records;
(c) schedule of feeding;
(d) control of feeding materials, seeds, fertilizers and other consumable materials.
By means of appropriate explanatory notes and a systems flow-chart show how ONE of these tasks may be planned.
You may assume that the computer installation is adequate for the purpose.

14. A mailing list is held on backing store. Each entry consists of a name and address preceded by up to 5 special characters, such as an asterisk (*). These special characters are used to convey information about the entry. For example, all names on the list where the household owns a car should receive mail offers for car radios. This information ('owns a car') could be indicated by

one of the special characters.
Make a flowchart for a program which will print out a selected
list of names and addresses.
You should explain any assumptions which you find it necessary
to make.

10

Computer software

As we saw in Chapter 6, a computer is a machine constructed to perform a specific range of basic operations, add, subtract, read, write etc., and the performance of each of these operations is initiated by communicating to the machine a unique code for each, a group of binary bits. These codes are known as the computer's *operation* or *function code*. In the ultimate, every task we require the computer to perform must be expressed as a list of these codes.

It is these lists of functions, whether expressed in basic machine code or assembled into some kind of computer language for eventual conversion to machine code, that go under the general title of computer *software*.

Software then is the list of instruction which, when communicated to the computer will enable it to carry out the procedure we require, usually known as computer programs. *Hardware* is the machines designed to carry out these tasks.

Types of software

There are a number of types of software for various purposes

(1) Application programs
(2) Application packages
(3) Sub-routines
(4) Utility programs
(5) Operating systems
(6) Assemblers and compilers.

The following is a review of each of these types.

Application programs

These are programs written to operate specific tailor-made local procedures and systems, for example, a sales ledger system, a wages system, a stock inventory system etc. They are usually written by programmers belonging to a specific computer installation and are designed to meet the particular needs of the organization the computer serves.

Application packages

In commercial data processing, a number of elements are found that are common to the needs of many users operating the same system. This is very evident in, for example, a wages system or a stock control system. To avoid programs having to be written by or for each individual user, manufacturers, software houses and computer bureaux offer standard application packages for a range of applications. The package consists of the programs covering the processing requirements of a given system or procedure and will include input and output formats, and file specifications as well as processing routines. The package can be varied within limits to suit a particular user's requirements.

Obviously, the acceptability of a package program will hinge on the extent of the changes that will have to be made to fit it in. These modifications could be either to the existing system or to the package itself. Should they be too extensive to be desirable or practical then a specially written program (an application program) would be called for.

The advantages in the use of application packages are

(1) They are economical.
(2) They are well documented, including a statement of objectives, detailed systems specification, identification of hardware requirements, input, output and file specifications and systems timing.
(3) They are available at comparatively short notice.
(4) They are easy to use.

However, the critical question is: Will it do the job required? If not, the above advantages become meaningless. One problem that may arise in the use of packages is that they call for a minimum hardware configuration which may not, in the event, be available. Application packages are usually supplied stored on a reel of magnetic tape.

Sub-routines

A sub-routine is a set of instructions within a main program designed to perform a standard procedure which may be required in a number of different programs or a number of times within the same program. To avoid writing the routine a multiple of times one version only is held in store and called in by the main program as and when required (see Figure 10.1).

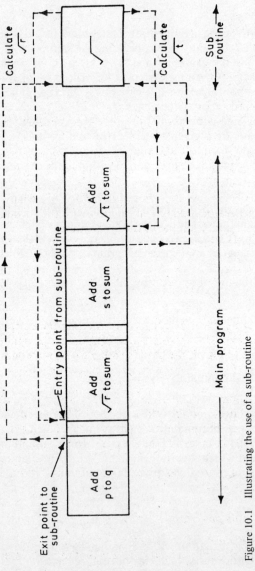

Figure 10.1   Illustrating the use of a sub-routine

Utility programs

Utility programs are designed to carry out standard routines that are common to most applications. They are usually part of the manufacturer's software library, and can be supplied to users as self contained routines. Examples of procedures that form the subject of utility software are:

File creation, maintenance and up-dating
Sorting
Merging
Information retrieval routines
Editing output records
Dumping of data to disc or tape
Data conversion routines, e.g. card to tape, tape to printer, tape to disc.

Again, as with application packages, the problem of compatibility with a given system may arise. In order to overcome this, these programs are often written in the form of *generators*. This means that formats can be fixed by the programmer for a specific application, and the generator used in conjunction with the format definition, to produce a utility unique to the application.

Under this general heading of utility programs may also be included *diagnostic routines* the object of which is to locate and define programming errors.

Operating systems

An operating system is a supervisory program, stored in the central processor that monitors and controls the execution of program instructions, assigns and controls the use of available hardware and, under some circumstances, decides which program is to be operated at a given time.

In the early days of computing a great deal of operator manual intervention was necessary to control the activities of the machine. An operating system to a certain extent has the effect of automating the operation activities and organizing the use of processing power in the most efficient way.

The following is a summary of the functions an operating system may perform (see Figure 10.2).

Communications with the operator

As we suggested above, with early computers the operator had to instruct the machine. An operating system means that the computer

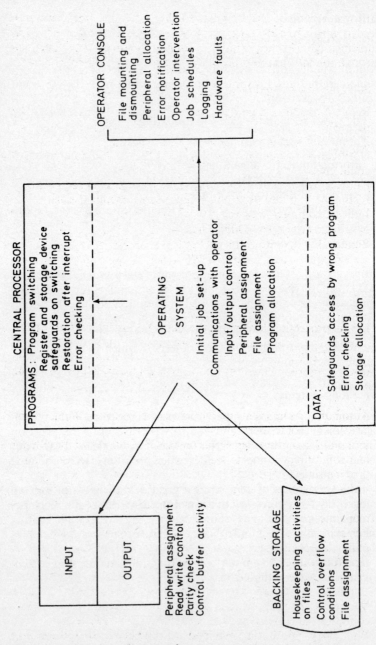

Figure 10.2   Functions of an operating system

can now tell the operator what to do, when his intervention is needed, and can inform the operator of actions the system itself has implemented. This information is usually conveyed to the operator through the medium of a printed message on the control console.

Such messages could include:

Request to load or unload data or program files to a specific peripheral device.
Automatic logging of machine time utilization.
Notification of opening and closing of files and making a record count check.
Notification of assignment of peripheral units to specified files.
Listing of files and programs required for scheduled jobs.
Indicate completion of job.
Notification of error conditions.
Request for operator intervention.

Hardware control

Efficient processing hinges on the harmonious interaction of the constituent parts of a computer configuration—input, output and storage devices as well as the central processor. To provide this the hardware control element of an operating system will perform the following:

Automatic assignment of peripheral units as demanded by processing requirements.
In a multi-programming situation, it will control switching from one program to another in the light of established priorities. When programs are interrupted it will safeguard the current records in store by transferring register and storage contents to temporary locations and will re-establish the position when the program recommences.
Perform house-keeping routines on files, checking header and trailer labels to check purge dates, continuation files, block or record counts etc.
Will dump the complete contents of CPU store and registers to enable a restart in the event of a processing breakdown.
Monitor storage in direct access devices to cope with overflow conditions and guard against unintentional overwrites.
Will carry out initial machine set-up checks to ensure that hardware is properly functioning and ready for processing runs.

Input and output control

The operating system will control the flow of input data from backing storage to CPU as demanded by processing requirements. It will also organize the allocation of storage space to receive the data, will perform standard checks such as parity checks and back-spacing instructions in the event of a mis-read, and organize the transfer of data temporarily held in buffer devices.

The system will organize the location of output data in store, supervise its transfer to an output peripheral automatically assigning a peripheral device for this purpose and will perform accuracy checks on the writing of data to the output device.

As a sub-set of an operating system, *communications software* must be included. By and large, communications software supervises the transfer of data between on-line terminals and the central computer in time-sharing and real time situations. It assembles and checks data flowing between the two, communicates programming requirements to the main operating system and keeps a check for faults in communication lines and the terminals.

Assemblers and compilers

These are discussed later on in this chapter when reviewing computer languages.

Computer Languages

Perhaps, at this point, it would be as well to remind ourselves of some basic concepts on programming referred to earlier in Chapter 6.

(1) A program instruction must contain two fundamental elements: an operation and an operand.
(2) The operation element defines the *function* the machine is required to perform.
(3) The operand quotes the *address* in which the data, on which the operation is to be performed, can be found.
(4) These instructions are held in word locations in store in the sequence they are to be executed.
(5) In the ultimate, the two elements must be communicated to, and held in store, as strings of binary bits.

Now we will turn our attention to the practicalities of writing a computer program, first of all reviewing the different levels of coding and language that may be used.

Machine code

A set of numeric codes designed to cover the whole range of machine functions (operation element expressed in binary) is known as a computer *instruction code* or *function code*. The unique address given to each storage location, when expressed as its numeric reference, is known as an *absolute address*. Program statements using machine function codes and absolute addresses are said to be written in *machine code*. A machine code statement could read:

Function   Address
  0100   1110

although in practice it would be more usual to write it using decimal numbers:

Function   Address
   4   16

and leave the input device to convert to binary expressions.

While early programs had to be written in this form, it was a very laborious business particularly as, in quoting absolute addresses, the programmer had to keep a log of the contents of each location to avoid duplicating their use.

Symbolic languages

The next development in programming, in order to simplify writing procedures was to substitute a mnemonic (an easily remembered group of letters) for the numeric function code—for example DIV (for divide) instead of 4—and a description of the data, say QTY (for quantity) instead of 16, the address at which quantity is held. The description QTY is known as the *symbolic address* in contrast to '16' the absolute address. In principle, symbolic languages depart very little from machine code statements. In as much as every individual step the computer has to take must still be listed, the number of statements required is exactly the same. The term *micro instruction* is used for this one-to-one relationship.

Assembly languages

In the course of programming experience, it was realized that certain groups of instructions designed to execute an often used procedure were recurring fairly regularly. To save keep rewriting these groups, single instructions were introduced to represent a whole group. The effect of this was that one single program statement would result in a whole range of machine instructions being executed. This type of instruction, with a one-for-many relationship with the machine code, is known as a *macro instruction*.

Of course, the major problem in using symbolic and assembly statements is that the programmer is no longer using a language the computer can understand. It becomes necessary, therefore, to interpose between the program and the central processor a translating device that will take the program statements and convert them into the binary numeric statements the machine code—the computer is designed to act upon.

This translation device, supplied by manufacturers for their own particular machines, is known as an *assembler program*. It contains, in effect, a list of all the permissible symbolic or assembly statements and their equivalent in machine code whether this be a single machine code instruction as in the case of a micro-instruction or a multiple number in the case of a macro-instruction.

The translating or *assembling* process takes place like this:

(1) The program having been written—at this point it is known as a *source program*—is prepared statement by statement in a machine readable form, for example punched into cards.

(2) The manufacturers assembler program, which may be supplied stored on disc or tape, is then read, in its entirety into the central processor.

(3) Source program statements are then read one by one, the identical statement traced in the assembler program and its equivalent in machine code written to an output medium (see Figure 10.3), usually magnetic tape. At the end of the process, the magnetic tape will hold the complete program in machine

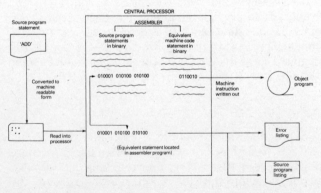

Figure 10.3   The assembling process

code form—now known as an *object program*—and it is this program that is used for future processing runs (see Figure 10.4).

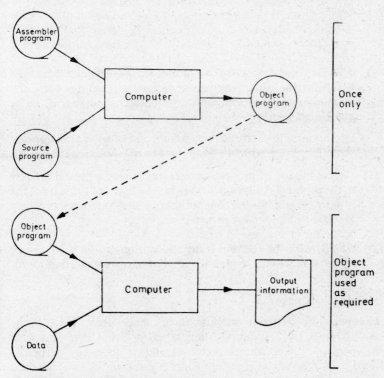

Figure 10.4   Assembling a source program

(4) Since the assembler program holds a complete list of all permissible statements, any *syntax* errors (grammatical errors) in the source program will be identified, rejected as invalid, and printed out as an error listing. At the same time it is usual to print out the complete list of source program statements for future reference.

The types of computer language we have discussed so far are usually referred to as *low level* languages. Three important features of these languages are:

(1) The statements do not materially depart from the machine instruction format. While mnemonic function codes and symbolic addresses are used, the construction of the statement is

still basically the same, each with its operation and operand, function and address. For this reason, languages of this type are said to be *computer* or *machine orientated*.

(2) While macro-instructions can be used to an extent in assembly languages, they are still predominantly based on the micro-instruction principle, and therefore time-consuming to construct.

(3) The range of statements is limited to a particular machines function code. Since the construction of the function code varies from manufacturer to manufacturer, the language tends to be *machine dependent*.

These features gave rise to the development of what are known as *high level* languages which:

(1) Enable the use of program statements having a greater affinity to the problem definition, i.e. within the limits of the rules of the program could be written in ordinary English statements. These are said to be *problem oriented* languages.

(2) Made far greater use of macro-instructions.

(3) Could, with the relevant translation program, be used on any make of machine having the required hardware configuration.

Standard languages

Co-operation between manufacturers and users led to the development of standard languages which were machine independent, i.e. their use is not dependent upon any particular make of machine. The following are examples of standard languages. Initially, separate languages were constructed to cover two main processing areas, business systems and mathematical problems. These are in widespread use today. One language COBOL (Common Business Oriented Language) was specifically designed for use in the business systems sector and two languages ALGOL (Algorithmic Language) and FORTRAN (Formula Translation) for application in the mathematical sector. The first of these two was a European development and the other its American equivalent. A later development resulted in the production of a universal language capable of dealing with both commercial and mathematical applications. This was first published in 1966 and is known as PL/1.

BASIC (Beginners All-purpose Symbolic Instruction Code) was originally introduced as a simple, easily written language for students using remote access time-sharing terminals. It has now become a very powerful and popular language while retaining its simplicity of construction. It provides a powerful tool for using computers in a conversational mode and its use with microcomputers is becoming widespread.

We saw earlier that a translation program, assembler program, is required to convert statements in low level language into machine language. It is evident that a far more sophisticated program will be required to convert statement in high level problem orientated languages. The program for doing this is known as a *compiler* program. This contains a list of all the permissible statements used in the language and for each statement a list of the machine instructions necessary to perform the statement. Thus by running the source (problem orientated) program with the compiler program, an object (machine instruction) program is produced for future use in processing runs.

Programming elements

The purpose of computer programming is to construct a list of instructions which, when executed by the computer, will result in pre-determined objectives being realized. While objectives will vary considerably, e.g. a program to print sales invoices, a program to up-date a stock ledger, a program to assemble production schedules, a number of elements can be identified common to all programs. These are

(1) Data transfer.

These are instructions to transfer data between the central processor and peripheral devices, input, output and backing Storage devices, and also to make transfers from one location to another within the central processor store.

(2) Arithmetic and Logic.

These instructions initiate operations by the Arithmetic and Logic Unit of the processor such as Add, Multiply, Compare etc.

(3) Conditional branch.

This occurs when alternative courses of action present themselves and a decision must be made which to follow, the decision being reached by testing the quality of a specific data item. If, for example, in a stock pricing process 15% was to be deducted from all items over £100, then the question 'Is more than £100?' must be asked of each item, the answer 'Yes' resulting in a different course of action to 'No'. The next instruction executed is conditional upon the result of the test applied and may involve by-passing the instructions that would otherwise have been carried out by making a *jump* to a new sequence.

(4) Unconditional Branch.

This diverts operations to an instruction out of sequence and does so automatically and without choice. It provides a means for repeating a sequence of similar operations each requiring the same set of instructions. This means an *unconditional jump* to the commencement of a routine providing a *loop* through which processing will continue to circulate until instructed to stop.

(5) Counters.

This provides a control mechanism for executing a defined number of passes through a procedure or routine. The counter will probably be set initially with the required number of passes, decremented by one for each pass, tested for zero at the completion of each pass and the program directed to another sequence of instructions when the contents of the counter is equal to zero.

Figure 10.5 illustrates these basic elements in a program flow chart designed to read in 100 records of examination marks, accumulate marks of 40 or more and those less than 40, divide by number of papers in each category to find average pass mark and average fail mark.

Development of a computer program

The following is an outline of the main stages involved in the preparation of a computer program:

(1) Program specification.

The object of this is to formally set down all of the information required to enable a programmer to write the program. It is usually prepared by a *systems analyst* in conjunction with a senior *programmer* and will include:

(a) An identification.
(b) The context in which the program will operate, i.e. its place within the system and the place of the system within the organization's overall processing activities.
(c) An identification of the program's objectives and its main functions.
(d) Detailed input and output specifications including precise field and record definitions.
(e) The precise detail of any master files the program will operate in conjunction with, e.g. files to be up-dated.

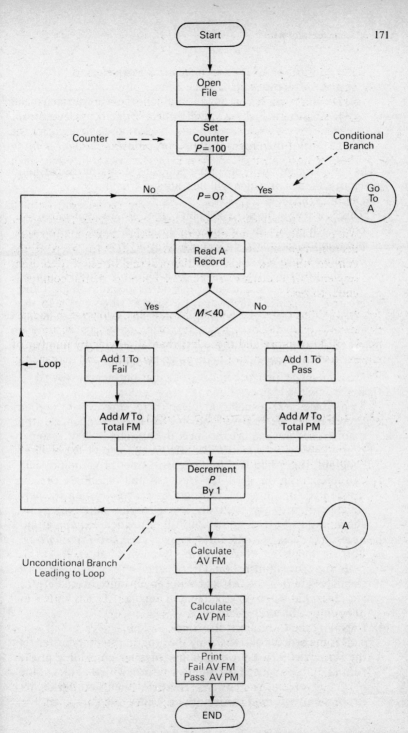

Figure 10.5 Flowchart illustrating branch instructions and a count

(f) Specification of the processing the program is to carry out and the relationship between input, output and master files.

(g) Details of accuracy controls that must be incorporated into the program such as validity checks, batch total controls etc.

(h) Details of the program testing procedures.

The specification will be prepared using both narrative and flowcharts, details of which will be found in Chapter 9.

(2) Defining the logic.

This is probably the most difficult part of programming, and the one which entails the greatest amount of creative thinking. The programmer is concerned with working out a logical sequence of operations that will cope with all combinations of the variables that the program must deal with to achieve the required results. While there are no standard procedures to induce logical and creative thinking, rough charting at this stage can help the programmer visualize alternative approaches to the problem, and to construct a picture of the logical flow of procedures. On the principle that two heads are often better than one it is often useful to exchange ideas with other programmers, especially those having experience in the particular problems involved.

(3) Recording the logic.

Two stages are usually involved here. Firstly an outline flowchart will be prepared showing the logical sequence of the main procedures required to meet the objectives. This is sometimes known as *macro-flowcharting*. Should it be a large program, this could well be done by a chief programmer who will prepare it in modular form so that modules can be distributed to a number of programmers to work on the next stage simultaneously. Secondly, a detailed flowchart is prepared showing step by step sequentially all of the detailed operations necessary. This is sometimes known as *micro-flowcharting*. Further details on flowcharts are given in Chapter 9. At this point the programmer should trace data items through the chart to make sure that the correct results are produced for all of the variables that will be encountered in the data. This is known as *dry-running* or a *table-check*.

(4) Encoding the Program Instruction.

This is the process of translating the program steps indicated on the flowchart into a programming language ensuring that the format of the language statements conform with the rules of the particular language being used. These statements are written on to special pre-printed programming sheets.

(5) Preparation for computer input.

This is the preparation of the encoded statements into a form that can be read in to the processor. For example, punched into cards or keyed to magnetic tape.

(6) Compiling the program.

As we saw earlier, the compiler is a program in machine language. It is stored in the central processor, and then the source program is read in as data. The instructions in the compiler govern the conversion of the computer language statements of the source program into the machine language instructions of the object program. As each source program instruction is read in, the compiler scans it for errors in the construction of the statements, syntax errors.

If any syntax errors are found, the compiler will give instructions for them to be printed out for the attention of the programmer. These error messages are known as *diagnostics*. In practice the complete source program is usually printed out with appropriate notes against each erroneous statements, and the number of errors shown at the end. When, after correction the program is free of syntax errors, the compiler controls the print out of the object program in machine code.

(7) Testing the program.

The diagnostic errors found in the compiling process are limited to errors of syntax. Logical errors in the construction of the program will not be revealed. It is thus quite possible for the program to be formally correct in its use of the programming language but still unable to process data correctly. It is, therefore, essential to test it using specimen data of the type it has been designed to process. To this end, the object program produced during the final compiling run is read into store and used to process a comprehensive range of test data specified by the systems analyst, the result having been previously calculated manually. If the correct results are not obtained amendments will have to be made to the source program. This means carrying out the whole process of compilation again until finally a fully proved object program is produced (Figure 10.6).

(8) Program documentation.

The program, having been exhaustively tested and proved is now handed over to the operations section of the computer installation for use on live runs. Before doing this, it is the programmer's responsibility to prepare a detailed specification of the program for future reference in the event of modifications or up-datings being needed to the program in the future.

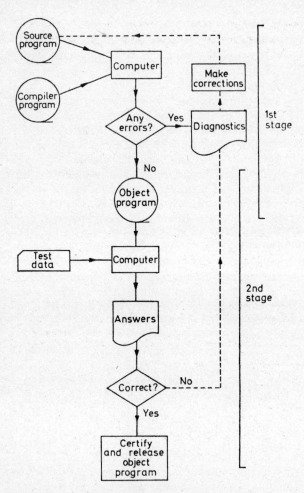

Figure 10.6   Compiling and testing a program

Such a specification will include:
(1) Program identification.
(2) Narrative explanations, logic flow charts and decision tables.
(3) Program coding sheets.
(4) Specimen input, output and file formats.
(5) Test data results with notes of corrected error conditions.
(6) Glossary of symbolic address names.
(7) History of program construction and testing.

(8) Operating instructions.

Details of any modifications to the program will be added to the specification as they occur.

Exercises

1. What do you understand by an *application package?* Discuss any problems which may arise if your company decided to use such a package to operate its Sales Ledger system.
2. Give an account of the functions you would expect an *operating system* to perform.
3. What is *utility software*? Suggest some purposes for which this is used.
4. Draw a flowchart illustrating the principles of
   (a) An unconditional jump
   (b) A conditional jump
   (c) A loop
   (d) A count.
5. Explain the relationship between a *source program* and an *object program* describing how the one is converted to the other.
6. A program may contain errors in construction and errors of logic. Distinguish between these two types of error and explain the methods that can be used to trace them.
7. List the stages involved in writing and documenting a program.
8. What do you consider to be the two essential components of a *machine instruction?* Give a short account of how these two components are dealt with in the central processor.
9. Distinguish between a machine orientated computer language and a problem orientated language explaining the main points of difference between the two.
10. Give an account of the function a *compiler* plays in preparing a program for use on a computer.
11. 'A programmer, writing in a high level language, need have no detailed knowledge of the computer's machine code.' Discuss this statement.

11

Collection, preparation and control of data

It could be said that data is the raw material of a data processing system. It consists of the facts and figures which record in detail the many and varied activities of a business. A data item, on its own, however, means little unless it is related to other items of data and interpreted within the context of the system as a whole. The aim of data processing is to relate and interpret data records to provide meaningful information in the form of output reports. One data record that Brown worked $40\frac{1}{2}$ hours in one week is of little use in itself while again a second data record that Brown is paid £1.50p an hour is similarly of little use. However, by relating these two records we can produce a report to the effect that the gross pay earned by Brown in that particular week was £60.75. If a further record is available that Brown spent the $40\frac{1}{2}$ hours making 6 tables we can begin to interpret these items of data in terms of specific production activities and production costs.

Types of data

Examining data in a little detail, we find that data items fall within a number of different but fairly well defined categories. If we use a simple illustration from a purchase ledger system, the basic information on record for each supplier could be as follows:

12345	A J Jones, 19 East Street, Weston	£297.00
(Account Number)	(Supplier Name and address)	(Balance outstanding)

In this record we can identify two main elements:
Firstly that part which identifies the supplier which is purely descriptive by nature. This is data we would not expect to change very frequently; in fact, unless the supplier changes his name and address it will always remain the same. This quality gives rise to data of this type being referred to as *static*. However, part of this

descriptive data is not strictly speaking necessary to the identification of the supplier, i.e. the account number. This is really an accountancy convenience to enable us to readily find an account when required and to provide a logical sequence in which accounts can be held on file. For this reason it is often known as *control data*.

The second element is the quantitative part, the balance, which we would expect to change quite frequently as more goods are purchased or as payments to the supplier are made. This is known as *dynamic* data since it is constantly being changed to provide a statement of the current situation. For example, later on in the month a transaction may be made with A J Jones as follows:

12345   A J Jones   Purchases   £250.00

which means that the original record will have to be amended to show a revised balance of £547.00.

This means that in data processing we are concerned with data records of two main kinds. On the one hand there is data which, while it records information relating to some business activity, remains unchanged for a long period of time—data we have referred to above as control and static data—but also contains a dynamic element, i.e. a statement of current quantitative values. This type of record is known as a *master record*. On the other hand, there are records relating to the periodic changes in values and quantities relating to the business activity such as the purchase of goods from a supplier as mentioned above. These are known as *movement records*.

There exists an interaction between these two types of record which we call *up-dating*, a process that amends the dynamic element of the master record by the transaction represented on the movement record thus bringing the master record up to date. In practice, not only does this amendment to the balance take place, but also details of the movement record are added to the existing master record so as to provide a history of transactions over a period of time.

A collection of data items relating to a particular procedure is known as a *data file*. A purchase ledger master file may well contain for each supplier, the following:

Identification of the supplier.
A number of data items representing transactions with the supplier over a period of time.
Balances outstanding on the account after each transaction.

A movement file will contain also the identification of the supplier, and details of those transactions that have taken place since the master file was last brought up to date.

The form these files take in an electronic data processing unit will, of course, depend on the hardware available, but master files are usually held on magnetic tape or disc while movement files are created initially by one of the input techniques discussed in Chapter 4 and eventually transferred to tape or disc for processing purposes.

Data origination

Data, whether movement or master, has to be obtained initially from one source or another. Recording master data is a once only operation, carried out when the system is first converted from manual methods, and subject to only occasional amendments, for example to add a new supplier or to alter a name and address. Recording movement data, since this represents a minute by minute record of the activities of a business, is a continuous process.

Data records may well originate at a number of different sources. We might have stock inventory movement data from a stores office, cash receipts from an accounts office, record of hours worked from a works office. Not only will the data come from different sources but will be in a number of different formats. Some may be hand-written, some prepared by machine, some containing information in both forms. The name we use for the medium on which this original data is recorded is a *source document*. These source documents will be created not only in the organization itself but some will flow into the system from outside—supplier's invoices, customer's orders and so on.

While some source documents may be prepared from the start in a machine usable form (e.g. MICR or OCR documents), most source documents will have to be manually entered through a keyboard device whether this be card punching, key to tape or disc recording or direct through a terminal.

It is important that source documents be prepared in a way which presents data in the most convenient way for conversion, and minimizes the need to refer back to the source department for checking.

To these ends the order in which data appears on the document, its legibility and accuracy, and the punctual despatch of documents to the data processing department are all very important.

Whatever the form of input, the order in which the data fields are to be entered must be rigidly defined and also, where applicable, the maximum size of fields. To simplify entry, the data on the source document should be arranged in the same order as that in which the fields are keyed in. Where possible the limitations in field size should also be indicated on the source document. Many data records contain non-variable information (such as a transaction code) which could well be pre-printed on the document. A way of preparing

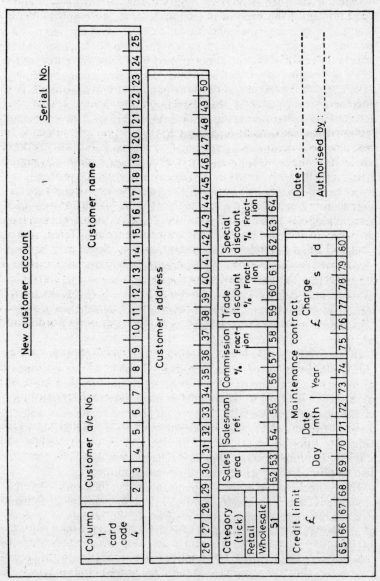

Figure 11.1 Specimen punching document

source documents to conform with these principles is suggested in Figure 11.1.

In a manual system, documents recording data usually pass through a number of hands, each person performing a given operation until the process is complete. A stores requisition, for example, might have the quantities and descriptions entered by one person, the unit price entered by a second, the calculations (unit price multiplied by quantity) performed by a third the entry into a stores issues summary by a fourth and posting to a costing system by a fifth person. By and large, the more people there are dealing with a document the greater is the chance of any inaccuracies being detected somewhere along the chain. In an electronic data processing system, once the source document has been prepared, there will probably be only one more reference to the data and that is at the conversion stage. From this point onwards, only automatic processes will be involved, so the opportunities for people to notice errors are much more limited. This emphasizes the need for a very high degree of accuracy in preparing source documents. Techniques for applying machine checks on accuracy are considered later in this chapter.

The conversion of the source document to a machine input form involves the operator in reading the document, possibly encoding the data, and then entering it into a keyboard. Illegible writing will result either in time being wasted while the document is checked back to source, or in inaccurate data being transcribed. The data processing department must insist on a high degree of accuracy and legibility when documents are prepared.

Given a satisfactory level of accuracy and legibility, there is still the possibility of error arising from a complete source document going astray. This makes it very necessary to impose some form of control over the flow of documents. Usually the most effective way of doing this is to serially number all source documents and to forward them to the processing department in batches arranged in sequence, quoting on the slip accompanying the batch the highest and lowest numbers in the sequence. The batches themselves should also be numbered in sequence and the batch number quoted.

The control section of the DP department can then check that the sequence is complete, making a note of the batch and the document serial numbers in a register. This method should reveal the absence of any individual document and also show if a complete batch has gone astray.

A further consideration is punctuality. A DP department works to a fairly rigid time schedule and it is important that source data should be received in time for the conversion process to take place, checks to be made, and the data assembled for the machine room by the time the machine run is due to take place. User departments must be informed of deadlines for the receipt of source documents. Finally, source documents should be accompanied with an authority for their acceptance into the data processing system. This may, in the case of routine documents, be the initials of the originating authority on the control slip, but for more important documents, such as requests to draw cheques, each separate document should be initialled.

Data conversion

In whatever form data originates, before processing can take place, it must be read into the computer. This may be done by direct entry or a second stage may be involved, the preparation of an intermediate document. Examples of the former are keyboard entry through a terminal or the use of OCR documents, and of the latter, punched cards or punched paper tape.

Details of the range of devices available for converting data to a machine acceptable form are given in Chapter 4 on input devices, in which emphasis is laid on techniques designed to preserve accuracy in the conversion process, an essential function if the results of processing are going to be reliable.

Identifying records

In order to distinguish one particular record from another it must contain some unique factor. This factor, referred to earlier as the control element in a data record, is known as the *record key*. Of course, a record in a movement file may contain the same key as one in a master file when the two relate to the same customer, supplier etc and so have to be related in a file updating process. Now the usual way of providing such a key is to allocate to each record a group of characters known as a *code*. It is a system with which we are all familiar in the form of bank account numbers and social security numbers. In fact, we find in most aspects of our lives requiring a clear identification, a number or code is used.

Coding design

Such a unique reference to records provided for any data processing system can also accomplish a number of useful factors, particularly in the area of computer processing where records cannot be identified, or examined by visual scrutiny. The code will give us:

(1) The means of identifying a record without reference to the descriptive data contained in the record.
(2) A medium for sorting records into a pre-determined order, or into defined groups based on some record characteristic, for example, geographical zones, or product groups.
(3) An easy way of matching records that relate to each other such as bringing movement and master records together.
(4) Economies can be effected in data recording. The use of a code can eliminate the need to repeat descriptive data. For example, there is no need to record a part specification on a stock control movement record since this can be copied, if required, from the master file record.
(5) It makes possible record indexing by associating the record key with a physical store location address.
(6) It can specify the processing routine. For example, the last digit could indicate whether cash or credit sales and so indicate the routine to be followed.
(7) A code may specify physical characteristics by relating elements of the code to factors such as size or volume.
(8) It can show relationships with other items, by for example, one element of the code being common to all parts of a sub-assembly, while the remaining elements defining each individual part of the assembly.

In fact, broadly speaking, a code can be made to do anything. It is simply giving a label or a series of labels to indicate a quality or a series of qualities about a commodity or a record of activity. Of course, the more we expect from a code, the more complex will be its construction and the more unwieldly its size.

Types of code

Codes used in data processing systems fall into two categories: (1) non-significant, (2) significant.

Non-significant codes, as the name suggests, do not attempt in any way to describe the factor to which they relate. In themselves, they are meaningless and the range of purposes they serve very limited. Such a code may be used to identify a record, as a medium for sorting records into code number sequence and for record matching purposes but little else. They are simple to construct, for example, all that is needed is a block of numbers, say 0001-9999. They involve the use of a minimum number of digits in their construction and make use of all the combinations in the sequence without leaving gaps. These are sometimes referred to as sequential or serial codes.

The construction of a significant code will be based on factors within a record that require to be identified. The combinations of such codes are infinite, but one or more of the following basic principles could well be incorporated.

Block codes

These are used to identify groups or blocks of records having a common property. The group is usually indicated by the first digit in the code and the remaining digits allocated serially to those records falling within the group. A simple geographical coding of sales ledger accounts could be:

Account Number	10000–19999 SW area.
	20000–29999 SE area.
	30000–39999 Home counties.

Such a coding principle allows for a more detailed grouping and the second digit might be used to signify a sub-group with the main grouping.

Account Number	10000–10999 SW area—Cornwall.
	11000–11999 SW area—Devon.
	12000–12999 SW area—Somerset.

It will be evident that the greater the degree of analysis required from the coding system, the greater the number of digits required to form the code. The range of number combinations used serially to allocate individual records within a sub-group, must be large enough to accommodate the largest group. Since the number of records in each sub-group is likely to vary considerably a large proportion of the codes will remain unused.

This block coding principle is used extensively in data processing systems having the advantages of simple construction and adaptability. It is comparatively easy to delete and insert groups, and the system lends itself readily to visual checks and provides a medium for sorting into the defined areas and districts and for retrieving information relevant to a particular area of district.

Significant digit codes

These are codes that incorporate a quantitative element in the form of an actual measurement of an attribute of a commodity. For example, the coding of copper piping could be

    264013   13 mm diameter
    264022   22 mm diameter
    264027   27 mm diameter

The significant digits of the code, in this case those defining diameter, are usually part of a longer code which may incorporate a second coding principle, and in this example the first digit 2 could represent plumbing fittings, the second, 6, copper fittings, the third 'pipe' and the last two the diameter of the pipe. While this type of code has the advantage that it accurately describes a commodity in detail and so is very useful in a visual context, there are drawbacks to its use in data processing systems. It is not always possible to define a measurement in purely numeric terms and this may result in a mixed alpha/numeric element in the code as would be the case with paper sizes, A4, A5 and so on.

Sorting and merging data records

Source data records, by nature of the activities that give rise to them, are usually generated in random order. For example, it is highly unlikely that issues of stock items from a factory or warehouse store will be in stock item number sequence. However, the master file for a stock inventory system will probably be kept in record key sequence. We then have the problem of 'marrying-up' movement records in random order with master records stored sequentially. Now, while at first thought, the obvious answer may be to sort the movement records into the same order as the master records and then to process the two files sequentially, merging and up-dating records when master and movement record keys coincide, there are, however, two factors which will influence this decision.

(1) The type of storage medium on which the master file is held.
(2) The proportion of movement records to master records in an updating run.

If records are held on magnetic tape the sequence of records, i.e. record key order, will be stored serially, i.e. one following the other physically. Under these circumstances, the movement records will also have to be sorted into the same sequence irrespective of consideration (2) above.

If master records are held on a direct access storage medium, e.g. magnetic disc, then they may be (a) stored at random with no reference to the record key order in which case there is no point in sorting the movement records but each master record will be located as required by reference to a word address/record key indexing system of some kind or (b) stored in sequence by reference to the record key.

In this latter case, the need for sorting movement records may depend on a factor known as the *hit rate,* i.e. the proportion of master records for which there are corresponding movements records. Should this hit rate factor be high, then it would be economical in machine time to sort the movement records into the same sequence and so process the files in record key order. Should, on the other hand, it be very low then the random selection of master records may be of advantage as in (a) above.

If sorting is necessary, as indeed is the case in most commercial data processing systems, there are two ways of doing this:

(1) To sort the data after its conversion but before reading in to the computer.
(2) To write the records on to the storage medium in random order and then use the computer to sort the items into sequence.

Sorting before processing

This method is only practical with input forms that contain one record only per document, i.e. unit record systems. Types of input documents that can be pre-sorted are punched cards (provided they contain one record only), MICR documents and OCR documents. Sorting is accomplished through a mechanical sorting device that will sense the record key contained in each document as they are passed through the device, finishing with a pack of documents in record key order.

Computer sorting

A number of computer techniques are used for sorting records into a required sequence and utility programs are available from manufacturers for this purpose.

It is not within the province of this book to describe all sorting systems but to illustrate how it may be done the following is a description of one technique known as a *two-way merge sort.* A magnetic tape containing the records in random order is loaded on to a tape deck and the records are read into the central processor one group or block at a time. The number of records in a block will depend on circumstances but will be constant throughout each stage of the sorting process. For this example we will take a block size of two records which is the smallest block size that can be used for this process. The first block of two records is read from the tape into the central processor where the magnitude of the sorting keys is compared. The two records are then written out, in the sequence required, to a second magnetic tape. This means that, if the required sequence is in ascending order the record with the smallest key will be written first but if the required sequence is in descending order the record with the smallest key will be written last.

The third and fourth records on the original tape are now read into store, again compared and written out in sequence but this time to a third tape so that at this stage we have three magnetic tapes, the original input tape containing the records in random order and two new output tapes each containing one 'String' comprising two records in key sequence. From this point onwards the two output tapes will be known as tapes 1 and 2. The term 'String' is used to indicate a number of records written to an output tape in the required sequence. This process now continues until the original tape is exhausted, two records at a time being read into store, compared and written out in strings of two, alternately to tapes 1 and 2. This completes the first pass.

For the second pass, tapes 1 and 2 having been rewound, become the input tapes and a second two tapes, 3 and 4, are loaded on to decks to receive the output from the processor. This time one string of two records is read in from each of tapes 1 and 2, the four keys are compared and written out to tape 3 in correct sequence as one string of four records. The second two strings from tapes 1 and 2 are then written as a string of four to tape 4. Thus at the end of the second pass tapes 3 and 4 contain a number of four-record strings written to them alternately. For the third pass tapes 3 and 4 become the input tapes from which strings of four records are read alternately, merged into sequential strings of eight records and over-written alternately to tapes 1 and 2, now used to receive output. The eight record strings are then merged in further passes into strings of sixteen, the sixteens into strings of thirty-two and so on until the one final string contains all the records in sequence. This is illustrated diagrammatically in Figure 11.2.

In the method described above, four tape decks are needed, but it is possible to manage with three by, at the end of each pass, writing the strings from the two output tapes alternately to a third tape which then becomes the one input tape for the next pass. In this case two strings are read from the one tape instead of one each from the two tapes. This, however, doubles the number of passes that need to be made to complete the sort.

Given a sufficient number of tape decks it is possible to speed up the sorting process by merging three or four strings at a time. These are known as 3-way and 4-way merge sorts, and require the use of six

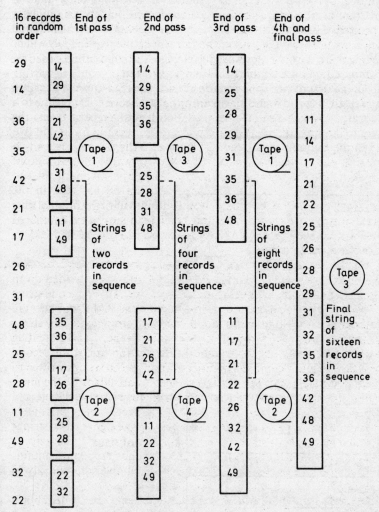

Figure 11.2   Illustrating a two-way merge sort

and eight tape decks respectively. Some other magnetic tape sorting techniques are known as *cascade sorting, polyphase sorting* and *oscillating sorting.*

It is possible to sort records into sequence by the use of the internal store of the processor alone, and this may be necessary if the configuration contains no form of backing store. However, the number of records that can be sorted in this way is limited by the size of store available to contain the records. The basic principle is to compare the keys of selected pairs of records and to exchange their position in store if the keys are not already in the sequence required. While there are different ways of selecting the pairs of records to be compared, in the example below pairs are taken in sequence starting from the first record. Thus records 1 and 2 are compared first, then 2 and 3, then 3 and 4 and so on until the last record. This process is repeated through a number of passes until all the records are in the required sequence.

In the example illustrated in Figure 11.3 there are six records in

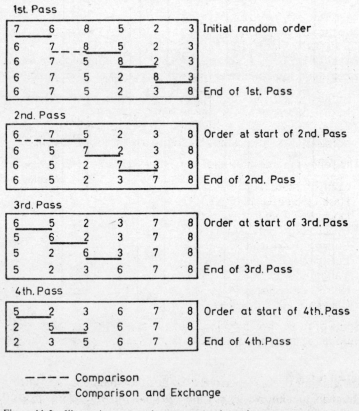

Figure 11.3   Illustrating a central processor 'exchange' sort

random order indicated by the six numbers printed in the top line. The first and second records are compared, 7 and 6, and since a final sequence is required in ascending order they are exchanged with each other so that the records are now in the order indicated in the second line. The second and third records are now compared, 7 and 8, but as these are already in sequence their order is left unchanged and the next two, 8 and 5 compared. In this case they are not in sequence and so are exchanged resulting in the order shown in line 3. This comparison of adjacent records is continued until the last record is reached. At this stage the highest record key must be in the final position. The process is then repeated through a number of passes until all the records are in sequence.

Checks on the accuracy of data

This section summarizes some of the techniques that are used to ensure the accuracy of data used in computer systems. Some of them are dealt with in more detail in other chapters.

Broadly speaking, as far as the input of data to a computer is concerned, we are concerned to ensure accuracy at three stages:

(1) In the preparation of source documents
(2) In the conversion of data to an input medium
(3) In the transfer of data to the central processor and, when necessary, its subsequent transfer to another form of store.

The following techniques are commonly used:

Control totals.
Hash or 'nonsense' totals.
Document sequence checks.
Check digit verification.
Punching verification.
Parity checks.
Validation.
Checks on reading.
Checks on data transfer.

Some of these checks may be used in only one of the three stages mentioned above while others may be applied at two or more stages.

Control totals

Source documents are collated in batches of a convenient size. Quantitative data is pre-listed on an adding machine and a total obtained. A note of this total is included on the control slip accompanying the batch. When punched cards or punched paper tape has been prepared from the source documents the quantitative data punched into these is totalled and checked against the total from the pre-listing (see Figure 11.4). An alternative method is to

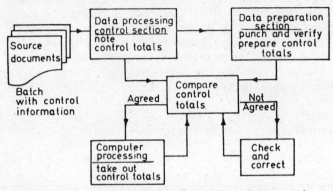

Figure 11.4   Reconciliation of control totals in a data processing routine

punch an additional card, or field in the case of paper tape, recording the control total as a minus quantity. The sum of the data on the cards or tape should now be zero. On reading into the computer, the machine is programmed to draw the operator's attention to a batch if this zero proof is not obtained.

Hash or nonsense totals

This consists of checking the totals of non-quantitative data taken before and after the punching process. This data may be the account reference numbers, or stock item numbers or indeed, the numerical value of alphabetical fields.

It should be noted that while control and hash totals ensure agreement on the total values of data recorded, they will not reveal compensating errors occurring within a particular batch of documents.

Sequence checks

This is a check of the serial numbers on source documents to ensure they are in continuous sequence. It is usual to note the range of serial numbers on the control slip attached to the batch of documents so providing a check on continuity from one batch to another.

Check digit verification

This is a mathematical method of checking the validity of numerical codes appearing on documents. It means giving each reference number unique qualities so that, when subject to a series of mathematical tests, the answer is always constant. This involves adding one or two digits to the reference number in order to make it conform with the criteria demanded by the method used. These additional digits are known as *check digits*.

The system basically involves weighting each digit in the number by a pre-determined amount, the digit being either multiplied by or added to the weight. The sum of the products or the additions is then divided by a pre-determined modulus and a test made of the remainder. To meet the requirements of the test this must be a constant.

While a number of different bases are used in check digit verification it is proposed to explain only one of these in detail. This is the method most commonly used in checking reference numbers in data processing systems.

In this example, the object is to provide reference numbers which, when each digit is multiplied by a weight that increases by one for each digit from the right, gives a sum of the products exactly divisible by 11, leaving a remainder every time of zero. Example: Taking a reference number 57342, find the digit that must be added as the last figure in order to make the resultant number conform with the above principles.

(1) Weight each digit by multiplying from the right by 1, 2, 3, 4, 5 etc.

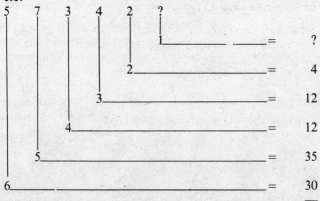

(2) Sum of the products (excluding the final check digit) 93

(3) Divide the total 93 by the modulus 11 = 8 remainder 5

(4) The check digit now becomes the difference between the modulus and the remainder, i.e. $11 - 5 = 6$

The reference number now becomes 57426 which conforms with these check digit verification principles, i.e. $(6 \times 1) + (2 \times 2) + (4 \times 3) + (3 \times 4) + (7 \times 5) + (5 \times 6) = 6 + 4 + 12 + 12 + 35 + 30 = 99$ which on division by 11 leaves a remainder of 0.

One disadvantage results from the use of a modulus 11. On an average, once in every ten times when the remainder is 1 the required check figure will be 10, and it may be impossible to accommodate two extra digits in the fields. In practice, when it is necessary to avoid increasing the length of the reference number by two digits, the numbers to which this applies can be discarded.

Check digit verification is carried out electronically, either in the central processor or by a check digit verifier linked to say, an adding or accounting machine, so that the check is made when source documents are prepared. The types of errors arising in the transcription of numeric data are given in the table below with the percentage of errors that will be revealed using the verification system described above.

Type of Error	Example	Percentage of Errors revealed
TRANSPOSITION	Reversing the position of digits 45678 becomes 54678 or 47658	100
TRANSCRIPTION	Mis-reading a digit and entering a different one 45678 becomes 49678	100
OMISSION	Leaving a digit out completely 45678 becomes 4678	100
ADDITION	Putting in an extra digit 45678 becomes 345678	100
RANDOM	A combination of two or more of the above 45678 becomes 9658	91

The above gives an average error finding ratio of 98.2. Assuming that an operator makes one error in every 50 entries, then this type of verification will give an accuracy ratio of 99.964%.

Verification

The verification process applied to input data is fully discussed in Chapter 4.

Parity checks

The principle of parity checking has already been discussed in relation to punched paper tape, but it should be appreciated that this form of checking is commonly applied to data held in any storage medium.

With magnetic tape, for instance, one track is reserved for parity purposes to ensure that the number of bits in each frame are either all odd or all even, and in addition the last frame in a block is used to ensure that the number of bits in each track are also either all odd or all even. Similarly, in other forms of external store and in the central processor, one bit in each word or block as appropriate, is used for parity checking.

Validation

While verification of punched cards and punched paper tape can ensure the accurate transcription of data from a source document it is no test of the accuracy of the original source data. Validation is a process of checking the validity of data against known factors, with which the data should conform. For example, stock item number 1234 appearing on a document is punched and verified correctly as 1234 but we know that all stock item numbers fall within the range 5000 to 5999.

Validation calls upon the program to check that all numbers fall within this range and to reject as invalid any that do not.

The general principle of validation, then, is to set tolerances against which the data can be tested. It might involve the definition of a range of reference numbers or impose limits on quantitative data, for example, regarding as invalid a record of wages earned in one week in excess of £50. It is also used to check the format of a record to ensure that the right type and correct number of characters appear in a data field, that there are the correct number of fields in a data record and so on. For example, a field programmed to contain six numeric characters would be rejected as invalid if only five characters were recorded or if one was an alphabetic character. It must be emphasized, however, that validation does not check the accuracy of data but rather ensures that data items fall within predetermined limits and conform to a predetermined format.

Checks on reading input

Checks to guard against mis-reading data are built into the hardware of the machine, usually in the form of checking stations. These have been discussed in detail in the chapter on Input.

Checks on data transfer

In addition to providing parity checks in the transfer of data to and from backing stores a 'read after write' check is frequently incorporated. This entails reading the data immediately after it has been written to store and checking back to the central processor store to ensure the accuracy of the transcription. It is recognized that mechanical failure within the central processor rarely happens, but as a precaution against fault in the transfer of records a parity check is usually made.

Security of data and files

As we have already seen, data records may be held either in files that are stored away from the computer such as punched cards, magnetic disc packs or magnetic tapes, or in files permanently on-line to the machine such as magnetic drums or fixed disc stores.

If magnetic storage media are stored away from the computer, particular attention must be paid to the environment in which they are stored. Although their magnetic state is quite stable, care should be taken to avoid exposure to stray magnetic fields, such as those from electric motors or from cables carrying heavy currents. Excess temperature and humidity should be avoided and the air kept as dust free as possible. Rigid control should be exercised over the use of files, a formal record being kept of issues and receipts of each file and a history of its mechanical performance. Magnetic tape files in particular should be handled with great care as a small mishap, such as creasing a portion of the tape could well result in the partial destruction of the magnetizable coating with the resultant loss of recorded data. It is important that the erasure of data on magnetic tapes should be controlled. A purge date, i.e. the date on or after which data can be over-written should be kept, and recorded in the header label, of each reel of tape.

Facilities should exist for the reconstruction of all types of file in the event of complete or partial accidental destruction. The method used will be determined by the type of file and the method of processing. For example, in a magnetic tape system where master files are held and up-dated by movement files, if the previous master and movement files are retained, the current master file edition can be reconstructed if necessary. As an additional safeguard, three generations of file are frequently kept.

Direct access files can be periodically copied on to magnetic tape, and movement files subsequent to copying retained. This again provides sufficient information to reconstruct the current file in the event of its destruction.

It should perhaps be remembered that the complete collection of computer records and programs constitutes a very costly investment. While it is impossible to completely insure an organization against the disruption which would be caused if they were entirely destroyed by a fire or explosion, it would certainly mitigate the situation if copies of all files were stored at a place remote from the computer installation.

Other security measures that may be taken are:

(1) The use of write-permit rings on magnetic tapes. The computer will only allow over-writing on the tape when the ring is in position.
(2) Software checks on file labels to ensure that correct files are loaded and that all records have been processed.
(3) Prevention of unauthorized access to computer installation.
(4) Use of passwords by computer users that will permit access only to those files relevant to the user's systems.

Exercises

1. What information would you expect to be held in a record of a customer's account on a sales ledger master file? Suggest the contents of a record that would be used to up-date the master file.
2. A stores requisition is received by the control section of the DP department holding data recording issues from store. Trace the progress of the data until the time it is held on magnetic tape ready for up-dating a stock inventory master file, mentioning any accuracy checks you think would be made during its progress.
3. Distinguish between (a) verification and (b) validation. A data field may be verified as correct but rejected as invalid. Why?
4. Calculate the digit that must be added to the following reference numbers to make them conform to a check digit verification check using a weighting 1, 2, 3, 4, . . . and a modulus 11.
      4963,   5633,   7100,   8368.
5. Distinguish between a non-significant and a significant record key. Give an example of how a significant record key may be used to identify specific factors in the data record to which it relates.

6. What is the difference between (a) master data (b) movement data. Using an example with which you are familiar describe the relationship between these two.

7. Suggest the safeguards you feel should be taken to prevent physical damage or corruption to a magnetic tape file.

8. Discuss the following statement: 'It does not matter if mistakes are made on source documents, the computer will find them'.

9. In preparing a source document the reference number 4636 is entered incorrectly as 436G, and the account number 83720 entered as 87320. While the value £87.63 is correct on the source document it is mis-read by both punching and verifying operators as £89.63. Explain how you would expect these errors to be found.

12

Systems considerations, design and implementation

While it is impractical to discuss in just one chapter all the implications in the design and implementation of computer systems, the object of this section is to give an overall picture of what a system is, and the stages and procedures incurred in evolving a computer system.

The question 'What is a system?' is not easily answered in a few words. Within the context of data processing systems, possibly the nearest definition we can get is 'An ordered set of procedures designed to organize, motivate, monitor and control an activity or series of activities to accomplish a pre-determined purpose'. As a basis to this discussion, we will take a system as referring to a discrete area of processing activity as one would generally find to fall within the spectrum of normal commercial usage, such as a stock control system, a wages system or a sales ledger system with however the reservation that such systems do not operate in isolation and they will have an inter-relationship with each other. In addition, the systems to a greater or lesser degree will in some aspects be integrated with each other, will operate within the same general business structure and work towards the same common purpose, i.e. that of the organization as a whole.

Systems environment

A data processing system does not just exist for the joy of being there. It exists as a result of some primary activity, manufacturing, servicing, research and so on, and its purpose in life is to record, control, promote and sometimes organize that activity. The activity that the system seeks to serve will have a bearing on the environment within which it works. While other environmental factors such as social, financial and legislative, are pertinent to the situation, the two factors we are going to consider at this point are *physical* and *organizational*.

Physical environment

This will be determined within the context of the way in which these activities are organized. The structure of the system will be influenced by such questions as:

(1) Are business activities concentrated into one location or are they dispersed over geographically widely separated units involving possibly a complex system of inter-communications?
(2) How is data emanating from the activities generated and how is it to be fed into the processing system?
(3) What response time is demanded from the processing system to provide the level of control called for?

It is suggested that these factors will have a material bearing on the following computer systems considerations:

(1) Centralized or distributed processing
(2) Provision of terminals as input/output media
(3) Data transmission facilities
(4) Computer operating modes: batch, time-sharing, real-time etc
(5) Collection, preparation and input of data
(6) Circulation or transmission of output reports
(7) Systems file structures: direct or serial storage devices
(8) Control: safeguards for security and accuracy.

Organizational environment

By definition, no automatic data processing system is an end in itself. It exists in relation to stimuli applied to it and information emanating from it in relation to the structure and objectives of the organization for which it provides a service. It is essentially part of the mechanics of a service that exists to provide information at the right time, in the right form and in the right place, promoting and guiding the controlling mechanism of the organization. This it does by monitoring, recording and processing data relating to the activities with which the organization is involved. It will, for example, provide information to guide management policy decisions, control production activities and optimize the use of available resources.

While it is not practical to lay down hard and fast rules, and indeed, exceptions will spring to mind particularly in the case of direct entry of source data through terminal devices, nevertheless, a data processing system can be looked at in three defined stages:

(1) Operations before entry to the computer system

(2) Computer operations
(3) Operations arising from computer output reports.

The first stage could well include originating, collating, checking, editing source data, and the third the implementation of action or policy based on output reporting (Figure 12.1).

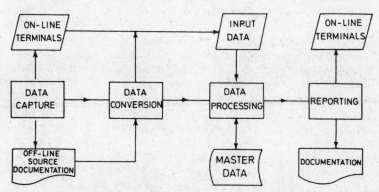

Figure 12.1   Progression of information through system

A system can, from one point of view, be looked at as a cyclical process (Figure 12.2), i.e. in the long term determined by, and in the short term influenced by, the activities taking place in the environment within which it is situated. By the same token, the information generated by the system will in turn determine and influence the activities of which the system is the subject.

At this point we may well ask ourselves, should the organizational environment determine the format of the system within which it works, or should the format of the system generate its own organizational environment. In practice, the solution usually falls somewhere between the two. The process of analysis of existing procedures and systems design does not necessarily sweep away the old completely, nor does it necessarily introduce a system to exclusively fit into the present order of things. It will seek, retaining where desirable present procedures, and introducing where necessary new or revised procedures, to formulate a system that, within the framework of available resources, will provide the most adequate service.

Systems design and implementation

As mentioned in an earlier chapter, in any organization systems already exist in one form or another for the processing of data before the decision to use a computer is taken. These systems have probably grown up over a long period of time with the development of the organization to meets its particular requirements, and have been

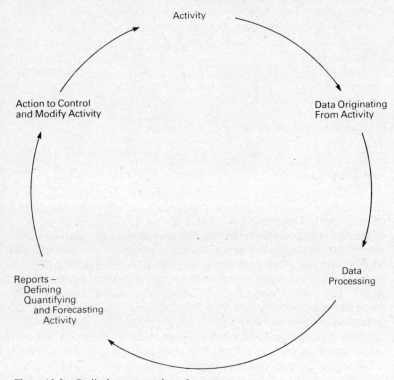

Figure 12.2   Cyclical representation of system

modified as these requirements have changed and also as the volumes of data to be processed have increased. Also, in all probability, the systems have developed within a departmental structure, individual procedures being geared to meet the requirements of particular departments, and so have a tendency to exist in isolation. This means that a variety of data processing methods are being used within the organization involving, in varying degrees, a combination of manual and machine methods. Serious consideration of the desirability of introducing computer systems is often triggered off by management's realization of the inadequacies inherent in this kind of situation.

Between the initial consideration of a computer installation and the time the systems become fully operational on the machine, a great deal of detailed work is necessary. This may be classified into the following areas:

(1) An initial survey to see if it is worth while to change to computer methods. This is usually known as a *feasibility study* and it will form the basis on which the decision is made.
(2) The investigation into, and analysis of, present systems and procedures.
(3) The design and detailed specification of systems in a form suitable for computer processing.
(4) Constructing and encoding the programs required to operate the systems.
(5) Implementation of the new systems.

Feasibility study

In the early days of computers, it was often not so much a question of assessing if it was worth while to introduce a computer but rather of seeing if the computer itself was able to do the job. With modern machines this question rarely arises, and we are more concerned with whether the use of a computer is justified. From this point of view, perhaps a better term for this initial study is a *justification study* rather than a *feasibility study*. While it would be safe to say that computer processing for all forms of commercial data is feasible, it might well be that the benefits accruing from the introduction of a machine do not justify the high expense and considerable re-organization involved.

Whatever we call this exercise, however, the main object is to ensure that a change over to computer methods is a workable project and is economically viable. Now the criteria on which the decision is based will vary from situation to situation. In one, expense may be the critical factor, in another time might be of prime importance and expense secondary, while other points of judgement may centre around staff shortage, accuracy, supply of management information and so on. Within the framework of a feasibility study, it is suggested that information could well be required on the following points to enable an objective decision to be reached by management:

(1) The overall objectives that will be attained, in terms of areas of work absorbed and the information that will be generated from the systems.
(2) The improvements that will result over present methods in accuracy, availability and control of data.

(3) The provision of adequate information for management control purposes. Will it place in the hands of management the information to enable it to run the whole organization more efficiently?

(4) Estimate of cost. This involves a cost evaluation of both present methods and the projected computer methods to provide a comparison, taking into account direct costs and any indirect savings that may accrue.

(5) The effect on the organization generally, including changes that will have to be made in departmental organization and in areas of managerial responsibility. The probable effect on staffing with an estimate of possible redundancies and the need for re-training.

(6) An estimate of the date by which the machine is expected to be installed and the systems to become operational. A computer is not the immediate answer to a current problem. It will probably be between twelve and eighteen months from the time the decision is made to buy that the first computer runs are made. The manufacturer's delivery date does not necessarily determine the implementation date. Time must be allowed for the development of systems and the necessary re-organization.

(7) How long can the machine be expected to give reasonable service? Change is costly and can be upsetting while it is happening. After the widespread change resulting from the initial conversion, no further major upheavals should be entertained for some time. Are there any technical developments round the corner that will make the processing techniques decided upon redundant or uneconomic in the near future?

Systems investigation

Having made the decision to go ahead on the basis of such a feasibility study, the next stages to set in motion are the detailed investigations of existing systems and the design of the new computer systems. This is known as a *systems project,* covering two main areas of work, *systems analysis* and *systems design.* Analysis is concerned with the investigation of the present position, fact finding, and recording the information found in such a way that a clear and precise picture is built up of what is going on. From this process, information is derived to help in the development of the new computer systems. Systems design is concerned with working out how the required objectives of the systems can be achieved in the most effective way, and specifying in detail all the processes involved.

Fact finding

Of the activities investigated by the systems analysts, he will be interested in the What, Where, Why, How, When and Who of the situation, and further than this, he will not only be concerned with what is actually happening but also with what should happen according to company practice and policy. There is quite often an appreciable difference between the two.

A number of techniques are used to find the facts of a situation,

(1) the examination of records, documents, files, organization charts, and procedure manuals,
(2) personal observation of staff as they carry out their work,
(3) getting staff to complete questionnaires and
(4) personal interviews and discussion with staff.

It is usually this last method that figures most prominently in a systems investigation.

The information the analyst is looking for can be classified under the following headings:

(1) Objectives. What is the system or procedure trying to achieve?
(2) Output. In what specific form are the outputs communicated, what are the contents of each? Is the output used and if so for what purpose and who by? Is it suitable for the purpose required and, indeed, is it really necessary at all? Is the same information being processed as the output of another procedure? Does the output of this procedure become the input of another?
(3) Input. What is the input? What forms does it take? Where does it come from? Is it the output of another procedure? Are all input records treated in the same way or are there exceptions? What is the detailed content of the Input?
(4) Records and Files. What files are kept? How often are they brought up to date? What purpose do they serve? How long are files kept before being disposed of?
(5) Processing. What is done to convert specific input information into the required output? Are any special skills required? How often is each procedure carried out? Could the job be done better if input was in a different form? Does processing anticipate further processes later on?
(6) Volumes and growth. What are current volumes? Are there any peak periods or seasonal fluctuations? What has been the rate of growth over the last two or three years? Is continued growth anticipated?
(7) Environments. What is the context within which the system operates? This will include research into the organizational structure of the departments involved, the adequacy of staff in

terms of both numbers and performance, communications within the department and with other departments and the degree of reliance on other services within the organization. A further important factor is to ascertain company policy in relation to the particular functions being investigated and any other factors such as trade practices and legal requirements that must be taken into account.

(8) Exceptions. Are there any exceptions to the general processing routine? If so, is it possible to classify them so as to bring them in to line for machine processing?

(9) Controls. What controls exist over the accuracy of the processing of the data processed?

In addition to these details relating to the procedures in the processing of the systems, there are four other things that the analyst will be interested in. These are:

(1) the equipment that is already in use, accounting machines, calculating machines and so on.

(2) estimating the cost of running the system under current methods, to provide a basis for comparison with the cost of any new methods proposed.

(3) the deadlines that have to be met by the output of the system and particularly why outputs have to be produced by these times.

(4) Which members of staff are responsible for making decisions, what type of decisions they are expected to make and the criteria upon which these decisions are based.

Fact finding, then, is the process of finding out how data is being processed within the organization. It enables the systems analyst to build up a picture of detailed requirements and ensures that he is conversant with all of the factors that must be taken into consideration when re-designing the system.

Fact recording and analysis

Information obtained during a systems investigation must be methodically recorded. It is usual to open a *systems investigation file* in which is kept copies of all documents relating to the system and the notes made by the analyst during his enquiries.

A number of methods that are used for recording and analysing facts are suggested below. While the circumstances of the situation and the individual preference of the analyst concerned will influence the recording techniques used, there are two basic factors that should be borne in mind. The first of these is that the object is to set down in a clear and concise form all of the facts that are relevant to the situation so that they can be referred to and understood during the design phase. The second is that the records in the systems file should be understandable by everyone concerned in the investigation, not just the analyst writing up the record. To this end, while there are no generally accepted standards, most firms using electronic data processing techniques extensively, evolve their own standard procedures for documenting systems so that should there be a change in personnel working on any particular project the problems of handing over are minimized.

Information flow diagrams   These are usually in the form of block or flow charts. The aim of this type of chart is to show the logical sequence of events that take place. Use is made of symbols representing activities, connected by flow-lines. A short description of the activity is contained in the symbol with, if necessary, additional explanatory notes appended. Block and Flow charts are considered in more detail in Chapter 9.

Procedure narrative   This is an organized descriptive account of procedures in a very detailed form. Usually it contains three basic elements

OPERATOR	OPERATION	OPERAND
Who does it	What is done	On what is it done

Organization chart   This shows the organizational structure of the departments responsible for carrying out the functions being investigated and defines areas of responsibility. This type of chart often also includes the numbers of staff engaged in each type of activity.

Document flow chart   This is a graphical presentation of the flow of documents and the procedures they are subjected to from the time they originate until they are eventually filed away. The detail should include the number of copies raised, how these are distributed and what happens to each copy.

Cost tables   In order to give a breakdown of operating costs of a system or a department, tables can be constructed analysing costs under main headings. The main cost factors usually involved are, staff, supplies, equipment and the cost of accommodation. These in turn can be broken down in terms of the procedures within the department or system.

Document description form   This contains a brief description of the document for identification purposes, a detailed record of the data appearing on the document with minimum and maximum size of data fields where applicable. It should indicate how the document originates, the volumes processed during a given period (with any periodic fluctuations) and how often the documents are processed (daily, weekly, or monthly). Finally it should state the use to which the document is put, for example, for up-dating a master record, or for distribution to customers.

Systems design

The general considerations in the design of systems are as follows:

(1) To generate the required information to the desired degree of accuracy, when needed, and in the form required.

(2) To be as flexible as possible. The system must be capable of change within a limited range as may be necessary with changing conditions and changing volumes. In other words, the system must not go to pieces if minor changes are made.

(3) As economical as possible. The analysts are not concerned with just one system in isolation but with the processing needs of the organization as a whole. The same inputs and outputs may be common to two or more systems. For example, an advice note could be the source document for the preparation of sales invoices in a sales ledger system and also for stock issues in a stock inventory system. The same consideration applies to output documents and to files. The analyst will be concerned with the cost of recording source data, its preparation in machine input form and the cost of computer processing time.

(4) Control requirements. The system must contain checks which will ensure the accuracy and security of data at all stages and have the capability of measuring its performance against the planned objectives. It should also be as 'fool proof' as possible so that no one person's mistakes will easily disorganize the system.

(5) Exception handling. Should there be any exceptions to the general routine of processing the analysts must decide how these should be treated. While a system could be designed to deal with all exceptions, this would not necessarily be the most efficient or most economical way of dealing with them. Consideration should be given to processing exceptions manually.

(6) Effective document design. A document is the vehicle for conveying information, and must be designed to do this in the most effective way.

(7) Effective coding design. Records processed by a computer are usually recognized by a 'key'. Coding systems should be designed so that the main activity to which the key relates is easily identifiable and so that the keys can be checked for accuracy.

(8) Constraints and legal requirements. Within an organization there are usually factors which over-ride purely internal systems considerations. These must be taken into account in systems design, even though they may make the system more involved than would otherwise be necessary. Such factors might include practices agreed with Trade Unions, custom and usage within a particular industry and, indeed, facets of management policy. All these impose constraints within which the analyst must work. In particular, when designing a system, allowance must be made for audit requirements and to this end, the analyst will find it necessary to consult with the firm's auditors while developing his systems in order to ascertain their requirements.

The situation as it now stands is that the objectives towards which we are to work have been specified in the feasibility study, information has been gleaned on the existing situation and more detail on the requirements of the system has been obtained through the process of fact finding and analysis. In addition to this we have a number of general considerations that have to be borne in mind.

We must now consider the development of an automatic data processing system to replace the old manual methods. While a number of stages in the design of a system are given later, two points should first be emphasized. One of these is that systems investigation and systems design are not completely consecutive activities in the sense that all of the fact finding and recording is finished before the design stage is commenced. While the analyst will usually make a start with investigating existing methods, continual reference back for additional information is necessary during the course of designing. Secondly, the design of a system tends to progress through a series of levels, each succeeding level specifying the requirements in greater detail until eventually a final and completely detailed systems definition is produced.

The following section breaks down the systems development procedure into a number of areas of work and presents them in the order in which they would probably be tackled by the analyst.

Output specification

By this time we will know in principle what is required of the system; this will have been decided upon at the feasibility study stage. If, for example, we are concerned with a stock inventory system, one of the outputs required could well be a list of goods to be re-ordered. At this stage in the systems design we are concerned with deciding the information that this list should contain. It may be, for instance that the list is to be passed on to a purchasing department where the orders are raised manually. In this case the output record content might consist only of an identification of the item, a statement of current stock, re-order level and re-order quantity. On the other hand a completely automated re-ordering system may have been decided upon, which will print out the purchase orders direct on the computer printer. In this case additional output information such as the name and address of the supplier would be required. Not only are we interested at this stage in the content of the records, but also in the order in which they must be produced, e.g. item number order, priority for ordering, product group order and so on. We also need to specify the frequency with which the reports are to be compiled and what is going to happen to them after they have been prepared.

File design

Having decided output requirements, we now have to decide the files that are needed to produce this information. Since, by this stage, the hardware that will be available will have been decided upon, the type of file available (magnetic tape, magnetic disc etc.) will be known. It remains to specify the content of the records kept on file, the sequence in which these are to be stored, the anticipated number of records in each file and the frequency with which the files will be processed.

Input specification

Next we are concerned with the input data necessary to generate the information on file that will in turn produce the output reports. As we saw earlier in the chapter on Data Preparation, this is usually a two stage matter, first recording the data at source and then converting it to a machine input form. For source documents the method of originating the data and recording it at source will have to be decided, the content of the input record, the controls that are to be imposed to ensure accuracy, and the routine for forwarding the documents to the D.P. Department for processing. As far as the conversion is concerned, here again a routine must be defined for preparing the data, controls established to ensure accuracy during conversion and the procedure for creating or up-dating files from the input medium outlined.

Procedure specification

This is concerned with working out the procedures necessary throughout the whole system, manual and machine, in order to produce the required outputs. While there are recognized methods for recording procedures (Block Charts, Flow Charts, Narrative etc.), there are no firm rules that can be applied to the actual procedure development process. This relies on the experience and aptitude of the analyst and his ability to bring creative and logical thinking to bear on the solution of the problems inherent in systems design. It is, to a certain extent, a process of trial and error—formulating a possible solution, testing this against known conditions, modifying and adjusting it if requirements are not met until eventually a satisfactory final solution is found.

Input and output form design

Having decided the content of source, input and output records, we are next concerned with the detailed design of the documents to contain the information. Source data is usually recorded on pre-printed forms. Design of these should take into account the next stage, that of data preparation, forms being designed so that data fields appear in the most convenient order for transcription to punched cards or punched paper tape. It is often as well, to ensure efficient recording at source, to specify on the source document the size, or maximum size of each data field, the type of field—alphabetic or numeric—and to incorporate any explanatory notes that are considered necessary for the guidance of the person completing the form. In addition to this, any non-variable data can be included when the form is initially printed. If machine input is punched cards, the cards will have to be printed showing fields and titles of fields to conform with the data appearing in the source document. However, whatever the input form the format of the input record must at this stage be clearly defined.

Much the same factors apply to the design of forms to contain output reports many of which, if the output is by way of a line-printer, can be pre-printed. The layout of data, position of fields within the output record, and size and content of fields must be clearly defined and communicated to the processor through the program, to control the format of the output reports.

Recording a new system

Having designed a new system as suggested above, the whole must be recorded formally and in detail. This formal record of the system is known as a system specification or a system definition. This should contain the following information:

(1) An overall description of the system, listing the inputs, outputs and files, and outlining the procedures involved and the aims of the system.
(2) A detailed specification of input, output and file records, accompanied by appropriate charts, specimen documents and explanations.
(3) A detailed account of all procedures again with appropriate charts and notes.
(4) For the guidance of programmers, a specification of each program required to operate the procedures.
(5) Details of how the system is to be implemented, specifying exactly how the change-over from the original manual system should be done.
(6) A note of the equipment needed to operate the system, not only for the actual computer processing and data preparation, but also any ancillary machines needed in the course of the preparation of source data and for dealing with output reports.
(7) Specification of testing procedures and test data for the programs and the system.

Finally, the complete systems specification should be formally agreed by management. After this the final stage is the implementation of the system.

Systems implementation

Since many of the problems associated with the initial setting up of a computer department are discussed in other chapters, we will consider implementation procedures on the assumption that a new system is being taken on to an already existing computer department. This will be considered under four main headings: staff training, pre-take-on procedures, file conversion and the actual change-over process from the original manual methods.

Staff training

Assuming the operations staff of the computer department to have been already trained, we are concerned with the problem of training those people outside the computer installation who will be involved in operating the new system. This includes both those who are concerned with the recording of source data and any manual processing this gives rise to, and also those who are going to use the output reports generated by the system. Some of the staff concerned will already have a good idea of what is going on as they will have been involved in the investigation and design stages of the project, but now it becomes necessary to give all the staff concerned a complete account of how the new system will operate, and individual members of staff a detailed explanation of what their particular role will be. This is not just a question of issuing instructions to everyone concerned, but also of enlisting their co-operation by involving them in the system and explaining the benefits that can be expected both to themselves and the company as a whole.

Perhaps the best approach is by personal discussion between the analyst responsible for designing the system and the staff who will work with it, with special discussions at supervisory and middle management level.

Specific training must be given to those people concerned in operating the new procedures to ensure that they are familiar with the new documentation, how documents are to be completed, what controls and checks are to be imposed and when information is to be forwarded to the computer department for processing. Not only should verbal explanations be made and demonstrations given, but the whole of the information should be collated in the form of a procedure manual, specifying in detail how each procedure is to be carried out and providing specimen forms with explanations as to their use. These procedure manuals must be made readily available to those members of staff concerned with carrying out the work.

Pre-take-on procedures

These are concerned with making the physical arrangements necessary for implementing the new system. The introduction of new methods will usually involve a degree of re-organization in offices, stores and so on. Adequate supplies of the new stationery and forms must be made available, and arrangements made to dispose of old files and forms no longer required. It may be necessary to provide additional machines both at the source data recording stage and at the computer output stage. For example, adding machines may be needed to prepare pre-lists for control totals, or where documents for distribution direct to customers have not previously been produced, a folding machine may be necessary.

File conversion

This is the process of transferring the information required for the system, from the old manual files to the new computer files.

The two major factors to bear in mind in file conversion are firstly the large volume of work to be done in a comparatively short time, and secondly the fact that records on files are not static but are continually being modified by records of business activity. It is hardly practical to stop all business activity while the conversion process is taking place. To help cope with the high volume of work it is often a sound policy either to engage temporary staff or to switch staff temporarily from other less pressing activities. For the conversion of the file records to punched card or punched paper tape form, the aid of a punching bureau can be enlisted.

The second complication, that of continually changing records, can be met by a two-stage conversion process. The first stage takes on the non-variable content of the records, which usually represents the bulk of the data, and then the variable content, a much shorter job, is taken on as the second stage. This means that the original files can still be up-dated while the conversion of non-variable data is taking place.

As an example of this, consider a stock inventory record containing the following information:

> Stock item number
> Description
> Minimum stock
> Maximum stock
> Re-order quantity
> Unit price
> Quantity
> Value

The first five data fields could well be taken on to the new files during the first stage since these are not likely to change in the short term, and then in the second stage the last three fields together with the stock item number for a second time, in order to marry-up the two parts of the record.

A file conversion routine usually consists of three stages. First comes the preparation of a document from the original file record, to be used for punching, second the preparation in punched card form, and third the computer runs to create the new files.

Change-over procedures

There are three approaches to the change-over to the new computer procedures.

Parallel running   This means that, for a period, data is processed by both the old and the new methods. Results of the two are compared and the old method discontinued as soon as the new one is proved.

Pilot running   In this case, the new method is proved with simulated or old data while current data is being processed by the old system. Using old data that has been previously processed manually has the advantage that the results of processing are already known and can be checked against the output of the new system. When the new system has been thoroughly tested and proved a switch is made, discontinuing the old procedures and operating the new.

There is, however, a second type of pilot running which consists of the gradual take-on of a system procedure by procedure. This, of course, is only viable with a system that lends itself to this piecemeal absorption. As each procedure is taken over, the output is fed back compared and used in the old system until progressively the whole system has been taken over.

Direct change-over   This means the closing down of the old system completely and starting up the new as soon as possible afterwards. It does not provide the safeguards of parallel and pilot running and is normally only used when there is insufficient similarity between old and new methods to provide a comparison. A direct change-over usually has to be implemented during a break in normal business activities, for example, at holiday time or a weekend.

Exercises

1. What do you understand by a feasibility study? Suggest the main factors on which you would report when carrying out such a study.
2. Discuss the techniques you would use in obtaining information about the operation of present systems in a company, with a view to using this information to help design new computer systems.
3. What are the main stages in the design of a new system for computer application?
4. The systems analyst must incorporate into his system, checks to ensure as high a degree of accuracy as possible. Suggest some of the methods he will use to do this.
5. What are the main aims a systems analyst has in mind when designing a new computer system.
6. Explain the three main ways of changing over from a manual system to a system processed by computer.

7. Describe a routine for converting records held on file in a manual system to a magnetic tape file.

8. Draw up a check list of the activities involved in designing and implementing a computer system.

9. What information would you expect to find in a systems definition?

10. List and comment briefly on the main activities in the design of a computer system to replace an existing manual system, placing these in the order you think they should be dealt with.

11. What is a computer feasibility study and how is such an activity carried out? Include in your answer details of the kinds of information which may be collected and the documents which result from a feasibility study.

12. You have just completed a feasibility study of the manual procedures in your company which was requested by the Board of Directors. You are now at the stage where you must prepare a report containing your findings and recommendations for submission to the Board. This report will consist of a number of headed sections, each dealing with a specific matter.

    Enumerate the section headings of your report and briefly say what will be contained under each heading.

13

Organization of a data processing department

We have already considered some of the processes that are applied to data in order to achieve the outputs that are called for by the system. The purpose of this chapter is to consider the organization of the department responsible for carrying out these processes, usually known as a *data processing department*.

Structure of a data processing department

While the detailed organizational structure of a DP department will depend to a large extent on the size of the organization it serves and the services it is expected to supply, it will be concerned with the following main areas of work:

(1) The investigation of present systems and procedures and the design of systems for computer application. This is done by *systems analysts*.
(2) The conversion of the systems specifications provided by the analysts into instructions that can be performed by the computer. This is the work of *programmers*.
(3) The performance of the operations and procedures within the data processing department. This includes such things as the acceptance and control of data, the preparation of data in a machine acceptable form, operating the computer and ancillary machines, the control of work flow, file and program usage and so on. This third area of work is the responsibility of the *operations manager*.

The whole of the department, systems analysts, programmers and operations, is under the control of a *data processing manager*.

The organizational structure of a department involved in these areas of work could take the form illustrated in Figure 12.1. While a more detailed account is given of some of them in other chapters, the following are comments on the functions involved.

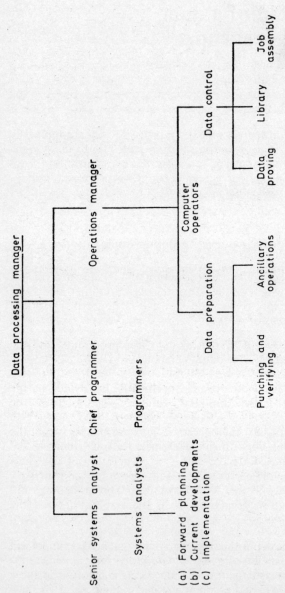

Figure 13.1   Organization chart of a data processing department

Data processing manager

It is evident that many departments of an organization depend on the data processing department for their processing needs. To carry out their function efficiently, they must be able to rely on the reports produced. Because of this, the data processing manager holds a key position in the organization. He should have the ability to be able to preserve good relationships between his own and the user departments, and have the tact and drive necessary to cope with the problems and difficulties that are bound to arise in these relationships.

In order to efficiently control his highly specialized staff he should have a good practical experience of data processing and a working knowledge of all the activities involved. He must keep up to date with current developments in the computer field and be able to advise management accordingly. He should have an open mind which is not intolerant of new ideas, and be capable of clear, logical and imaginative thinking. The ability to communicate effectively is most important, not only with technicians but with laymen, bearing in mind that he will be dealing with his Board of Directors, the heads of other departments, his own staff and the computer's manufacturer.

Systems analysis

As we saw earlier, data processing is a means to an end. Data is raw material consisting to a great extent of a mass of unrelated facts and figures. Processing is the technique of relating all these, and the required end is the provision of meaningful information. The context within which this is all carried out is known as a *system*, and the system comprises all the detailed rules and procedures which must be observed to give the required end product. By usage, the term system usually applies to a major activity of the business, for instance, a sales ledger system, or a stock inventory system. In the latter case we are concerned with relating a mass of data recording stock issues, stock receipts, minimum stock levels, unit prices etc. When processed these will provide up to date statements of current stock levels and values, re-order lists, analysis of material usage and so on.

These systems exist in every business but usually not in a form suitable for processing by computer. The *systems analyst* has as his aim the design of a system that can be so processed. This entails three main functions:

(1) Investigation into, and analysis of existing systems.

(2) The design of systems for computer application to attain predetermined aims.

(3) The implementation (or putting into action) of the new systems.

The range of work and techniques with which the systems analyst becomes involved is very wide, so he needs a lot of general experience in commercial systems as well as a good knowledge of data processing and computers. He should also have a detailed knowledge of the policy and organization of the company with which he is working.

As it would be unusual to find any one person with this wide range of experience and knowledge, it is usual for analysts to work in a team. Ideally each member of the team would possess specialist experience in one or more areas of work. The combined 'know-how' of the team can then be brought to bear on the wide range of problems inherent in systems design. The team is usually led by a senior systems analyst who is responsible to the data processing manager.

Success in the investigation and design of a system depends to a large extent on the ability of the systems analyst to enlist the co-operation of members of staff involved who, indeed, may not (for one reason or another) welcome the changes brought about by the introduction of a computer. The analyst must, therefore, be a person able to mix easily with people and to communicate effectively. Other qualities required by an analyst are a capacity for logical thinking, a high standard of accuracy, patience, tact and the ability to record his work clearly and concisely and to work to target dates.

Systems analysts will have three main tasks:

(1) Forward planning, i.e. investigation of systems that are planned for the fairly distant future.

(2) Current development, i.e. the detailed specification of systems planned for implementation in the near future.

(3) Implementation, i.e. supervising the testing and taking over by the computer of systems when design has been completed.

Programming

Programmers usually take over when the analyst has completed the design of a new computer system and has documented the design in the form of a *systems specification*. Basically the program is a series of coded instructions that can be stored in the central processor and executed in the appropriate sequence. Two qualities required of the programmer are the ability to reason logically and to pay very careful attention to detail. The need to document programs with complete accuracy and to conform with recognized standards imposes additional disciplines on the programmer. Systems analysis and programming are discussed in more detail in Chapters 12 and 10 respectively.

Data processing operations

Analysts and programmers are concerned largely with work of a 'once only' nature. They may be responsible from time to time for amendments and alterations to a system, but once it has been designed, documented and programmed, and starts to be used for routine processing operations, it becomes the responsibility of the operations section. While the structural organization of this section will depend to a great extent on the size of the department and the volume and variety of data processing work, the following basic functions fall within its area of responsibility (see Figure 13.2).

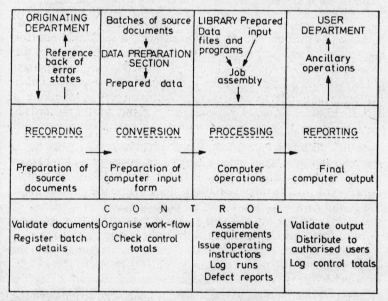

Figure 13.2   Basic functions of a data processing department

Recording-conversion-processing-reporting

Because it provides a service for user departments, the operations section has a continuous two-way flow of work: source data flows in and reports flow out. As well as this, there is a considerable movement of data within the section itself. Source documents go to data preparation, input documents to the computer machine room, output reports from the machine room and so on. Also, the operations section must work to a quite rigid timetable to ensure that reports are available when required, input data is ready for processing when needed and to ensure efficient usage of available machine time. To co-ordinate all of these activities to meet specified deadlines and to ensure the accuracy and security of processing generally, an effective control must be imposed on the work of the operations department. This is usually done by forming a *control section* which is responsible for organizing the flow of work through the department, co-ordinating its activities and imposing standards to ensure the accuracy and security of data processed.

Recording

While it is not the responsibility of the data processing department to originate source data, since this is done in the other departments of the organization, it is the province of the control section to check that data is originated in a way that conforms with procedures laid down when the system was designed and accepted.

As a basic principle, all source data coming into the installation must be handed to a reception clerk. This is the link between the computer and the user departments. The staff of the departments which originate the data should not have unrestricted access to the rest of the computer staff.

Source documents are usually handed in at reception in batches at the frequency and times specified in procedure manuals. Each batch should be accompanied by a *control slip* which gives, where appropriate, an identification of the documents, the number in the batch and their sequence numbers, any control totals obtained by pre-listing and the initials of the person authorized to release the documents for processing. One of the responsibilities of the control section is to check at this point that the documents contained in the batch conform with the details on the control slip and to check as far as possible that they have been accurately completed and are legible. Registers are maintained by the control section in which batch details (date, sequence numbers and any control totals) are recorded.

So that queries may be quickly resolved, there should be a defined procedure for reference back to the originating department of any question arising when checking source documents. The aim should be to ensure that source data is correct before it is passed on from reception to the data preparation section, since the sooner an error is detected, the less trouble is caused in correcting it.

While the principle of batching source documents is discussed in detail in Chapter 11 the following advantage of this procedure are mentioned in connection with data preparation:

(1) It presents punch operators with reasonable sized jobs.
(2) It facilitates the tracing of errors. The reason for failure to reconcile control totals is more easily found if the error occurs in a fairly small batch.
(3) It allows errors to be traced in one batch while processing continues with those batches that have been proved correct.

Conversion

We have already seen that it is usually necessary to convert source data to an input form suitable for machines. This is known as *data preparation* and is the work of the data preparation section of the data processing department. This section contains the machines for converting source data (usually punched card or punched paper tape machines) and operators who are under the control of a *punch room supervisor*. The control section is responsible for the flow of work through the data preparation stage, to ensure that prepared data is available in time for scheduled computer runs. Batches of source documents are handed to the supervisor who allocates work to the operators and supervises the punching and verifying. Punch operators must be supplied with clear written instructions for the preparation of each card form and a specimen of the card format. Other than punching and verifying, the data preparation section may be involved with the extraction of control totals by passing cards through a punched card tabulator and with using punched card sorters to put the cards in a required sequence.

Once they have been punched and verified, source documents should be cancelled, to prevent their re-entry into the system. This is often done by requiring operators to stamp source documents with a numbered rubber stamp. This serves the purposes both of cancelling the source document and of identifying the operator who punched the data from it.

Control totals taken from the prepared data are compared by the control section with the totals previously noted from the source documents control slip. This process of comparison of totals helps to detect errors made in the data preparation section.

The general process of controlling the accuracy of punching and verifying, the correction of errors and reconciliation of totals is usually known as *data proving* (see Figure 13.3).

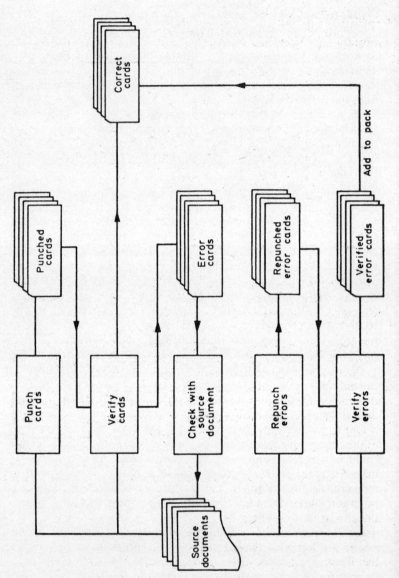

Figure 13.3   Routine for preparation of punched cards from source documents

Processing

Before a processing run takes place, the computer operators must be supplied with all the materials necessary for the run. Getting all these requirements together, another function of the control section, is known as *job assembly*. It is usual to specify the requirements for individual runs in the procedure manuals prepared when the system was first designed. While, of course, these will vary with the type of run, the following is a typical list:

(1) Operating instructions stating exactly what processing is to take place.
(2) The program necessary for the run.
(3) The job input data.
(4) Any pre-printed stationery for output.
(5) Any files required. Assuming magnetic tape files are used, this would include any master files for up-dating and any tapes for taking on the results of processing. These latter may be completely blank tapes, or tapes containing data no longer required that can now be over-written.

Staffing arrangements for the computer room will depend on the size of the installation and on work volumes, but will consist basically of a computer room supervisor and a number of operators. As it is desirable to run computers for as many hours a day as possible, shift working may often be involved, with a number of operating teams each under the control of a shift leader.

Operators are expected to keep a 'log' recording the utilization of the machine time and to report any defects resulting in the loss of machine time, whether these arise through mechanical failures or defects in input data or programs.

One function vitally important to smooth processing is the control of the storage and use of data files and programs. A large installation could well be concerned with the storage and use of hundreds of magnetic tapes. These contain programs and master data representing the information requirements not only of the processing department but of the whole organization. It is essential, therefore, that suitable physical conditions are available for maintaining the tapes in good order and that controls are imposed to ensure the use of the correct tapes in processing and the security of the information they contain. The section of the department responsible for this is known as a *tape library,* and is under the control of a librarian.

The conditions necessary for storing magnetic tapes are basically those required in the computer room itself. These are discussed in

Chapter 15. For this reason it is often convenient for the library to be situated in a section of the computer machine room that has been fitted with storage racks on which the tapes, in their individual dustproof containers, can be stored.

The control of the use of tapes centres around the upkeep of records designed to identify the contents of each tape and to record their issue to and receipt from the machine room. Notes must also be kept on the physical condition of each tape. Most important, a note must be kept of the date until which recorded data must be preserved. This is known as a *purge date,* and on or after the purge date the tape can be over-written with new data.

Reporting

Another of the functions of the control section is to accept output reports from the computer machine room and arrange for their distribution to the departments authorized to receive them. Before distribution the validity of the report should be checked against the format specified in procedure manuals and any control totals noted in the appropriate register. In addition to this, ancillary machine operations may be called for such as bursting continuous stationery, collating, folding and so on. A description of these ancillary operations is given in the chapter on output.

Finally, in relation to the general organization of a data processing department, the following points should be noted:

(1) Staff duties should be clearly defined in writing and an organization chart prepared for the department.
(2) The organization should be arranged to guard against the possibility of the whole department grinding to a halt through the absence or irregular conduct of one member of staff.
(3) Allowance must be made for the observance of any legal requirements, such as auditing, and also for any special constraints imposed by management.
(4) Computer department staff should not be allowed to take part in the preparation of source documents or, other than the control and data preparation staff, have access to them.
(5) For security purposes the various sections of the department should, as far as possible, be physically separated, access to the records controlled by each section being strictly limited to those people responsible for them.
(6) Strict control must be imposed over important documents, such as blank cheque forms and wage payment slips.
(7) Access to the computer machine room and to the library files should be strictly limited.

(8) The general aims of the control section of the department are:
  (a) To organize the flow of work through the department as smoothly and efficiently as possible.
  (b) To conform with the times set for the production of output reports.
  (c) To ensure as far as possible the detection and correction of errors thus saving time and money otherwise wasted in re-processing.
  (d) To keep the records and to ensure the procedures that satisfy legal and auditing requirements.
  (e) To prevent any deliberate malpractices.

The working environment

Apart from the organizational structure of a DP department, another important consideration is the environment in which processing activities take place. Experience has shown that there is frequently a matter of compromise between fitting hardware and personnel into modified existing accommodation rather than new tailor-made premises. In either case, there are a number of factors worthy of consideration in providing the environmental conditions that will promote an efficient working unit.

Some of these considerations will be self evident—adequate lighting and heating, noise control, minimum working areas—and will be mandatory within the framework of legislation. More specific considerations when designing the accommodation in which a computer department will work are as follows:

(1) An arrangement of units within the department to facilitate a logical flow of work and at the same time minimize the distances over which work has to be carried.
(2) The provision of pleasing working conditions and rest areas, bearing in mind the repetitive and often boring work in data preparation procedures.
(3) Provision of support services to ensure conditions essential to the efficient working of the machines, air conditioning, temperature, humidity and dust control.
(4) Adequate facilities for supervision and control of both machines and data.
(5) Security of access to machine rooms and stores and also to confidential records and potentially valuable documents such as cheque blanks.
(6) Provision of facilities for machine maintenance staff.

(7) The provision of adequate communications network for peripheral/computer interface.
(8) Controlled environment facilities for off-line storage of files held on magnetic media.
(9) Provision of adequate office accommodation for management, systems design, programming and operating staff.

Data processing standards

In an organization as complex as a DP Department it is important that work should be carried out in accordance with pre-determined rules and procedures, that all personnel should be aware of the framework of the department in which they are working and familiar with the relationships within the department and with the requirements of the users the department serves.

To help achieve these aims, a set of uniform practices and techniques are set out, in other words standard working practices, and these, together with information of departmental structure and relationships compiled into a *standards manual*. Standards may be of two kinds: (a) Those laying down rules and guides as to the method work in the department should be carried out. (b) Those stipulating targets against which the actual performance of the department can be measured.

Why standards?

A number of advantages are claimed for the use of standards as follows:

(1) To promote efficiency within the department.
(2) To ensure a reasonable return on the very high capital and revenue costs of running a computer department.
(3) To ensure an effective induction of new members of staff by adhering to common documented work routines, thus preserving continuity.
(4) To provide a comprehensive reference document for all members of staff.
(5) To safeguard the interests of both the DP staff and the organization as a whole.
(6) If standards are observed the control of activities is that much easier.
(7) Budgeting for departmental costs and planning for future developments become more objective and more easily formulated.

(8) To safeguard agencies outside the organization against errors, e.g. suppliers and customers, and also to safeguard the company against the non-payment of accounts.
(9) To protect against the criminal use of information and fraudulent practices by members of the DP staff.
(10) To meet auditing requirements.
(11) To comply with current legislation.

The standards manual

While a standards manual will be compiled to meet the requirements of a specific data processing department and the contents will, therefore, vary from situation to situation, the following are sections a typical manual will contain:

(1) Details of machine resources available with notes on their purpose, their capacities and throughput speeds.
(2) An outline of the organization of the department, its aims and responsibilities and job descriptions of departmental staff.
(3) Details of departmental administration, including reporting procedures, maintenance of departmental records, training facilities, support services (secretarial, clerical etc) and the maintenance of discipline.
(4) Details of departmental staff: systems analysts, programmers, data preparation staff, control staff, computer operators, librarian.
    In respect of these staff the standards manual should detail:
        methods of work
        the standard documentation involved in each task
        procedures for testing and maintaining systems and programs
        specification of control procedures and accuracy checks.
(5) Performance standards for departmental staff and for machine and equipment resources.

All in all, the standards manual should represent a detailed and complete picture of what is required by and from each member of the departments staff and from the department as a whole.

Computer bureaux

In this chapter up until now we have assumed a situation where the processing requirements of an organization are met by its own data processing department. This, however, may not always be the case and an organization may make use of an outside agency to provide these, or some of these, requirements. This kind of agency known as a *computer bureau* is usually an independent company aiming to provide services within the range listed below. It is also possible to obtain some of these services from manufacturers, Software houses and even from some computer users who have spare capacity to sell.

A computer bureau will provide services from the following range:

(1) A complete processing service in which the bureau does the same range of work for a client as would be done if the client had his own installation.

(2) Software services.
Writing application programs to a client's specification
Writing and supplying standard specialized application package programs, e.g. sales ledger, purchase ledger, stock control etc
Providing sub-routines and utility packages

(3) Hardware services.
A 'do it yourself' service where machines are made available for use by the client's own staff
A processing service where data is accepted by the bureau, processed by its own staff and the results returned to the client
Time-sharing facilities by siting terminals in the client's premises for use over a communication link

(4) Systems analysis and design

(5) Data preparation, e.g. conversion of source documents to a machine acceptable medium such as punched cards.

(6) Consultancy, e.g. advice on buying, installing and running a computer.

(7) Specialized activities, e.g. microfilming, MICR and OCR services.

Why use a bureau?

A number of circumstances may give rise to an organization deciding to use the services of a bureau:

(1) Economic, since the installation of a computer is a very expensive project. It may be that a company either does not have the resources available or feels that the resources it has can be used to greater advantage in other areas.

(2) Work load, for example, the total work volumes may not justify an 'in-house' computer and even with a company having its own machine there may be very busy times when it becomes necessary to off-load some work to a bureau.

(3) To gain experience before a final decision to purchase computer equipment.

(4) To take advantage of specialized services offered by the bureaux.
(5) As an insurance by having available stand-by facilities in the case of major machine failure.
(6) To cope with the problems and work volumes associated with a manual to computer changeover.

It will be appreciated that the range of services provided by bureaux will vary from one to another. When choosing a bureau it is important to ascertain that it has the expertise, the hardware and software facilities to provide the required services and that its past record proves its ability to meet the levels of confidentiality, security and dead-lines demanded.

Exercises

1. What main sections would you expect to find in a data processing department? Give a short account of the work of each.
2. Describe the flow of any processing job of your choice through a data processing department from the time the source documents are handed in at reception until the distribution of the final reports.
3. What qualities would you look for in a person applying for the position of data processing manager?
4. Describe the work of the data preparation section of a DP department.
5. (a) Show diagrammatically the structure of that part of a typical data processing department which is the responsibility of the operations manager.
   (b) Indicate the functions of each section shown in your answer to (a) by describing briefly the events that occur between a user department submitting data to the computer department and receiving their results.
6. Draw a functional organization chart for the personnel of a large commercial data processing installation using a computer.
7. What do you consider to be the main considerations when designing and arranging accommodation for a DP department to provide efficient and harmonious working conditions?
8. Give reasons why you feel the setting of standards to control the work in a DP department is desirable.
9. What major areas of information would you expect to be contained in a standards manual for a DP department.
10. Give an account of the services a computer bureau will provide.

11. Suggest circumstances that may give rise to a commercial company employing the services of a computer bureau.
12. Suggest any disadvantages you feel may accrue from the use of a computer bureau.

14

Applications

The computer applications described in this chapter have been deliberately kept fairly simple, since the object is to illustrate the type of work that is commonly the subject of electronic processing and to demonstrate some of the techniques and devices described in this book. The descriptions of these applications are not intended to represent complete systems definitions.

If we start by considering one main business function, that of Sales, we find that in dealing with and in recording a credit sale to a customer the following main areas of work are involved:

(1) Receipt of customer's order.
(2) Vetting for credit control purposes, with procedures for opening new accounts where appropriate.
(3) Preparing the documents relating to the transaction: stores despatch instructions, advice note, invoice etc.
(4) Calculating the price of the goods sold.
(5) Packing and despatching the goods.
(6) Up-dating stores inventory.
(7) Up-dating sales ledger and preparation of customer sales statements.
(8) Sales Analysis.

Now the range of work within this main function, sales, that is performed by computer will vary from situation to situation. For instance, the entry point for computer processing could be at (2) which means that the credit control procedures, preparation of documents, stock inventory, sales ledger and sales analysis would all be performed by the machine. On the other hand perhaps all the stages up to and including the preparation of the invoice are manual procedures and the entry point for the computer is at (6) stock inventory.

From this series of procedures it is proposed to select just two routines. The first assumes the entry point to computer processing to be a manually completed invoice, and is just concerned with up-dating a sales ledger and the production of sales statements and a analysis. The second assumes the point of entry to be a completed advice note and is concerned with

(1) Daily   Customer Invoices
                Re-order list of Stock Items
(2) Monthly   Customer Sales Statements
                Sales Analysis by Areas.

Sales ledger application

The first routine is described below and also shown in chart form in Figure 14.1. It assumes that data is prepared in punched cards, is sorted off-line and that backing storage is magnetic tape.

The output requirements are

(1) Customers' Sales Statements.
These will contain the balance outstanding at the start of the month, a list of movements during the month in date order, and finally the balance outstanding at the end of the month.
(2) Sales Analysis over areas.
Records that need to be kept on file to produce these outputs are:
  (a) Master Records. Each record containing the customer's name and address, customer account reference number, balance on the account and the date of the balance. In order to provide an area sales analysis, the first digit of the account number is the key to the sales area.
  (b) Movement Records.
These record all movement items, details of sales being obtained from invoices, returns and allowances from credit notes, cash received and discounts from cash books and so on.
  (c) Change Records.
These are needed for opening new accounts, deleting from files accounts that have been closed and making amendments such as of address, to customer details.

Master records are held in account number sequence on magnetic tape files. Movement data and changes are prepared on punched cards from batches of source documents received daily at the DP department. In this application, we are only considering the sales ledger and analysis over areas, i.e. we are not interested in the individual items on the invoices as we would be for a routine to prepare invoices or to up-date a stock inventory system.

For each movement item a card will be prepared containing the customer account number, the date, a code to indicate the type of transaction—invoice, credit note, cash etc.—and the amount. Cards recording changes will have to be designed to include full customer

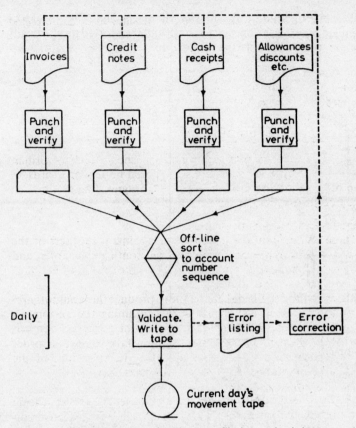

Figure 14.1   (a) Preparation of movements file in a sales ledger application

details, name, address, account number, to provide the information to open a new account on the master file. The batches of source documents will be pre-listed and control totals obtained before punching and these in turn will be checked against totals obtained from the batches of cards after completion of the punching operation.

We now have available, prepared daily, the movement data and the changes in machine input form. Now a number of ways suggest themselves by which the up-dating of the master file can be accomplished from these, bearing in mind that what we are aiming at is a file or files containing the master data and opening balances, and the movement data in date order within account number. Cards could be sorted daily on a punched card sorter and then used as a direct input to up-date the master file each day. They could be assembled over a week or even a month and then sorted mechanically and then used to up-date the master file.

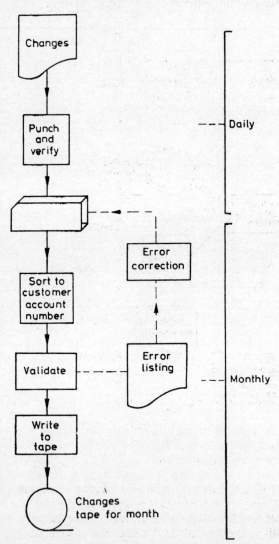

Figure 14.1 (b) Preparation of changes file in a sales ledger application

Another way would be to write them in random order to magnetic tape and then sort them on the tape to the required sequence, using this sorted movements tape to up-date the master file. All these represent possible ways in which the problem could be tackled and the method chosen will depend on such things as volumes of data, available hardware and the amount of computer time available.

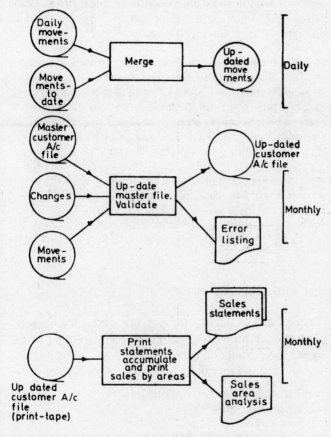

Figure 14.1   (c) Computer runs in a sales ledger application

For the purpose of this example we will assume that the daily output of movement cards is mechanically sorted into customer account number sequence. The cards are then written to a magnetic tape that we will call a movements tape. The cards recording changes, since these will be fairly few in number, will be kept on a punched card file for processing at the end of the month.

Each subsequent day's movement is applied to the movements file in a daily up-dating run on the computer. This means that at the end of the month we have a file containing all the movements in date order within account number. Next the monthly changes cards are sorted mechanically and written to a further magnetic tape. This now leaves us with three tape files, the master file containing opening balances, a movement file and a changes file. The next procedure is to process these three tapes on the computer to merge all the data they contain on to a fourth tape. This we can call a *print* tape, which will in turn be used to print out the information we require. During the preparation of the print tape any errors, for example, movement items for account numbers not appearing on either the master or changes files, will be printed out so that a manual check can be made.

The final stage, then, is to run the print tape to produce on a line printer the sales ledger accounts and the customer statement. At the same time, customer master data and closing balances are written to another tape, this becoming the opening master tape for the next accounting period.

While the records are being processed and printing is taking place, the value of those records carrying a code indicating 'sales' are accumulated in store locations according to the first digit in the account number indicating the sales area. At the end of the run the totals in these locations are printed out to provide the Sales Analysis.

Sales ledger and stock inventory

For this procedure we assume that the source documents are advice notes prepared by the despatch department, one copy sent to the customer and the second copies, containing the following information, batched and sent daily to the computer department:

(1) Customer account number, name and address
(2) Date and advice note number
(3) Part numbers and descriptions of goods despatched.
(4) Quantity of each item in (3) above.

We will also assume that data preparation is again in punched cards although, of course, other methods may be employed such as key-to-tape or disc. Of course not all of this information needs to be keyed in as much of it is already held on sales ledger and stock inventory master files from which it can be copied when required. The essential information required is (a) Customer account number, for customer identification, (b) Date and advice note number, which will be quoted on the invoices, (c) Part numbers and quantities of goods despatched.

Computer files

These are held on magnetic disc as follows:

(1) Movement File.

This holds daily movement items read in from the data preparation stage. Initially the records will be in no particular sequence other than the order in which they are prepared by the despatch department. Since it will be necessary later on to sort records by stock item number for pricing and for stock-inventory up-dating, to avoid losing the identity of each item with the correct customer account number, it is necessary to prefix each item with the customer reference. This is done when the records are read to disc.

(2) Master Sales Ledger File.

This will hold records for every customer on the file containing the following:

(a) Customer identification: account number, name and address
(b) Balance outstanding at the start of the month's trading with a list of Invoice numbers and amounts making up this balance.
(c) Movement items to date for the current month showing date, Invoice number and amount.
(d) Balance outstanding to date.

(3) Stock Inventory Master File.

This will hold a record for each stock item containing the following:

(a) Stock item identification: stock code and description.
(b) Control information: minimum and maximum stock levels, stock re-order level and quantity etc.
(c) Unit prices
(d) Records showing issues and receipts during the current period.

Having outlined input and output requirements of the system it is now proposed to examine the computer runs with master files organized sequentially. From many points of view, processing in this mode is very similar to magnetic tape file processing. Master records are held on disc in key sequence order in a continuous set of addresses and, before an up-dating run, movement records must be sorted into the same sequence. From a storage point of view, two approaches need to be considered: (a) Up-dating records and writing them back to the original disc file area, and (b) Completely rewriting the file during up-dating to a completely separate disc or file area.

As we saw in Chapter 7, up-dated records may outgrow their location in store and have to be placed in overflow areas with their new addresses tagged. This makes possible the use of storage as in (a) above. However, with a high hit-rate and where records are likely to be substantially expanded in the up-dating process, a situation might well arise when a large proportion of the records have been diverted to overflow areas and home addresses contain a high proportion of tags. Under these circumstances much of the advantage of fast processing with sequential file organization is lost, and it could well be that more rapid processing would be achieved by adopting (b) above. It is this principle (b) that is illustrated in Figure 14.2 in which the following computer runs are shown.

(1) Data from source documents is punched into cards and written in random order to disc (DI). Validation and editing procedures are carried out and an error list printed so that corrections can be made and fed back into the system. Editing procedures will include the pre-fixing of each stock movement item with the customer account number to enable reassembly later in customer sequence for invoice preparation.

(2) The unsorted movement records are now sorted into stock item code sequence. While this can be done by using the same disc file area and over-writing the unsorted records, a more secure way is to rewrite the sorted records to a separate disc file area D2.

(3) Sorted movements are then processed against the stock inventory master file D3, from which stock item description and unit price are extracted. Calculations are performed to give the product, quantity times unit price, and the record rewritten in its expanded form

ORIGINAL RECORDS

Customer a/c number	Stock Item Code	Quantity
12345	2469	24

EXPANDED RECORD

Customer a/c number	Stock item code	Description	Quantity	Unit price	Value
12345	2469	Jug	24	2.50	60.00

In the same run the master stock inventory record is updated to give revised stock balances. These new balances are compared with the control criteria governing re-order conditions for each item of stock and a re-order list printed. The updated master stock inventory file is completely rewritten to disc file area D4 and the expanded movement records to another area D5.

(4) A sort is then made of the records on D5 into customer account

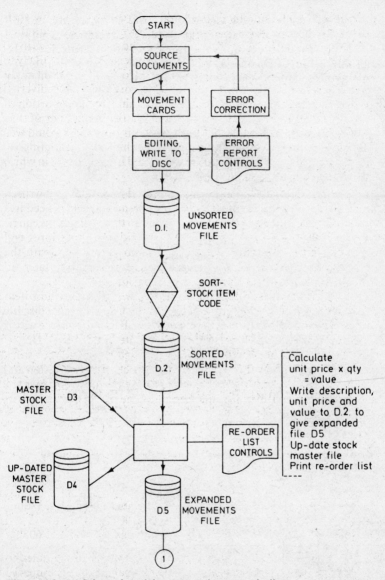

Figure 14.2 (a) Sales and stock inventory using magnetic discs

number sequence, D6, grouping back together the stock items originally appearing on the advice note.

(5) File D6 is then run against sales ledger master file D7 from which

the relevant additional information required for the preparation of invoices is extracted. For example, customer name and address and details of discounts and settlement terms. From the interaction of D6 and D7 a print file D8 is prepared from which Invoices can later be printed. Master sales records are updated

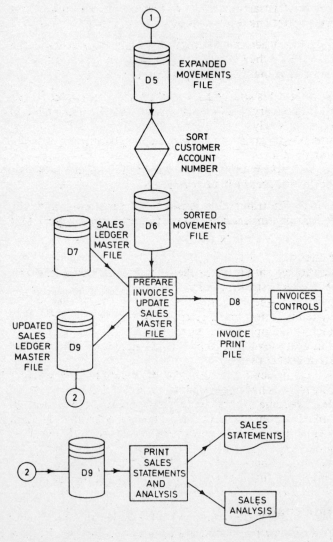

Figure 14.2   (b)

being expanded to include invoice identification and total value, and revised sales ledger balances calculated.

(6) At the end of the month the sales ledger master file will contain records of all transactions relating to the period, from which customer sales statements can be prepared. At the same time totals can be accumulated on the first two digits of the account number for transactions made during the current month and printed to give a monthly sales analysis by area.

As suggested earlier, an alternative way is to over-write the original record with the updated record in the same location on the same file area. The main points of difference are:

(1) Updated record is written back to the same location on disc or placed if necessary in an overflow area with the home address tagged accordingly.
(2) Records not updated can remain unchanged in their original location on disc.
(3) By and large, the number of runs will be the same but a smaller number of file areas will be required.

Figure 14.3 illustrates this method of processing and the procedure for updating records shown in chart form in Figure 14.4 as follows:

(1) Open files
(2) Read in to central processor the records contained in the first bucket of the first file cylinder.
(3) Read in a movement record.
(4) Compare movement and master record keys for a match.
(5) If match found update master record.
(6) Read in next movement record. If key higher than that of last record in bucket then
   (a) If creating new file write bucket out to new file area whether any records have been updated or not.
   (b) If using same file area write bucket out to original location only if updating has taken place. If overflow situation results tag and place unaccommodated record in overflow area.
(7) Read in second bucket of first cylinder.
(8) Continue until final bucket in final cylinder is processed.

Production control

Let us move on now from applications in purely commercial data processing. A significant proportion of the computers used in this country, probably amounting within a short time to one-sixth of the total, are used in production control. It is apparent that very great benefits can arise from the use of computers to ensure the optimum utilization of production resources. If we say that production control techniques have as their aim the completion of specified

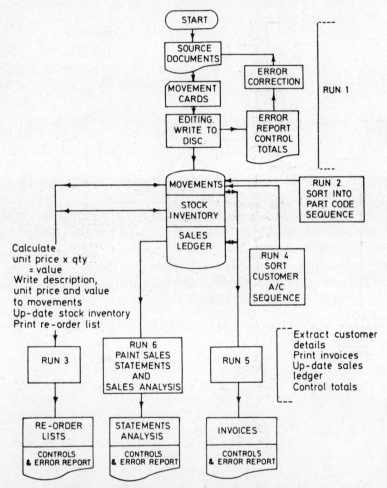

Figure 14.3   Alternative sales and stock inventory using magnetic discs

work at the right time with the greatest economy in the use of resources, we can see that it might be impossible, using a manual system of control to achieve all these aims at the same time. For example, delays in production might be insured against by carrying over-large stocks of components, thus achieving production at the right time but at the expense of the economical use of resources.

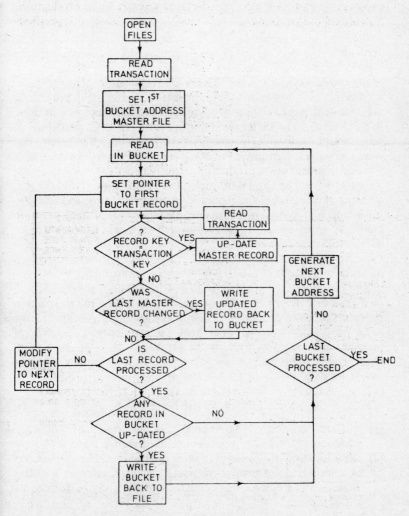

Figure 14.4   Updating records on magnetic disc

In large scale production so many variables are involved (work priority, availability of stock, utilization of available machines and manpower, and so on) that reliance on human skill and experience to make all the information on these variables available, to take it all into consideration and to reach the best decision every time is asking the impossible. The computer comes into its own in this field not only by its capacity to store the mass of statistical data involved in production and to make this available in the required form very quickly, but more important by its capacity to weigh up a situation and arrive at a decision. This decision, moreover can take into account all the information the computer has on all the variables and is based on a review of every combination of these variables.

In production control, the first area to feel the impact of computer methods is usually that of stock control. By this we mean not merely a convenient mechanism for recording issues and receipts, in other words keeping a stock ledger, but the control of stock quantities at their optimum level. This means taking into consideration such things as market trends with seasonal fluctuations in the demand for finished goods, future production requirements for raw materials, the cost of tying up capital in stocks, the cost of storage and the cost of being out of stock, the reliability of suppliers, the necessary re-order time and so on. For a firm keeping thousands of stock items, to manually apply each of these variables to each item of stock would, of course, be an immense task. Given the criteria on which to judge these factors, to the computer the setting of optimum stock levels to meet the conditions prevailing presents no major difficulty.

The computer having determined what stocks are required, its next area of concern is in planning and controlling the production processes necessary to make these stocks available. Usually, in large scale production, the product progresses through a number of production levels. For example, raw materials become component parts, components become sub-assemblies, sub-assemblies become major assemblies which then make up the finished product. The output at each level can be regarded as the 'stock' for the input to the next level. Two main problems arise here:

(1) the maintenance of the correct stock quantities at each production level to provide a continuous work flow, and
(2) the allocation of resources to meet the production requirements at each level. We have already seen earlier, that control of this first factor, stock quantities, can be successfully performed by the computer.

The second factor involves the analysis of finished products into the requirements at different production levels. This means that the computer must keep on file a record of the components, assemblies etc., that make up each standard finished product. By a process of analysing the make-up of each product, relating this to demand and to already existing stocks, the computer is able to produce a production schedule. In producing this, another factor the machine is able to take into consideration is that of components and assemblies common to two or more finished products so that these can be batch produced to ensure economic production quantities.

The third major area of work the computer is concerned with is that of scheduling production and allocating resources. We saw earlier that one of the aims in production control is to achieve the greatest economy in the use of resources. One of the most difficult problems in scheduling production on a multi-level basis is to ensure the full utilization of resources at all levels. A bottle-neck at one level of production could well lead to the use of resources at subsequent levels at less than their full capacity. Again, the computer is able to take all the variables into consideration and to schedule production in the most efficient manner. Having implemented the production schedule, there remains the task of comparing performance with plans. This monitoring can be done through the computer by feeding back to it data recording performance. For the information of management, the computer will then report on any failure to meet planned requirements.

Finally, in a fully integrated computer production control system, the effects of changes in scheduled production can be quickly assessed. In a manually controlled system, the effects of a management decision to squeeze in an urgent job are often virtually impossible to assess. However, with computer control, these effects can be quickly and accurately foreseen thus providing the information management needs to make its decisions in a rational and calculated way.

Rates accounting

One of the earlier computer applications in this country was in public administration for the processing of rate accounts. In fact a large number of local authorities have now changed, or are in the process of changing over to computer methods for this purpose. While the detail varies from authority to authority, the basic requirements of a rating system are as follows; it must be able to:

(1) Maintain an up to date file of records of properties
(2) Periodically calculate the rates due in respect of each property
(3) Prepare and circulate rate notices
(4) Keep personal accounts recording amounts due and amounts paid
(5) Record receipts of cash

(6) Periodically list outstanding balances

(7) Prepare reminder notices as appropriate.

Initially a master rate file is prepared, usually in two sections. The first section contains records of all properties within the rating area, and the second, records of those properties where the owner, rather than the occupier, is the ratepayer. We will assume that these records are held on magnetic tape in property reference number sequence and that the first type of record contains the following information:

(1) Property reference number. This is usually based on the geographical location of the property and refers to the district, street and number within the street.

(2) The basis of the rate assessment—net annual value and rateable value—with records of any revision of these.

(3) Occupier's name and address.

(4) A code number to distinguish successive occupiers.

(5) Dates of commencement and/or termination of occupation.

(6) Owner's reference if occupier is not the rate-payer.

(7) Coding to indicate the type of property.

(8) Occupier's personal account showing amounts due and recording cash received.

The second type of record, the owner's record, contains much the same information, but the sequence key is the owner's reference rather than the property reference. Since one owner may be responsible for the rates levied on a number of premises, the record may contain a schedule of premises. However, it is more usual in computer processing for a multiple number of records to be held for one owner, each containing details of one property. In either case, the record will identify the property by the property reference number and address, identify the owner by the owner's reference, name and address and will also include details of the rates assessed and the owner's personal account.

With this master rate file as our starting point, the following is a brief description of the processing necessary to achieve the requirements listed earlier. These are shown diagrammatically in Figure 14.5 (a) to (f).

(1) The revision of the master rate file by changes, e.g. change in basis of assessment, in owner or occupier, addition of new premises or deletion of demolished premises etc. Changes are punched into cards, written to magnetic tape, sorted into key number sequence and applied to amend the master rate file, resulting in master rate file (2).

(2) Calculation of rates due and preparation of rates notices for

distribution. In this case the declared rate in the £1 for the various categories of property are read into store from punched cards (the number of rates being very limited). Codings are

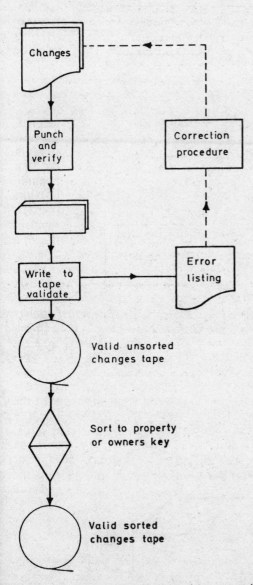

Figure 14.5   (a) Treatment of changes in a rates application

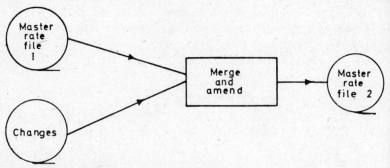

Figure 14.5   (b) Amending master rates file with changes

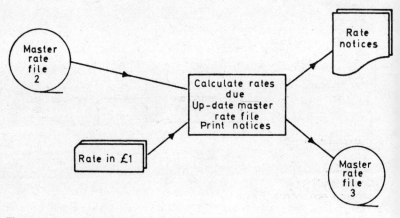

Figure 14.5   (c) Calculating rates due and printing rates notices

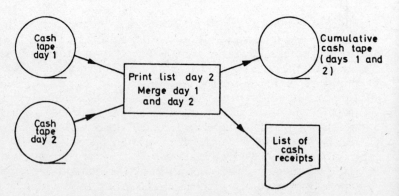

Figure 14.5   (d) Treatment of daily cash receipts

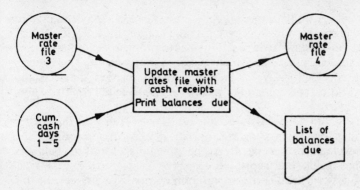

Figure 14.5   (e) Posting cash receipts for the week and producing list of balances

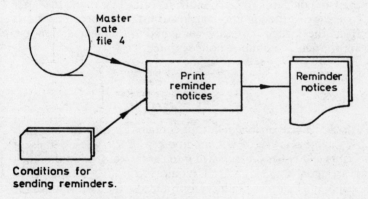

Figure 14.5   (f) Printing reminder notices

matched with the property code in the master record on master rate file (2) and the rateable value multiplied by the rate in the £1 to calculate the rates due. The rates notices are printed and at the same time the rates due written to the record in the master file, producing an updated master rates file (3).

(3)   Next we deal with cash receipts. We will assume the treatment of these will require a daily printed list of cash received and a weekly run to update the master rates file with the accumulated receipts for the week. To this end, cards are punched daily to record the amount received and the property or owners reference number. These cards are in turn written to magnetic tape and sorted into key sequence. This tape is then used in a print run to prepare the required listing for the first day of the

week. A similar tape is prepared for the second day and used to print the second day's receipts, and at the same time the records are merged with the first day so as to produce a cumulative tape containing the first two days' records in sequence. This process is repeated for days 3, 4 and 5 thereby producing at the end of the week, a tape containing records of the receipts for the whole week.

(4) This cumulative cash receipts tape is now run with the master rates file (3) updating the appropriate records and producing a new master rates file (4). At the same time a list of the balances due at this stage is printed.

(5) The final stage is the preparation of reminder notices. In this case the specified conditions in which reminder notes are to be sent may be written into the program or, on the other hand, be prepared on cards for each individual run. Assuming the latter to be the case the conditions are read into store where the records from the master tape are compared with them and where appropriate, a reminder notice printed.

Exercises

1. A stock file held on magnetic tape contains a sequence of records in ascending order of commodity key. Each week details of receipts and issues are punched into cards. Records on the stock file are updated weekly and it is required to produce an analysis of receipts and issues by product group and also the total value of the stock after updating. Draw a flowchart to illustrate these procedures.

2. Describe a routine for producing customer invoices by computer assuming the following to be available:
   (a) Advice notes containing customer name, address and account number, and a list of items supplied quoting stock item number and quantity.
   (b) A magnetic disc file of stock records in item number sequence, each record containing item number, description and unit price.
   (c) Assume a central processor, card reader, line printer and magnetic disc backing storage to be available.

3. Describe a routine for dealing with (2) above but to cope with three categories of customer A, B and C who are given 15%, 25% and $33\frac{1}{3}$% trade discount respectively.

4. Using any computer configuration of your choice describe a

routine for dealing with student enrolment in a college in order to produce:

(a) A list of students on each course in alphabetical order.

(b) Lists of students in alphabetical order with two or more A level passes.

(c) The average age of students on each course.

5. Describe in outline the uses of a computer in any specialized field with which you are familiar such as education or traffic control.

6. Suggest, giving reasons, the type of backing store you would use and the way you would expect records to be organized on file, in the following applications:

(a) Customer sales accounts in an electricity board.

(b) A hotel room booking system.

(c) A sales ledger system recording the sale of heavy engineering equipment on which there is only movement on 5% of accounts each month.

Some management aspects of computers

'Going computer' has far reaching effects on an organization. It is not just the buying of another accounting or calculating machine to fit in neatly with established procedures, but rather the introduction of a key factor around which the whole administrative machinery could well revolve and, upon which it may well depend. Only the highest level of management will be able to authorize the financial outlay, re-definition of responsibilities, and the structural re-organization necessary to use a computer to the full. It is, therefore, imperative to the success of a computer project that management at director level should be actively involved. This chapter is concerned with the part played by management in relation to the use of computers in an organization. This will be considered under two main headings, management policy and management problems.

Management policy

The immediate difficulty that faces management in connection with a change-over to computers is that on the one hand they must make decisions, while on the other they cannot be expected to have the necessary expert knowledge. With this in mind we shall look at the complete computer project in three stages. First the situations that suggest installation of a computer, then the initial investigation or feasibility study, and finally the installation of the machine and the implementation of systems.

Later on we will give more detailed consideration to the circumstances which may make the installation of a computer desirable, but the first essential is to decide whether it is worth incurring the cost of a feasibility study. Management should therefore, even at this early stage, have some idea of what a computer can and what it cannot do. The feasibility study is usually conducted by experts, either from independent consultants or from a manufacturer. It is their responsibility to advise management on the desirability of using a machine, to recommend the areas of work that should be taken on and to specify the configuration of the installation needed. Management should be in a position to make a critical appraisal of the report by having a good idea of what they require from the installation and, as far as possible, some idea of the capabilities of computers. As far as the third stage is concerned, for this management will have appointed their own expert staff, computer manager, systems analysts etc. From this point onwards, active participation of management at director level is again necessary to provide the authority for implementing the changes that must be made. One workable approach to this is to give a director who is not involved in any one particular department of the business, overall responsibility for computer services.

At this point it would be as well to examine the position of the manager of a computer installation. It is impractical to make him responsible to the head of any particular section of the business, because, as we have seen, the effective installation of a computer requires decisions to be made which will affect the working of several departments. In the interests of the business as a whole, these decisions must not be subject to veto or modification by the head of any one department. The computer manager must therefore be directly responsible to the director responsible for computer services. As far as the mechanics of director participation are concerned, a logical solution would be control through a committee with the director as chairman and as members, the computer manager, a representative of the manufacturers supplying the machine and the departmental managers who are, from time to time, directly affected by the planning. While the computer manager would have responsibility for the detailed organization of his own department and the take-on of the areas of work as these are decided by the committee, the committee should make decisions affecting areas of work outside the computer department and be concerned with overall planning. Another important function of the committee would be to review periodically the progress of the project as reported by the computer manager.

Having emphasized the need for the involvement of management at director level, while the expert technical know-how of the manufacturers and the computer manager cannot be expected of the director concerned, management should not be completely dependent on the experts. The director concerned should make a point of learning all that he can on the subject so that he is able to bring a degree of discernment and critical appraisal to bear on the proposals formulated by the experts. There are a number of ways of going about this of which, perhaps, the two most useful are by attending courses put on by manufacturers for executives at this level and by visiting other firms who have installed computers in similar circumstances to find out what their problems have been.

Having discussed the need for management participation in a computer project we should now examine in greater detail the factors that may give rise to consideration of a computer installation. Where does a computer fit in to an organization?

Since the introduction of computers, not much more than 30 years ago, the general approach to their use has gone through three stages. Initially the computer was designed as a specialist tool for solving a particular problem. The first machines were built to solve problems in aeronautics and ballistics. The realization that a computer could be used to process routine jobs very quickly led to the second approach, sometimes known as a 'hardware' approach which regarded it as just another machine to perform existing clerical procedures. The attitude during this phase was that the machine should fit into the existing systems environment by taking over the routine repetitive-work done mainly by junior clerks. The third, sometimes known as the 'systems approach' takes a far wider view. It looks on the computer as a management tool, involved in decision making formerly performed by middle management, and providing the information to guide policy decisions. In fact it becomes the 'peg' for the re-structuring of the organization. To some extent, the attitude that a computer is just another grey box to tuck away in the corner of the accounts office still exists, although this is soon dissipated when an investigation into its use starts. In order to get the greatest benefit from the considerable expense involved, management policy must look towards the realization of the full potential of the machine.

Initial thinking

We have already considered under the heading of Feasibility Study in Chapter 12, the detailed considerations that management will take into account in reaching a decision, but what factors prompt thinking in terms of computers in the first place? It is suggested that the following four motives play their part.

(1) To resolve a problem situation.
(2) To generally increase performance and profitability of the organization.
(3) To provide a base for re-organization.
(4) Prestige. not really relevant now

While it was suggested previously that an early and very limited approach to computer use was for solving specific problems, never the less, the existence of a problem situation is a valid reason for thinking in terms of a computer providing that the potentialities of its wider use are also considered. While it is impractical to itemize all the problems that arise in a business, situations do arise which just cannot be coped with by existing resources and methods, due to such things as complexity of work, shortage of trained staff, or increase in work volume.

A firm with such a problem should of course investigate all possible solutions, of which a computer installation is only one, but it may turn out to be the most promising one.

The second situation arises, not so much from a specific problem, but from conditions which make it apparent that the general use of resources, processing methods and control techniques are such that the organization is not producing either the performance or the profit it could. Investigation into the use of a computer to generally tone-up business activity is again, a sound enough proposition.

The situation we have in mind in the third case is the one in which organizational structure of a business has 'just grown' with the firm's development. This frequently results in recognition at some point that the whole structure is far too complex and top-heavy. Not only is the introduction of a computer a valid reason for carrying out a complete re-organization but it will also have the effect of streamlining and simplifying processing methods.

Finally, to be realistic, it must be realized that the day is still not past when computers are installed mainly for prestige purposes. It has been said that 40% of the machines used in the USA were bought mainly from motives of prestige. To the directors concerned this is doubtless a valid reason, but it is doubtful if, under these circumstances, the best is got out of the machine.

Buy, rent or bureau?

Management, having decided to adopt computer methods are now faced with a choice between three ways of going about it: (a) to purchase a machine outright from the manufacturer (b) to rent from a manufacturer or (c) to enlist the services of a computer bureau to process the work they have in mind.

Thinking of a computer bureau first, the decision will mainly revolve around the prices charged and the volume of work involved. For a computer to earn its keep it has to put in a lot of hours a day; in fact many installations work round the clock. Obviously, if the volume of work will only be sufficient to keep the machine occupied for a few hours a week, the use of a computer bureau is probably the best approach. It must be remembered that apart from the cost of the machine the cost of creating a computer department can be very high. The provision of accommodation, staff, salaries, systems and development costs and the cost of ancillary equipment all have to be taken into consideration. Although when buying time from a computer bureau, a degree of reorganization and staff retraining is still necessary, the other main items of cost are not directly incurred. The services provided by computer bureaux are discussed in detail in Chapter 13.

As far as a decision to rent or buy a machine is concerned, this again is largely a question of balance between economics and volumes of work but a third factor, technical development, should also be considered. Because of the very rapid developments in technical performance of machines, many firms have in the past been reluctant to purchase one outright, taking the view that it was better to hire one and change it when technical advances made this desirable. An argument perhaps particularly valid in the light of mini and microcomputer developments.

However, this last consideration apart, assuming the availability of resources to purchase a machine outright, comparative costs should be obtained of the annual hire costs, including maintenance, and the annual capital cost of buying assessed over the useful life of the machine plus, again, the cost of maintenance. Other points to bear in mind if hiring are (a) the minimum length of time the manufacturer will contract for and (b) any restriction on the number of hours the machine may be operated in a week. Additional charges may be incurred for more than the number of hours stipulated in the agreement.

User satisfaction

It must be remembered that the success of a computer system is measured in terms of the value of the service it provides to the people on the end of the system, i.e. the user, and not in terms of its operational efficiency to the computer department staff—although, of course, these two may well coincide. An essential prerequisite to user satisfaction is user involvement. A system designed and imposed upon a user department without reference, through its staff, to departmental requirements, is hardly likely to succeed.

While user involvement will necessarily take place during the systems investigation stage, the principle must go further than this. Involvement must promote co-operation on the part of the user, otherwise the system will fail. The user department is essentially part of the system. From here, source documentation will probably originate, output reports will be used, and modifications to the system arising from policy changes will be determined.

In order that users appreciate the purpose and the value of their part, they must be aware of the working of the complete system. It is particularly important to make key user staff aware of the capabilities and limitations of the computer. In the early stages of a project, user education is a most important factor not only in relation to basic computer and systems concepts but also in the advantages expected in their own particular area of work.

Involvement may not necessarily lead to co-operation and indeed co-operation may not necessarily lead to satisfaction; in fact two other ingredients are necessary, goodwill and expertise. The provision of the latter is a managerial function, and the former relies on the enthusiasm, persuasion and the general ethos generated on the part of both user and computer staff.

Performance monitoring

While, in the feasibility stage, the justification for computer systems will have been established, the performance of the factors on which such justification has been determined must be clearly monitored during development and implementation. This will mean checking on budgeted costing, and realization of aims, the accuracy, timeliness and usefulness of outputs. The valuation of performance should be a regular periodic process while the system is operative.

The computer project

The following are the main steps management must take to introduce computer methods.

(1) Establish firm objectives. Motives for introducing a computer need to be examined, the uses to which it is to be put decided upon and an estimate made of the date at which the installation will become operational.
(2) Make a preliminary study, including (a) investigation into alternative ways of achieving the same objectives (b) the education of the director made responsible for computer services, (c) getting as much information as possible on the problems likely to arise in transferring to computer operation the areas of work decided upon.
(3) Conduct research into the consequences. Analyse the effect on the actual work that will be taken on. What benefits will arise? What changes in organization will have to be made? What will

be the effect on staff—redundancy, re-training, shift in responsibilities.

(4) Make plans for introducing the changes. Draw up a time-table for implementing the changes. Allow reasonable time for staff re-training and attitudes to become accustomed to the idea of a computer. Plan communications and decide which members of staff are to be consulted. Plan staff movements and staff training.

(5) Put the plan into action. Where possible do this in phases, reviewing each completed phase before moving on to the next. Leave room for flexibility to cover any unforeseen circumstances that may arise.

Management problems

We now move to a review of some of the problems faced by management in putting computer systems into operation. Introducing a computer means change: changes in organization, in areas of responsibility, in work load, in work flow, in work discipline and in physical environment. Change is not only unsettling while it lasts but it may also, in the long term, produce conditions that are unsatisfactory or unacceptable to some people. Management problems, by and large, centre around attitudes to, and the results of, the change brought about by the adoption of computer methods.

Attitudes to change

As was mentioned above, change is unsettling both from an organizational and from an individual point of view. Attitudes to change are determined by a number of factors and vary very much from person to person. Some members of staff may well welcome change while others view it with grave misgivings. While it is hardly the province of this book to go deeply into the psychology of change, some of the factors affecting peoples' attitudes are worth mentioning. Age is significant, younger people generally accepting change more readily than older. Social responsibilities, upkeep of a home, care of children etc., may lead to an over-riding desire for security. A person's standing in the organization, the prospects opened up by change and the rewards offered, and his individual personality will directly affect his attitude. Some of these factors are, of course, outside the control of the management but, nevertheless, management will want to implement changes as smoothly as possible and, as far as they can, to engender in their staff a favourable and enthusiastic attitude to the proposed changes. Factors within an organization that will have an influence on staff attitudes are:

(*a*) *Past policy to change.*
Has the management dealt fairly and reasonably with members of staff involved in change in the past?

(*b*) *Relationships within the firm*
Are management-staff relationships such as to produce an atmosphere of confidence and co-operation, or, on the other hand, are staff suspicious of management motives?

(*c*) *Communications*
Knowledge that change is to happen without knowing the effects it will have on individuals gives rise to a great deal of speculation and rumour. A computer having been decided upon, while it may not be possible at this early stage to define the role each member of staff will play in relation to it, they must be kept informed of general aims and policy. However, a general statement of what is happening and why, is of less importance than being told 'what will happen to me?' Wherever possible, staff must be reassured about their continued security and standing within the organization. Unless they know where they stand, key personnel will be tempted to 'play it safe' by getting a job elsewhere.

(*d*) *Participation and identification*
In planning the detail of the change-over, existing staff should be involved as much as possible. This has both a practical aspect, as the people doing the job often know best what is going on, and the purpose of identifying them with the planning process.

(*e*) *Rewards*
Of course, a rational reaction to change is 'What am I going to get out of it'? Change will probably be welcomed if the end product is a more interesting or comfortable job, or greater financial reward. Planning policy must take into account that incentives may need to be offered.

(*f*) *Timing*
If any change is unsettling, hurried and unplanned change is very much more so, and repeatedly postponed changes only add to the confusion. Allow time in planning to ensure that all the requirements of the change can be met, and having set a date, keep to it.

Generally, then, management at director level must realize that the introduction of a computer will mean change. This change may not be welcomed by some staff and so management has a responsibility to encourage the acceptance of change and to plan its implementation with the minimum amount of upheaval.

The computer and middle management

It is not unusual for the impact of the change-over to be felt most at middle management level, particularly by heads of departments. This problem needs special attention by management. The general effect of computer processing in relation to departmental structure is that some departments are completely eliminated, the staffing of others may be considerably reduced and departmental divisions tend to break down. In addition to this, since routine decision making will now largely be the province of the computer, the responsibilities of middle managers in this field are very much reduced.

Departments that are mainly concerned with routine processing will tend to disappear altogether. For example, an invoicing department that, having received advice notes from the stores, prices them, extends, deducts discounts and types a sales invoice for dispatch to the customer, need no longer exist when this processing is carried out electronically. In other departments, some functions may still be performed manually, while the bulk of the work is processed by computer. In a Wages Office, for example, the bulk of the work is concerned with the routine calculation of wages and the preparation of a pay-roll, all of which can be coped with by the computer, but a small amount of the work may be retained as manual procedures—individual tax statements for employees leaving, tax and pension returns to Inland Revenue etc. However, does the retention of this small amount of manual work justify the continued existence of a separate wages office?

In manual systems, work flow tends to progress from department to department. For example, details of a credit sale are recorded in the stores on an advice note, the advice note passes to the stock control department to record the issue, then to an invoicing department to price, extend and raise an invoice. Copies of the invoice then go to the sales department for sales analysis and to accounts department for ledger posting. In a computer system, the one record prepared from the source document, in this case the advice note, will be used within the one department, the computer department, to prepare the invoice, update the stock records, update the sales ledger and provide the statistical information. This eliminates to a great extent the need for separate departments each processing the separate jobs within the one main business function—sales.

This all leads to the complete elimination of some departments and a tendency to merge the manual processing left in other departments on a more functional basis. The number of management posts at departmental level is reduced, and responsibilities are changed.

Another major effect on middle management centres around the ability of the computer to make routine decisions. Notoriously, a great deal of the department manager's time is taken up in sorting out problems arising from routine work. These decisions are often necessarily subjective, sometimes based on experience and know-how but without the detailed information necessary to reach an objective decision, or sometimes because too many variables are involved for adequate consideration. The human mind finds difficulty in making a decision if faced with more than two variables. The computer suffers from neither of these disadvantages. It can have all the information available at very short notice that is necessary to reach a decision, and it can take into account any number of variables. If correctly programmed the computer will not only make routine decisions far more quickly but also far more objectively. Not only are the routine decisions of the middle manager reduced, but also his role in making major policy decisions is diminished. Top management rely on middle management for the information on which they base policy decisions. With a computer in operation this reliance is to a great extent eliminated, the information being supplied direct from the computer department. Not only this, the computer eliminates to a great extent the time lag experienced with manual systems as information is gradually passed up through a chain of command. For example, if control totals are produced by a number of ledger clerks, summarized by the accounts office manager, edited by the accountant and then passed on to the financial director, even assuming each person in the chain does his work quickly (a large assumption) the results may well arrive at the top too late for quick corrective action to be taken. The computerized reduction of the time lag between performance and reporting, enables management to reach policy decisions in time for them to be effective. As a by-product of this, some policy decisions previously left to lower levels of management because of the time element and the information requirements, can now come within the province of top level management.

To summarize then, one important effect of a computer is, at high management level, to widen the area of decision making and to ensure that the information required to support policy decisions is available in time for them to be effective. At middle management level, it eliminates to a great extent the need for routine decision making and also eliminates the preparation of control information to support policy decisions made at top management level. Looked at from another point of view, however, one important advantage for middle management is that more time is available for supervising the work under their control and for planning and for developing new ideas.

Staff

We have seen that the reorganization inherent in the introduction of a computer will eventually lead to the displacement of staff. Experience shows that large scale redundancy is unlikely to result from the new processing methods. This is due largely to the fact that most of the routine manual processing is done by unskilled labour in which there is usually a fairly high labour turnover rate. Thus the problem of redundancy at this level has a tendency to solve itself. The problem of more highly skilled and therefore more permanent labour, however, has to be faced. Within a computer department a number of new posts will arise, of systems analysts, programmers, control staff, computer operators and so on. Most firms make a practice of recruiting much of this staff from within their own organization and providing the necessary facilities for training. While it may be argued that it is better to recruit skilled programmers and analysts from outside, existing staff have the advantage of an intimate knowledge of the organization and the policy and practices of their own firm, and they are known quantities as far as the management is concerned. In practice, the best policy is often a compromise between the two by appointing from outside the senior systems man and chief programmer, and recruiting the rest of the computer department staff from existing employees. Recruitment of staff for data preparation, that is, operators for punched cards, punched paper tape machines etc., usually presents no initial difficulty. Most firms employ operators for one kind of machine or another in connection with manual systems, and usually the operators displaced by the introduction of computer methods are prepared to be retrained.

Computer department staff

There are two problems that management should be aware of as far as the staff of the computer department itself is concerned. The first is that the shortage of skilled computer staff. This, while being very evident at the moment, will probably be cured in time. There is still a fair amount of competition between computer users for trained staff which means that fairly high salaries must be paid to attract and keep the computer manager, systems, programming and operating staff. There is also a tendency for staff to be attracted by the capability of the machine. A firm with a new powerful machine can often attract staff more easily than a firm operating an older and less versatile machine.

We have already seen that one effect of a computer is to reduce the power and responsibilities of middle management, but the reverse side of the coin to this is that in doing so a great deal of power is placed in the hands of the small group of specialists staffing the computer department. The whole organization can well become completely dependent on the computer staff for its routine processing needs and the management dependent for the control information required to make decisions. Perhaps one can go even further than this and say that even a small section of the department, for example the data preparation section, has the power to bring the whole processing and therefore the operation of the firm to a stand-still.

Environment

The physical conditions demanded by the computer itself—temperature, humidity, air filtration etc.—will be stipulated by the manufacturer concerned. Perhaps it would be as well to mention in this section on management problems more specifically those parts of an installation concerned with data preparation. This tends to be repetitive, uninteresting and boring but the whole processing service depends on the accuracy and punctuality with which this work is performed. Working conditions should be such as to promote efficient preparation of data. Apart from a pleasant physical environment, work loads and work flow should be organized so as to get the best out of the operators. In particular, the more exacting punching jobs should be fairly distributed, and should be kept reasonably small so that punch operators are presented with jobs whose end is quickly attainable rather than ones seeming to be endless.

Increased work load during implementation

Another problem faced by management is the very heavy work load during the change-over period, occasioned by the transfer of manual records to computer files and the probable need to run both manual and computer systems for a time in order to check the latter. Unless plans are formulated well in advance to cope with this extra work, take-on dates could well be delayed. A sufficiently interested staff, will often be prepared to help by working overtime although the temporary transfer of staff from other less vital activities or the employment of temporary staff are other ways of dealing with the problem.

Machine failure

Modern computers regularly and efficiently maintained and in the hands of adequately trained operators, are very reliable pieces of equipment. However, even in the best run installations the possibility of a lengthy breakdown cannot be ignored. To insure against this, most firms enter into a reciprocal 'stand-by' agreement with another firm operating a similar machine. This ensures that with the machine out of action vital jobs can still be processed.

Costs

While it is impractical to quote prices of individual computers, either purchased outright or rented, the following is an attempt to set down the main items of cost other than the computer itself, when setting up a computer department. It should be emphasized, however, that it is much more difficult to accurately assess the costs incurred, and indeed the benefits derived, than for most other forms of capital investment.

Costs can be classified under the main headings of accommodation, hardware, investigation and development, and maintenance.

(a) Accommodation

Basic requirements are a computer room, data preparation section, accommodation for file and paper storage, offices for systems analysts and programmers, control room and reception centre, computer manager's office and work-room for maintenance engineers. Over and above this provision will probably have to be made for air-conditioning equipment for at least the computer room and library.

In practice it is found that the space required by a computer installation is less than that needed to accommodate the personnel, machines and materials used for manual systems for an equivalent work load. Also, whereas in manual systems, accommodation requirements tend to increase in proportion to increase in work volumes, a computer is able to considerably increase its turnover of work with only need, perhaps, for extra space for the additional machines to cope with data preparation.

(b) Hardware

Hardware, of course, is the major cost element, and usually these requirements are assessed at the feasibility study stage. However, it is as well to bear in mind from the outset that detailed systems investigation may indicate a need for more equipment than that considered necessary at the feasibility study. For example, it may be found that additional backing storage is required. Hardware costs fall into four main groups (a) The computer itself, i.e. the central processor, and peripheral equipment which would normally consist of input and output devices, and backing storage. (b) Data Preparation equipment. (c) Ancillary equipment for output handling, guillotines, bursters, collators, folding machines etc., and (d) the provision of storage equipment, racks, cupboards, safes for high security documents, desks etc.

(c) Investigation and development costs

This is the most difficult cost item to estimate. As far as the feasibility study is concerned, if the manufacturer takes this on, on the basis of obtaining the order for the machine, then there will be probably no charge. A firm proposing to spend £100 000–£200 000 on equipment, rather than relying on one manufacturer, would probably prefer a completely independent investigation by a consultant. For a full scale investigation a fee of £10 000 or more could well be incurred. An alternative approach, to cut costs at this initial stage, is for the prospective user to appoint a team of say three people from his own staff, possibly from an existing Organization and Methods department, to carry out the investigation, and call in consultants to check through and advise on the report they prepare.

As far as systems development and programming costs are concerned, while the number of analysts and programmers to be employed can be fixed fairly accurately, the time they will take to bring systems to an operational point is very difficult to estimate. A number of variables are involved. The experience and know-how of the staff, unforeseen complications in design, the degree of turnover within the systems and programming teams. As a generalization it must be said that this cost had a tendency to escalate, resulting in performance costs being well in excess of estimates. This can be mitigated to a certain extent by making sure that at least one team member has previous practical experience in developing similar systems.

(d) Operating costs

Once the system has settled down and become fully operational, discounting rental charges for the machine should this be appropriate, the main cost elements are, of course, accommodation, staff, supplies and machine maintenance. Systems having been implemented, the requirements for systems and programming staff will very much decrease. The need for systems maintenance, however, still exists although the systems and programming staff required for this purpose is probably only in the region of 20% of that required during development.

It is not easy to assess objectively savings that arise through using a computer. As has been pointed out, the argument that computers result in staff savings is not usually borne out by experience, except, perhaps when very high volumes of routine processing are taken over from unskilled clerical labour. But even then it must be kept in mind that the cost of trained computer staff can be individually two or three times as high as the unskilled labour they replace. Other direct savings may be in the cost of equipment no longer needed—accounting, calculating machines etc.—and in savings in accommodation.

Generally speaking, cost benefits tend to be of an indirect character. For example, a computer Sales Ledger system will probably get customer sales statements out earlier, thus encouraging earlier payment and so improving cash flow. A computer stock inventory system may lead to lower stock levels being maintained resulting in savings in storage costs and releasing cash otherwise tied up in stocks. This type of saving however is difficult to measure in advance.

Exercises

1. It has been suggested by members of your firm that a digital computer would be a valuable asset.
   Briefly suggest the constitution of a committee that you would set up to examine the project.
   What points would you look for before agreeing to the installation?
2. Why do you think it desirable that management at director level should be actively involved in implementing a computer project?
3. What are the probable effects on management at departmental level of the introduction of computer systems?
4. What main advantages would you expect to accrue from the

introduction of a computer installation to carry out routine clerical procedures?

5. What main items of cost would you expect to be incurred in the introduction of a computer department for processing commercial systems?

6. List some of the circumstances that you feel might give rise to management initially thinking in terms of a changeover to computer methods.

7. As a manager responsible for implementing computer systems, what actions would you take to minimize the disruption caused by the changeover.

8. What are the main steps involved in planning the installation of a computer.

9. 'Electronic digital computers can be programmed to make decisions and to carry out processes which will in the long term change the nature of the tasks allocated to middle management and executives'. Discuss this statement giving reasoned and logical arguments for any assertions you may make or examples which support your case.

10. 'The introduction of a computer tends towards the breakdown of departmental barriers'. Explain why this is so.

11. What investigations should a company make before a decision is made whether or not to purchase a computer for its commercial work?

Some social aspects of computers

The suggestion has been made that the advent of the computer heralds a second Industrial Revolution. Be this as it may, it is certainly true to say that the developing use of computers is having very far reaching effects in Commerce, Industry and the Public Services. The computer is a most powerful tool, and if used wisely can do much to alleviate the burden of repetitive donkey-work, increase efficiency in commerce and industry, speed new developments in technology and by virtue of the vast amounts of information and the extremely rapid processing power it has at its command, provide benefits to mankind in an ever-increasing range of services.

Some of these services in which computers are proving to play an important part are

(1) Education
The development of computer-aided learning systems over a whole range of both arts and sciences.
(2) Medicine
Not only as a rapid and effective aid to diagnosis by reference to stored clinical data but also in the field of monitoring techniques of patients.
(3) Traffic control
As an aid to providing a smoother flow of traffic on our road systems.
(4) Meteorology
To provide more accurate and detailed weather forecasts.
(5) Information services
Through the medium of television displayed data on demand, e.g. the Prestel service.

On the other hand, like any other tool, the use of computers can be abused to the detriment of the individual. It could make easier the imposing of stricter controls over, and increasing interference into, the lives of people and also the promotion of changes in working conditions and environment for which people have not been fully prepared.

Social effects

Perhaps, at any rate in their early stages of development, computers were endowed by the public with an air of mystery probably fostered by the use of such descriptions as 'electronic brains' and by an emphasis on their capacity to remember and to make decisions. This gave rise, and indeed still does to a certain extent, to fears that computers would take over both in the organizational 'big brother' sense and by performing a great deal of work previously manually performed thus making many workers redundant.

Essentially a computer is an automative device and will, therefore, by definition automatically do jobs that would otherwise have been performed manually. Does this mean that the fears of large scale redundancy have been or are being realized? Although a different story may emerge in the field of microcomputer controlled technology, experience to date in the area of computer data processing is that these fears are to a large extent unfounded. It would be difficult to argue that the total number of people employed in commercial and public service administration has declined since the advent of the computer.

The introduction of these machines have, in themselves, opened up new areas of work both for their users and their manufacturers, and it is often possible for the user to absorb some of his staff, whose work has been taken over, into the new computer department. However, to be realistic, there will be people in individual organizations who cannot be so absorbed and who are faced with losing the work they may have been doing over a long period of time. To mitigate this situation, many organizations provide

(1) Re-training facilities with the object of transferring displaced employees to other areas of work within the organization.
(2) Offer financially attractive early retirement schemes.
(3) Policies for putting a brake on the recruitment of new employees until all the people disturbed by the introduction of the computer have been re-settled.

As far as the take-over in the 'big brother' sense is concerned, perhaps this concern is not quite as unfounded. Central and local government departments are making increasing use of computers to store income tax records, health records, car records, national insurance records, census records and records concerning any relationships we have had with the law. Furthermore, in the commercial spectrum, computerized records are held of our credit worthiness, our banking history, credit card transactions etc.

Perhaps all this makes it understandable that fears should arise in many peoples minds that a point may be reached at which our lives are too much of an open book to any person with access to the computer files. It would seem to be reasonable that safeguards should be provided to guard against the misuse of information stored centrally in computers.

Apart from the fears that may arise through the widespread use of computers, the practical effects of their introduction have been becoming more apparent over the past few years. Our electricity, gas, rates accounts etc, have taken on a new form. When we pay them we are instructed 'do not fold', otherwise the computer will be unable to digest them. Our signature, on its own, is no longer sufficient for many transactions, we have to quote numbers as well. We are presented with documents printed in strange characters with which we are unfamiliar. These are some of the more noticeable effects of computers in our daily life and we must expect their influence to become more marked as their use extends.

Computer privacy

As we saw above, an increasingly wide range of data relating to our personal lives is being held on computer files. Some of the fears and problems associated with this practice are

(1) Data may not be accurate and therefore incorrect conclusions may be drawn from its use.
(2) It is possible for an organization to sell data from its computer files to a third party and its use put to a purpose for which it was never originally intended without the consent or even the knowledge of the person to whom it relates.
(3) There is no guarantee that a person with access to computer files will not access and retrieve data, using it to his own advantage and to the disadvantage of the person it concerns.

These problems associated with the storage of personal data are giving rise to a great deal of thought and discussion and it would seem reasonable that some mandatory safeguards along the following lines should eventually be formulated

(1) The right of the individual to obtain and inspect a printed copy of data relating to him held on computer files.

(2) If data is to be used for a purpose for which it was not originally intended, the right to know and to veto its disclosure to a third party.

(3) The right to have any errors coming to light corrected and where the bare facts might unfairly or unjustly reflect upon the individual, the right to insert some kind of explanation.

(4) The exclusion of data relating to personal convictions e.g. religious or political.

(5) A periodic review of some kinds of records with a view to their deletion if the passage of time has rendered them no longer relevant. For example, records relating to criminal or civil legal actions or records of credit worthiness.

(6) Strict controls to limit access to records by only authorized personnel.

Taking this problem of computer privacy to its ultimate, if we reached a situation where an individual's unique identifying reference number, say national insurance number, was used in all the records relating to him in all the data banks linked together, then the total information relating to the person could be retrieved through that one reference. A rather frightening thought!

Exercises

1. What measures do you think should be taken to safeguard against the abuse of the use of data records held in computers on individuals?

2. Give an account of how computers are proving to be of benefit to people in areas other than Industry and Commerce.

3. 'More computers—more unemployment'. Discuss this statement.

4. Give an account of how you feel computers have had an effect on our domestic lives.

5. Suggest reasons why the holding of personal records on computers could represent an invasion of our privacy.

Index